MA

High Noon of Empire

High Noon
of
Empire

The Diary of Lieutenant Colonel
Henry Tyndall 1895–1915

Henry Tyndall

Editor: B.A. James
Foreword: John Laffin

Pen & Sword
MILITARY

First published in Great Britain in 2007 by
Pen & Sword Military
an imprint of
Pen & Sword Books Ltd
47 Church Street
Barnsley
South Yorkshire
S70 2AS

ISBN 978 1 84415 546 0

A CIP catalogue record for this book is available from the British Library

Typeset in Ehrhardt

Printed and bound in England by Biddles Ltd, King's Lynn

Pen & Sword Books Ltd incorporates the Imprints of Pen & Sword Aviation,
Pen & Sword Maritime, Pen & Sword Military, Wharncliffe Local History,
Pen & Sword Select, Pen & Sword Military Classics and Leo Cooper.

For a complete list of Pen & Sword titles please contact
PEN & SWORD BOOKS LIMITED
47 Church Street, Barnsley, South Yorkshire, S70 2AS, England
E-mail: enquiries@pen-and-sword.co.uk
Website: www.pen-and-sword.co.uk

Contents

Preface

Henry Stuart Tyndall was a typical product of his age. It was the late Victorian age when the British Empire covered a fifth of the earth's surface, proudly demonstrated in school classrooms by reference to a large Mercator projection on which the considerable amount of land area coloured red was disproportionately magnified to north and south giving sure credence to the claim that 'the sun never set on the Empire'.

Tyndall served in the brightest jewel in the crown, India, and fought in one of the most troubled and far-flung outposts, the North-West Frontier. At the start of his career he took part in the Malakand Campaign of 1897, of which he gives an eyewitness account, including his meeting with Winston Churchill, then a young war correspondent. Thereafter Tyndall spent many years in military cantonments in India; a life he chronicles at first with meticulous precision. He was obviously very sociable and took a keen interest in his fellow men to the extent of recording lists of names of those whom he met whether in the Mess, Club or on shipboard – an aide-memoire perhaps, but a habit, nevertheless, ingrained in the good military officer who should remember all the names of the men on his unit.

He was a keen patriotic, and somewhat stereotyped, Indian Army officer of that period although, at the same time sensitive and artistic, he painted, played the piano and wrote short stories which were published. He was also something of a poet. Secure in his social class, his vision was largely limited to the military caste into which he had been born; his father was a general who had also served in India, and he seemed to have little interest in the wider issues of Indian politics (no doubt a taboo subject in his Mess!) or in the 'natives' as the Indians were called in the days of the Raj. Indeed, the Army officers' life in India was circumscribed compared with civilians. It was a small world centred on the military cantonment, nevertheless it was a privileged existence with rare opportunities for sport, travel and action. Most officers, with their wives, felt that they were part of a family, a family of brother officers, and a young officer, wishing to marry had to get permission from his colonel who usually vetted the young lady as to her suitability.

In contrast the British soldier in India was uniquely underprivileged and underpaid; he was virtually confined to barracks, all Indian villages, bazaars and shops were out of bounds and he would often not have the opportunity of speaking to a white woman during his entire service of five years. But it was not resented. The officer was accepted as one of the warrior caste or samurai, a leader of men, set above him, *primus inter pares* were the 'Heaven born' Indian Civil Service officials who ruled the country. The commercial people or 'box wallahs' were further down the social scale although better off financially. India was a great place for precedence. Its origins in Mogul times and not uninfluenced, perhaps, by the Hindu caste system which divided society into Brahmins, (priests), Kshatriya (warriors), Vaisha (traders) and Sudra (other castes), and excluding the Untouchables.

The sepoys or native troops like the enlisted men in Tyndall's regiment, the 40th Pathans, (poachers turned gamekeepers), were often recruited from the same village, class or tribe resulting in closely knit bonds of blood, speech, religion or caste. They had considerable status in their villages, and were able to send money home to their families, receiving pensions if they served long enough and grants of land at least until the end of the nineteenth century.

Beneath the formal picture of cantonment life which emerges in the diary – British Indian society in the high-noon of Empire: the endless calling, un-sophisticated jokes, shikar (shooting and fishing) and regimental ceremonial – there is a man hardened by the tough foot-slogging soldiering of those days. Tyndall's yearning for action is evident in his frequent requests for transfer to more active spots, and in his chagrin when the 40th Pathans were not included with the troops sent to China in June 1900 to quell the Boxer Rising. His ambition for action was fulfilled towards the end of his career; on the Western Front in 1915, in East Africa most of all and in the 3rd Afghan War.

The historical introduction has been written for the general reader. In dealing with the complicated and colourful tapestry which is Indian history, it is only possible in a short space to present a general picture weaving in the main events influencing the tumultuous course of political developments, from the early invasions to Kipling's India and eventually Independence. Within this frame-work I have laid most emphasis on Afghanistan and the North-West Frontier, where the 'Great Game' was played out, to help in placing the Malakand Campaign in the right context as it was indirectly one of the closing episodes, and is where Tyndall's story starts.

I have arranged the events of Tyndall's career from 1915, when his diary finishes, to 1924 when he proceeded on a year's leave pending retirement, in diary form and, indeed, included are two reports written by Tyndall himself. These have been extracted from the Regimental History of the 40th Pathans, (Major R.S. Waters OBE who served with Tyndall). The Campaign in East Africa 1915–1917 as it affected Tyndall, who won a DSO and Croix de Guerre, and the 40th Pathans, can be followed quite easily by reference to the map.

This marching soldier of the Queen was a gallant officer who conscientiously served his sovereign wherever duty called – on the hot dusty plains of India, on the North-West frontier of India, in France or the dense malarial bush of East Africa. It was a chauvinistic time of Imperial grandeur, but Colonel Tyndall's diary deserves attention as it reflects the manners, customs and attitudes of this vanished age.

B.A. James, Ludlow, Shropshire.

Foreword

John Laffin

B.A. James, 'Jimmy' to his friends, has a feeling for history. As an RAF Squadron Leader in the Second World War he became a prisoner of the Nazis and, as one of the officers who made a break for freedom during 'the Great Escape' he played a part in shaping history. He wrote about his adventures in *Moonless Night*, one of the most significant books by a prisoner of war to come out of the appalling conflict.

Jimmy again demonstrates his affinity for history by editing the diary of a British Army officer who served during the extraordinary era of the Raj.

Henry Tyndall's diary begins in 1895 and ends in 1915. Jimmy, realizing that a segment of an interesting life limited to twenty years is inadequate, has provided us with a lengthy and absorbing account of British imperial interest in India. Britain gave up India in 1947, an enormous national emotional wrench after an investment of 2 million British lives over the decades and centuries.

To take Tyndall's diary forward after 1915, James has, in effect, written entries for him until 1924. Here is an officer's life of loyal service to the Crown, from the lowly rank of second lieutenant to lieutenant colonel commanding a regiment. Tyndall fought not only in India but in East Africa during the First World War, where he was awarded the Distinguished Service Order and the Croix de Guerre.

Jimmy James's editing of Tyndall's diary is knowledgeable and efficient. The reader is not left wondering what a sangar might be and there is adequate information about, for instance the Malakand Campaign in 1897.

Tyndall himself comes across as an alert, observant man with a sense of humour. I wonder if he was one of the perpetrators of a practical joke played on an amorous couple on board the RMS *Arabia*, en route to India. Tyndall records that the pair 'pleased with each other's society, found their deck chairs tied together'.

Reading Tyndall, through Jimmy James's sympathetic treatment of his diary, is rather like looking at sepia photographs of his period.

* Tyndall in a 'delightful Regimental Mess' – bungalow covered with creepers, the rooms full of skins and trophies, Grecian and Buddhist remains.

* It was a 'fine sight' to see the tribesmen in their flowing garments attacking fearlessly and Tyndall found it hard to realize that he was not looking at a play.

* The Swat Valley, where there was plenty of shade, through which green-banked irrigation channels 'trickles coolly amid wild olive and fig trees.'

* One Mess had a complete set of folding camp chairs and tables; aluminium cups, plates and boxes which became tables after they were unslung from mules at the end of a day's march.

Campaigning comes vividly alive – the blazing heat and occasionally the bitter cold, the choking dust, the mountains, deserts and jungles, the wounds and deaths in action, the disease and the tremendous effort. And all for a distant sovereign. Tyndall served Queen Victoria, Edward VII and George V in his time. Thank goodness that Jimmy James has brought his diary to the attention of a new generation of Britons.

Acknowledgements

Old diaries come to light in strange ways. Tyndall's Diary was no exception. Some years ago my wife and I were in Sussex where we used to visit a splendid inn called the Wheatsheaf between Horsham and Crawley run by a no less splendid couple called Jerry and Kay King Tours. Jerry had been a Fleet Air Arm pilot and had a great interest in military history, the walls were festooned with flags, RAF and Naval wings and crests, swords, kukris, badges, photographs and militaria of all sorts. Jerry knew that I had written a book about my war experiences *Moonless Night* and one night he pushed over the bar a bulky volume of photocopied material telling me that he had been given this by a Caledonian air line pilot called Jim Hopton who had told him that he could do what he liked with it, an injunction which Jerry passed on to me. I must, therefore, give special thanks to Jerry for bringing the diary to my attention. I am also grateful to Gilly Hopton, the widow of Jim Hopton, for making available the original diary found with other Indian artefacts in the house bought by the Hoptons.

I have to thank Joanna McKinnon, Tyndall's great niece and nearest living relative for permission to publish the diary and for help and encouragement, together with her husband Colonel Ian McKinnon, and for loan of photographs of Tyndall's parents.

I am particularly appreciative of David Blakeway Smith's help in typing the entire text on his computer; he had an interest in that he had been a housemaster at Haileybury College where thirty-three members of the same family had been pupils, the first having died in the Black Hole of Calcutta. I have to thank Glenda and Eiddon Rees for use of photocopying facilities of Glendaph Nursing Home; also Chris Williams for similar facilities in his estate agency.

I am very grateful to the late Dr John Laffin, the distinguished military historian, for writing the foreword.

I am indebted to the Imperial War Museum for their interest and help with the text especially Dr Christopher Dowling and Elizabeth Bowring, and also at the National Army Museum, Dr Massie and Juliet O'Connell in particular, for their assistance with photographs and relevant information.

I must thank my old friend the late Lt Colonel Jack Churchill DSO, MC who served in the army in India in the late 1920s – not far off Tyndall's time – for guidance on Indian conditions.'We had to march the devil of a long way,' he said. Little did he imagine that he would be my companion nearly twenty years later when we were marching 'the devil of a long way to the Baltic ports in Germany' after escaping from a Nazi death camp. My wife deserves an accolade for putting up with the long preparations for the publishing of this diary. Also I must thank her for her discerning and helpful comments.

I am indebited to Major David Thomas, formerly of the 7th Gurkha Rifles, for information about the Gurkhas.

The *Illustrated London News* derserves grateful recognition for the excellent reproduction of Tyndall's sketch of the Malakand area which appeared in their issue of 1897, shown on the dust jacket of this book.

Finally I have to thank Rupert Harding of Pen & Sword, my commissioning editor, for putting it all together.

B. A. 'Jimmy' James

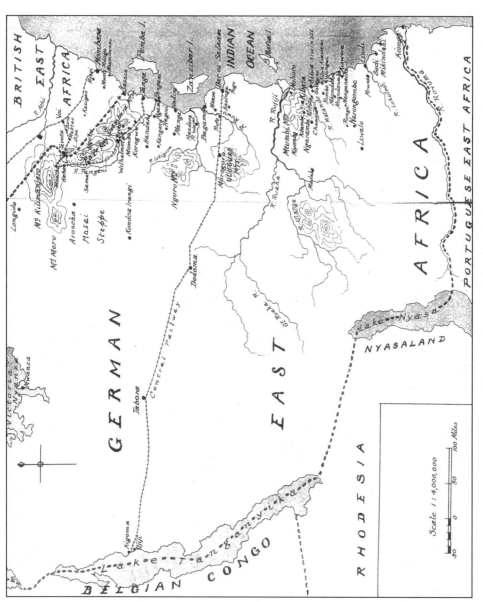

East Africa during the First World War

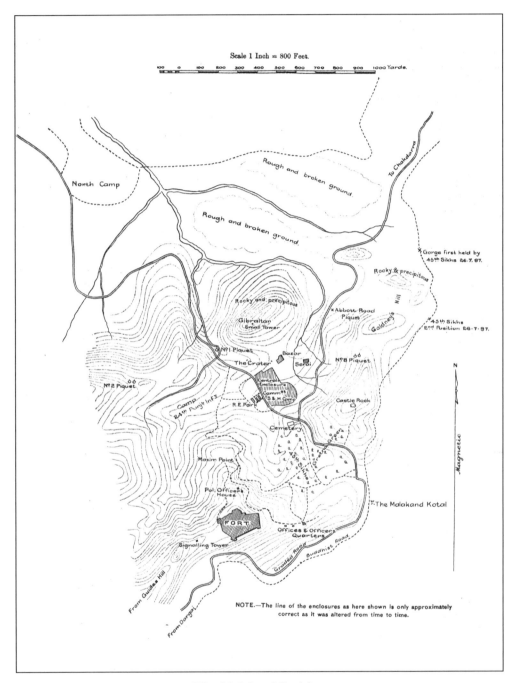

The Malakand Position

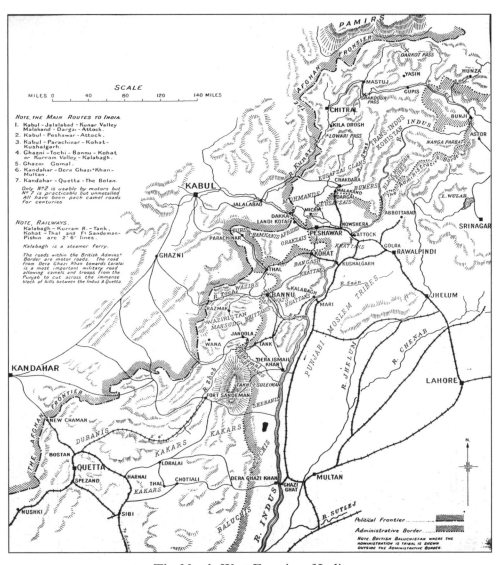

SCALE

MILES 0   40   80   120   140 MILES

NOTE, THE MAIN ROUTES TO INDIA

1. Kabul - Jalalabad - Kunar Valley
   Malakand - Dargai - Attock.
2. Kabul - Peshawar - Attock.
3. Kabul - Parachinar - Kohat -
   Kushalgarh.
4. Ghazni - Tochi - Bannu - Kohat
   or Kurram Valley - Kalabagh.
5. Ghazni Gomal.
6. Kandahar - Dera Ghazi·Khan -
   Multan.
7. Kandahar - Quetta - The Bolan.

Only Nº2 is usable by motors but
Nº7 is practicable but unmetalled
All have been pack camel roads
for centuries

NOTE, RAILWAYS.
Kalabagh - Kurram R. - Tank.
Kohat - Thal and Fᵗ Sandeman -
Pishin are 2' 6" lines.

Kalabagh is a steamer ferry.

The roads within the British Admins
Border are motor roads. The road
from Dera Ghazi Khan towards Loralai
is a most important military road
allowing camels and troops from the
Punjab to cut across the immense
block of hills between the Indus & Quetta

Political Frontier
Administrative Border

NOTE. BRITISH BALUCHISTAN WHERE THE
ADMINISTRATION IS TRIBAL IS SHEWN
OUTSIDE THE ADMINISTRATIVE BORDER.

The North-West Frontier of India

Historical Sketch

India, Afghanistan and the North-West Frontier

The natural boundaries of India are mountains and sea. A great semicircle of the highest mountains on earth sweeps around the northern frontier from west of the River Indus to the Bay of Bengal, a distance of over 2,000 miles. The sea washes the southern shores. This has had a very significant effect on the history of the country.

For centuries the destinies of Afghanistan and India were shaped by invasions from the north-west. It was the only practicable route and remains the most difficult – featureless deserts, barren plateaux and tremendous mountain ranges barred the way to the lush plains and riches of India. Conquering armies came this way because no sea route from the west had been discovered. Driven on by the ambition and burning desire for conquest by their rulers and generals, armed hosts trudged across the Karakhum and Kizil Kum deserts, struggled over the Hindu Kush (Hindu Killer) mountains in central Afghanistan and fought their way through the Khyber, Bolan and other passes into the Indian sub-continent. They conquered the native populations and pushed them to the south then, succumbing to the debilitating atmosphere and climate, they were themselves overcome by a fresh wave of invaders.

From about 1500 BC Aryans thronged through the passes and left their legacy of Hinduism and Brahminism, later Buddhism. Earliest proven influences were Persian, by tradition amongst the Afghans, once called Pushtoons (from which Pathan is derived), suggests that they originated in Palestine in the days of King Saul and were scattered by Nebuchadnezzar with the tribes of Israel settling in the mountains of Ghor in western Afghanistan.

The Medes and Persians appeared on the scene about 600BC. The Medes, under Cyaxares, established a powerful empire which was overthrown by the Persians under Cyrus the Great, whose rule by 550 BC embraced a vast territory, including what is now Afghanistan, founding the Archaemenid empire, the next ruler of which was Darius (522–485 BC) whose generals subdued the Indus valley.

Next came the Greeks. Alexander the Great in five years (330–325 BC) led his army of 35,000 in a series of astonishing marches to Babylon, Susa and

Persepolis, defeating Darius III of Persia. He invaded northern India and defeated King Porus in 327BC. A mutiny in his army prevented him from advancing to the Ganges and he returned reluctantly to Babylon where he died of a fever in 325 BC. His cavalry commander, Seleucas Nikator, then founded the Seluicid dynasty. Bactria to the north-east of the Hindu Kush was colonized by Greeks and became one of the most important provinces of the Seleucid Empire.

In this period Ashoka, one of the most famous monarchs of the Mauryan dynasty, ruled from the Hindu Kush to Mysore. His bloody conquest of the Kalinga country, now Orissa in north-east India, disturbed him and he embraced Buddhism, renounced armed conquest and adopted a policy he called 'conquest by dharma' (principles of right life). Many engravings on rocks and pillars bear witness to his faith. He died in 238 BC.

Selucids and Mauryans disintegrated about 160 BC and were overwhelmed by invading forces from Asia: Sakas, Kushans who propagated Mahayanna Buddhism and Parthians. Persians again made their appearance when the Sassanids ruled Afghanistan for about two centuries.

The Ephthalites or White Huns broke out on the stage about 425 AD and carved their name on history with the sword, but little else remains for posterity. The Sassamids ruled again until they were eclipsed by Islam.

The Ghaznavid empire, Mamluk Turks, began in 962 AD and Mahmoud of Ghazni made expeditions to the Indus and the Ganges, among many others, and took the Islamic faith to Kashmir. He sacked the Temple of Shiva at Somnath in Gujarat.

Ghazni became a centre of learning and art, but in its turn it was sacked and burnt by King Alaudin of Ghor (the world burner) in 1152. Ghorids were really Tajiks, the Ghorid Dynasty being founded in 1186: they ruled northern India from Delhi. Moslem dynasties were extended to much of northern India and they also penetrated far into the Deccan.

A savage interlude occurred in 1220 with the murderous onslaught of the Mongols under Genghis Khan, until the rise of Hitler and the Nazis, the greatest catastrophe to befall mankind. In Afghanistan they plundered cities, massacred the inhabitants and ravaged the land. Bactria, which had been a prosperous territory, never fully recovered. 'There is no greater joy than to kill one's enemies and take from them everything they had', said Genghis Khan. One method of killing prisoners was to crush them to death under boards laid over them as they lay trussed on the ground while the Mongols danced, feasted and sang on the boards above them. The Mongols halted at the Indus, as Genghis feared the heat of the Indian plains on his horsemen, one of the most fearsome and disciplined fighting machines the world has seen; to drop a bow on parade meant instant death.

Tamberlaine or Timur was a Barlas Turk with his capital at Samarkand. He was another scourge from central Asia and carved out an empire the size of Australia, founding the Timurid dynasty with his capital at Harat which became a centre of art and commerce. Although he invaded India in 1398 and sacked Delhi, leaving massacre and desolation, he did not conquer the sub-continent and his sprawling state split up into squabbling principalities.

In 1504 Babur, a Barlas Turk and a descendant of Genghis Khan with a few followers, set out on a journey which was to end in the conquest of India and the establishment of the Moghul dynasty. His most decisive battle was fought at Panipat in 1525. By the brilliant tactical employment of 12,000 cavalry and the new Turkish artillery, he defeated the sultan, Ibrahim Lodi, routing his army of 100,000 with 100 elephants. Before he died in 1530 he had established his capital at Agra and extended his kingdom over northern India to Bengal. Besides being a military commander of genius, he was also an engaging personality with an eye for beauty, a Turkish poet of considerable gifts and a diarist. His memoirs *Babur Nameh* have become a world classic. His grandson, Akbar, 1556–1605, was the greatest of the Moghul emperors; he subdued most of India, and created an administrative system which was to survive for two centuries, indeed not a little of this was to be adopted by the British. But after centuries of invasion from the Asian land mass, the Europeans started to arrive by sea and a yet greater empire was to rise up.

Portuguese seamen, trained and inspired by Henry the Navigator, crept down the west coast of Africa and Bartolomeo Diaz discovered the Cape of Good Hope in 1486. Vasco da Gama sailed round the Cape in 1487 and blazed the sea route to India.

By virtue of the Papal Bull of 1493 the Portuguese enjoyed a monopoly of trade to India. All undiscovered countries east of a line drawn through the Cape Verde Islands were assigned to Portugal and all countries to the west of this line to Spain. Throughout Catholic Europe any pronouncement by the Pope on political issues was regarded as the highest expression of international law. Not for 100 years did the Protestant nations feel strong enough to challenge the Latin monopoly of trade and exploration.

In the meantime they tried fruitlessly to find the north-west passage to India and also the north-east passage, which were not covered by the papal Bull. Finally they rebelled against the spiritual and temporal power of the Pope. The forcible annexation of Portugal by Spain in 1580 led to a declaration of war on Spain by England, who had been on friendly terms with the Portuguese since the Treaty of Westminster 1386, as also had the united Netherlands.

In 1579 Sir Francis Drake sailed round the world and visited the Moluccas or Spice Islands. Thenceforth both England and Holland made a simultaneous assault on the Spanish-controlled Portuguese monopoly, and then fought each other.

Queen Elizabeth had already declared to the Spanish ambassador in 1580 that 'the ocean was free to all, for as much as neither nature nor regard for public use do permit the exclusive use thereof', when the East India Company was incorporated on the last day of 1600 with twenty-one subscribers and exclusive trade with India for fifteen years. It was in the East Indies – Java-Sumatra and the Moluccas – the first vessels made a landfall. They had left London eighteen months before after a hazardous voyage – one of the five vessels had had to be abandoned, her crew decimated by scurvy. The Dutch, who were well-established, proved formidable competitors and the English perforce fortuitously turned their attention to India. The first vessel called at Surat in 1608 and Captain Hawkins stepped ashore in the face of much hostility from the Portuguese who controlled the port; although they did their best to murder him, he finally managed to hire a large retinue and travelled to Agra to visit the court of the Moghul Emperor, Jahangir, son of Akhbar. Hawkins presented the Emperor with a letter from King James I and remained at the court for many months trying to get an agreement on trade and to open a factory, really a warehouse at Surat. However, the Emperor cared nothing for trade and, as a Moghul Emperor, considered himself above agreements which he would break anyway. Furthermore he was an alcoholic and a slave to opium. He was cruel and controlled his court with the lash. Hawkins however, as a bluff, hard-drinking seaman, appealed to him and he became a great favourite at court, being given command of 400 horse in the cavalry at a huge salary. Jahangir insisted that Hawkins marry, and produced an Armenian girl to whom Hawkins was 'married' by his servant Nicholas, the marriage later legalized by a chaplain at Surat. In the end Hawkins accomplished very little but at least he had opened the channel of communication with the Emperor and had shown the Portuguese that the English could go ashore if they wanted to.

It was not until 1612 that the East India Company obtained permission to build a factory at Surat. In the early days the Company possessed little knowledge of the East, and received no help from the state; it relied on individual effort – a group of subscribers dispatched a vessel to India and on its return wound up the venture and realized the profits from pepper and spices such as cloves, nutmeg, cinnamon and ginger, then of great importance for partial preservation of food, exchanged in part for English goods and, in the early days for loot from Portuguese and Spanish ships. There was little inkling then that the activities of these merchant adventurers would lead to the burgeoning of the brightest jewel in the British crown. During the next 300 years the East India Company gradually annexed and conquered the subcontinent.

Development of British power through the East India Company was not a conscious thrust of deliberate aggrandisement and expansion; it followed a varied and changing pattern of trade – aggression, diplomacy, defence and opportunism, all played a part. The EIC became, in effect, the British Government in India with its own army. The impetus of trade and with it the expectation of profits was the motivating force behind the Company's policy – peaceful expansion if possible, but if obstacles were in the way, or if other nations or peoples became aggressive and attacked the Company's forts or installations then, depending often on who was directing the Company's fortunes on the ground, force would be applied and sometimes more than required. The Court of Directors was, in general, opposed to military adventures as these cost a lot of money, but they were often, willy-nilly, led into them by ambitious and aggressive commanders over whom they could exercise little control due to the very long and poor communications.

The arrival in 1615 of Sir Thomas Roe, paid by the EIC as Ambassador to the Court of Jehangir, was a fitting prelude to the Imperial pageant that was to follow. He was a big man with a powerful personality and held a fiat from King James I to conduct full negotiations, carrying a message seeking 'quiet trade and commerce without any kind of hindrance or molestation', at the same time drawing attention to the strength of English Naval Power. When he was brought before Jehangir he declined to touch the ground with his head, saying he had not come as a servant. He did much to foster good relations, was instrumental in improving conditions for the Company's staff at Surat and Agra, and established the right of the Company to trade permanently. His parting words were 'my sincerity toward you in all my actions is without spot; my neglect of private gain is without example, and my frugality beyond your expectation'; a rather pompous and self-righteous opinion of himself but, perhaps, justified by his achievements at a difficult time. He had negotiated a firm base for the Company's future operations, had advocated trade and not war and, after he left in 1619, the Company remained peaceful and mercantile for seventy years. There were few such exemplary servants of the Company in the years to come.

During the seventeenth century Portuguese possessions in the East were gradually whittled away mainly by the Dutch. The British also had a hand but Portugal's independence from Spain in 1640 reduced English hostility and recalled the old tradition of friendship based on the Treaty of 1386. Charles II married Catherine of Braganza in 1661 and Bombay was acquired as part of her dowry

The Viceroy of Goa remarked prophetically, 'India will be lost on the same day on which the English nation is settled in Bombay'. Indeed, less than ten years later Bombay was styled a Colony and twenty single women of 'sober and civil lives' were sent from England on a year's engagement and provided with one suit of wearing apparel, presumably to cheer up the male employees. Unfortunately we hear later that some of these women 'are grown scandalous to our nation, religion and government'.

In 1640 the Company procured a narrow strip of land on the Coromandel Coast where they built a fortified factory which was named Fort St George, around which grew up the great city of Madras.

The policy of the Court of Directors in London was peaceful expansion. For most of the seventeenth century this was the case. Two of the Company's great bases had been procured peacefully, but they were narrow strips of land set on the coast of an oriental country teeming with dark forces. They served the purpose, for the time being, of the London Trading Company whose subscribers were looking for profits from the long sea voyages of the Company's ships which, even if they survived storms and battles with the Dutch and Portuguese, took two years for the round trip. Cromwell gave the Company a Charter in 1657 and it received Royal patronage. In this period it became a joint Stock Company and was empowered to raise its own troops for defence of its forts and trading posts. All ships were manned but the Royal Navy Sea Power provided the shield for the development of trade and the flag which it followed.

The steaming delta of the mighty Ganges and Brahmaputra Rivers in Bengal was the unlikely location for the establishment of the next major trading post. This was set up at Kalikata by Job Charnock, the English agent at Hughli, with the agreement of the Moghul Emperor, Aurangzeb, who had previously opposed the idea, but became suitably impressed by English Sea Power which kept the pilgrim routes open to Mecca across the Arabian Sea.

With a new Charter from James II the Company felt itself 'in the condition of a sovereign state in India' and this moved the directors to send their prophetic Dispatch (1697) 'to establish such a polity of civil and military power and create and secure such a large revenue . . . as may be the foundation of a large, well-grounded sure English Dominion in India for all time to come'.

In 1699 the trading post at Kalikata, now named Fort William, became the Company's third Presidency and from a collection of huts in a malarial swamp it grew into a vast city of 3,500,000 – Calcutta, the capital of India until 1910.

In England the Company had its opponents who inveighed against the 'unjust and wicked war with the Great Moghul'. No doubt there was some jealousy as the Company had a virtual monopoly of trade with the East.

The Moghuls had extended their power over most of India and Aurangzeb, the last great Emperor, had even subdued the Deccan, the home of Marathas. However Aurangzeb died in 1707 and this marked the beginning of the decline of the Moghul Empire.

The Maratha armies were already on the march under their great leader, Sivaji. These hardy peasants and mountaineers from the Ghats travelled light, were well disciplined and formed the infantry and swift-moving cavalry of the great Hindu Confederacy which attacked the Moghul Empire to the north, and in 1740 burst into the Carnatic and slew the Nawab Dost Ali in battle. Had the

Company not concluded a Treaty with the Marathas in 1739 allowing free trade throughout their dominions, their position at Fort St George might have been difficult.

Now arose a new and far greater threat to the position of the British in India. The 'Compagnie des Indes Orientales' had been founded in 1664; the French were late on the scene. Pondicherry was one of the first settlements. The progress and development of the Company's policy in many cases was left to the men on the spot who often led it into adventures disapproved at home, as in the case of the EIC. Two such men were Dupleix and Clive.

Dupleix launched a campaign against the Marathas and as a result gained control of the whole of the Deccan. He then carried the war into the Carnatic against the English settlements. Madras was captured in 1746 but returned to the English by the Treaty of Aix la Chappelle, which terminated the war of the Austrian Succession in 1748.

Robert Clive, destined to be one of the greatest figures in British Indian history, then a young clerk in the East India Company's Fort St David, stepped on the stage in time for the next round against the French. He was of a melancholic disposition: bored counting bales and adding up invoices, depressed by the climate and monotony, he tried to shoot himself but each time the pistol failed to fire. He concluded that he must be reserved for a special purpose, joined the military branch of the Company's service and set about laying the foundations of British power in India.

Under Major 'Stringer' Lawrence, considered the founder of the Indian Army, Clive received valuable guidance in military affairs, and the pupil soon outstripped his master. The French had pressed forward into the Carnatic again and Trichinopoly was besieged. Clive, with 200 English soldiers and 300 Sepoys, seized the fort at Arcot, the political capital of the Carnatic, in 1751. This obliged the French to withdraw a considerable force from Trichinopoly to attempt recapture. The siege of Arcot lasted fifty days and was the rock upon which French influence in the Carnatic foundered.

In 1756 the Seven Years War broke out and, as always, the fighting between the British and French in Europe was reproduced in India. Clive was now, at the age of thirty-one, Governor of Fort St David, and so that he could command both Royal and Company troops, was commissioned as a lieutenant colonel in the Army. The capture of Calcutta by the Nawab Siraj ud-Daula and the infamous 'Black Hole' obliged the Company to order Clive to recapture Calcutta – nothing more. He sailed with a fleet of twelve ships under Vice-Admiral Watson, and command of the sea ensured that they sailed unmolested up the Ganges Delta. Calcutta fell on 2 January 1757.

Fearful that the French would attack in the Carnatic, the Directors ordered Clive back to Madras. He refused, arguing that Madras could look after itself with the resources available; on the other hand, as he pointed out, there was a serious risk of French intervention in Bengal, with the probability that Calcutta would be recaptured if his forces were to leave.

The letter took a year to reach London. In the meantime Clive got on with Empire building. With Watson, he took Chandanagar, the main French station in Bengal, and fought the Battle of Plassey.

The battle was won by a combination of intrigue, daring and luck. Mir Jaffa, an uncle of the Nawab, and a general in his army, was anxious to snatch his nephew's position, in return for 1764, a hard fought battle which resulted in a decisive victory for the Company's forces. Baxar is considered by some to be the real origin of British power in India. For the first time in the history of the long rule of the Moghuls the once great Emperor made submission to a foe who was soon to supplant him.

What had been a small trading company now controlled Bengal, Bihar, Orissa and Oudh. Clive reorganized the Company's army in Bengal, splitting it into three brigades with the most up-to-date military equipment. 'John Company' was now the most formidable military power in the East. Clive left for home in 1767, broken in health; in spite of his faults, the real founder of British power in India.

Warren Hastings became Governor General of Bengal, Madras and the Bombay Presidencies. He was one of the greatest administrators in British Indian history, and laid the foundations of the Civil Service; he was also – a fact not always recognized – a great war leader. The Court of Directors again stated limits of expansion, but was really powerless to have much influence on affairs six months and 6,000 miles away. The Marathas had spread over most of North India and occupied a large part of the former Moghul Empire – a puppet Emperor sat on the throne at Allahabad. In 1773 they invaded Rohilkand (the home of the Rohillas) and Hastings sent a force to join the Nawab of Oudh in throwing them out, in fulfilment of a Treaty whereby the Rohillas were to pay a sum of forty lakhs in such an event; payment was evaded and the Nawab of Oudh understandably took exception and requested a British brigade to help chastise and conquer the Rohillas; a penalty for their breach of the Treaty. Hastings reluctantly agreed, a brigade was sent and Rohilkand was overrun and incorporated in the territory of Oudh, thus virtually extending the Company's dominions to the foot of the Himalayas. Hastings did not lack for enemies and this action formed one of the main counts against him later in Parliament.

On the other side of the world, a war started which had a direct influence on events in India. The American Colonies were revolting; among other things they objected to the tax on tea from the East India Company and there ensued the Boston Tea Party when they threw chests of tea into the harbour – and so was born a great Republic's aversion to tea. The war with the Colonists started in

1777. They were joined by the French who, at the same time, took the opportunity to renew hostilities with the British in India, and urged the Marathas to continue harassing the British. The Marathas allied themselves with several native states notably Mysore, of which Haider Ali was the Nizam, and his hordes thundered down the valleys into the Carnatic, creating the utmost terror and confusion. Eyre Coote was sent by Hastings to deal with the Carnatic and his disciplined squares routed Haider Ali's army of 60,000 at the Battle of Porto Novo in 1781. French and British warships fought a number of naval actions off the coasts of the Coromandel and Ceylon in the years 1782–83. Hostilities were finally brought to an end by the Treaty of Mangalore in 1784.

Although Hastings' power as Governor General had seen the extension of Company territory and the demise of the powerful Maratha Confederacy, he was not an Empire builder in the mould of Clive and Wellesley. He saw that it would be possible to achieve the 'dominion of all India', but added, 'it is an event I never wish to see'. He treated the people of India with consideration and endeavoured to make all servants of the Company do the same.

Warren Hastings returned to England in 1785 and was impeached in 1788 – the trial lasted until 1795 when he was acquitted on all counts. There have been various explanations of this scandalous affair of the impeachment of a man of principle and high achievement; it perhaps stems from the bitter party politics of the time. The final judgement on him has to be left to the House of Commons where he was called in 1813 to give evidence once more in the place where he had suffered so long. When it was ended 'all the members by one simultaneous impulse, rose with their heads uncovered, and stood in silence till I passed the door of their chamber'.

In the latter half of the eighteenth century the feeling had been growing that the nation itself through Parliament, rather than through a private trading company, however powerful and wealthy, must ultimately be responsible for British rule in India. In 1784 Pitt forced through the India Act which practically made the East India Company a subordinate department of State.

The Trading Company was slowly creating the framework of the Raj. Lord Cornwallis arrived as Governor General in 1786 and organized the Company much on civil service lines. He laid the foundation of the present Indian Constitution. Still the men at home drew back from further conquest. 'To pursue schemes of conquest and extension of dominion in India are measures repugnant to the wish, the honour and policy of this nation.' So ran the declaration of Parliament made in Pitt's Act of 1784 and Cornwallis was anxious to concur with this. However, Tipu the Sultan of Mysore, who styled himself 'the Tiger' was making trouble and Cornwallis was obliged to act against him in 1792, resulting in a large accession of land to the Company.

Sir John Shore was the next notable man on the spot for the Company. He became Governor General of Bengal with authority over Madras and Bombay in 1793 and was memorable mainly for his continuation of the policy of neutrality with non-intervention in Indian affairs. He was probably lucky that no wars were forced upon him. The Marathas controlled the whole of central India and much of the North. The Moghul Emperor, Shah Allam, was under the protection at Delhi of Mahadji Sindhia, the greatest Maratha Chieftain, 'the nominal slave, but his right master'. The unfortunate Shah Allam had been imprisoned and blinded by a savage Rohilla Chief when Sindhia had temporarily lost his hold on Delhi in 1788. Shore was very happy to go on mulling over revenues, playing cricket and translating Persian classics into English. 'I could form alliances that would shake the Maratha Empire to its very foundations. I will rather trust to the permanence of our dominions to a perseverance in true principles.' The Directors had a well-trained and docile dog. They were not long to be left with this comfortable state of affairs.

Richard Wellesley, Earl of Mornington, arrived as Governor General in 1798; his brother Arthur, later the Duke of Wellington, had arrived shortly before to take command of the 33rd Foot at Madras; a forceful combination ensuring a good deal of aggressive action which was to change the face of India.

Wellesley saw that Great Britain could no longer play anything but a prominent part in India. In 1799 Tipu, the 'Tiger' of Mysore who hated the English, and had plotted with the French, was defeated and his country divided between the Company and the Nizam of Hyderabad. There followed the Maratha Wars stemming from the Treaty of Bassein in 1802 between the Peshwa (Prime Minister) of the Confederacy and the British, and objected to by Sindhia and Holkar, two powerful Maratha Chieftains, on the ground that it was an open surrender of independence, as indeed it was, allowing for the permanent stationing of the Company's troops at Poona and control of foreign policy inter alia; a hard bargain struck between a cornered Peshwa and Richard Wellesley. The Maratha states were essentially predatory, but they were very tough well-organized fighters, and they assembled an army of 250,000, besides 40,000 troops organized into brigades and trained and disciplined by Frenchmen. Arthur Wellesley in the Deccan and General Lake in the north, conducted a brilliant campaign and with no more than 55,000 troops between them defeated the Maratha armies in less than two years – Assaye being the most notable battle.

The Maratha States were brought under British control, dependant ruler-ships such as Surat and the Carnatic were absorbed, and general control was secured over all the native states from Cape Cormorin to the Sutlej. The territorial dominions of the East India Company had been widely extended while the directors were wringing their hands in despair. The frontier of British India had been carried to the upper reaches of the Jumna, which flowed out of the foothills of the Himalayas.

It was time to give some specialized training for the Company's Civil Service and for the Army which now numbered well over a quarter of a million. Haileybury College was opened in 1806 and trained a number of fine administrators for the Company's Indian Empire. Addiscombe near Croydon was opened in 1809 to train young men for the military service, and included such famous graduates as Field Marshal Earl Roberts of Kandahar and Field Marshal Earl Napier.

The Company was becoming financially stretched and the directors were relieved to have a period of peace after Wellesley's expansionist policy – commerce and not military adventures. Lord Cornwallis, now sixty-six, was sent out again to straighten things out. He handed back to astonished Maratha Chiefs much of the territory taken under Wellesley. Anarchy followed but no more than there had been before in the non-British controlled territories.

In 1807 Lord Minto was appointed Governor General and at first followed a policy of non-aggression. He believed that 'good government of the people is the great end' and warned the directors, 'Your rule is alien and can never be popular'. He recognized that the duration of British rule would be limited, and foresaw that when we had unified the diverse and fragmented peoples and states of India under one government then we would depart, as he put it 'leaving the natives so far improved from their connection with us as to be capable of maintaining a free, or at least, a regular government amongst themselves'.

Napoleon, however, was at the height of his power and, as always, French military moves in Europe were reflected by similar activity in India. Minto feared that the French might invade India either through Persia or Afghanistan. He dispatched three able men on diplomatic missions to create buffer states in the north-west; Malcolm to Persia, Mountstuart Elphinstone to Afghanistan and Metcalfe to the Punjab. The Shah of Persia agreed to dismiss the French Ambassador and resist the passage of European troops in return for money and assistance. Elphinstone met Shah Shuja, the Afghan King, in Peshawar and he also agreed to resist the passage of French troops. Charles Metcalfe had the most difficult task. He was an old Etonian of only twenty-five years, but he was also an intellectual who translated Rousseau and read Lucan, Homer and Juvenal, among others, for relaxation and kept a diary noting down thoughts on self love, duty, and sin and suffering. This complex, introspective young man was pitted against the wily and unscrupulous Sikh leader Ranjit Singh, Maharajah of Lahore, the Ruler of the Punjab, a hard-drinking, shrewd barbarian whose political acumen, nevertheless, led him never to quarrel with the English and to tolerate Muslims, of whom there were many in the Punjab, who therefore fought for him. This unpromising confrontation produced the Treaty of Amritsar, in 1809, which guaranteed the territorial limits of the Punjab, provided Ranjit Singh did not encroach on

Company territory east of the Sutlej, in return for an alliance against the French.

The Earl of Moira (later Marquess of Hastings) was sent out as Governor General in 1814 and instructed to keep the peace; but he was a soldier – besides, extreme provocation came from two main sources.

Usually there was a threat from the north. From the fastnesses of Nepal some extremely tough little fighting men, Gurkhas, descended onto the plains and occupied territory claimed by the East India Company in 1814. After some very hard fighting Kathmandu was occupied and the Treaty of Sagauli was concluded with the Gurkhas in 1816. Some Nepalese provinces were surrendered and Simla was acquired as the future hot weather capital. Ever since the Gurkhas have been proud to be recruited into the Indian Army, and have proved themselves to be among the finest soldiers anywhere.

Soon after this, the Pindaris burst upon central India, torturing, burning and looting. They were the remnants of the Maratha armies, but embraced many desperate men including a number of Pathans. Hastings gathered a very large army to oppose them, since war with them involved fighting the Marathas to whose lands they retreated, and the hunt for the Pindaris became merged in the Third Maratha War. The Treaty of Poona, June 1817, almost marked the end of the Maratha power in India.

Faint rumblings foreshadowing the Mutiny, still a quarter of a century in the future, occurred in 1824 when there was a Sepoy Mutiny at Barrackpore near Calcutta. The causes need not be dwelt on here; it is sufficient to say that the values and relationships of the old army were passing. Loyalty, fidelity and courage between British officers and Indian men had created a special relationship, helping to forge an Indian Army which had conquered an Empire. A new type of British officer, stemming from the Wellesleys' elitist philosophy, self-confident and often arrogant, refused to hear complaints put to them respectfully by their men. A breakdown of trust and respect was beginning to permeate the EIC's army, now the biggest in the world.

Lord Amherst arrived as Governor General in 1823 and was greeted with the usual pomp in Calcutta. It was the greatest event in Anglo-Indian Society, crowds lined the banks of the river, guns pounding out salutes, troops drawn up on the bank with members of the Council lined up to receive the new Ruler of the EIC's empire and his lady. It was often a great surprise to newcomers. 'Surprised we were,' wrote Lady Amherst, 'at the well-fashioned dress and manners of the ladies'.

The new Governor General had ambitions to being another Wellesley but he was not in the same mould. He got embroiled in a stormy interlude in Burma, on which he declared war in 1823 following Burmese infringements of British Indian territory. The Peace Treaty gave us Assam, Arakan and Tenasserim.

The directors viewed this with icy reserve because the war had cost £13,000,000.

The next Governor General, Lord Bentinck, was far more to their liking. The son of a Whig Prime Minister and former Governor of Madras, he was told that he must economize. A real Liberal, he espoused the philosophy of utilitarianism and during his nine years in office it could certainly be said that he tried to achieve the greatest good for the greatest number of people. He was the first Governor General openly to act on the theory that the welfare of subject people was a main, perhaps primary, duty of the British in India.

He made economies in the civil and military services. He enlarged the jurisdiction of native judges and increased their salaries, and he carried out a number of social reforms such as abolishing Sati or Suttee, the immolation of widows on the funeral pyres of their husbands, and the breaking up of the Thugs who went about the country strangling and robbing peaceful travellers.

Bentinck scrupulously upheld the policy of non-intervention pressed on him by the directors. His only annexations of Indian territory followed from his hatred of maladministration and corruption; in particular the Raja of Mysore, who had been set up by Wellesley on the understanding that he would govern well, was deposed when this did not happen, and his country was then administered by British officials.

In 1835 on the eve of his departure, he pronounced the Russian advance to the Indian frontier as the greatest danger to which our Empire in the East had been exposed. It is time now to turn to Afghanistan and the north-west approaches to India.

Russia's sphere of influence had been drawing nearer over the previous 200 years, and the focus of political interest in India was to shift to the North-West Frontier. 'The Great Game' was about to begin, and for the next 100 years Britain was to be preoccupied with this wild frontier region and the untamed tribes who lived there – the Pathans. 'This prickly and untrimmed hedge,' as Sir Olaf Caroe put it.

This period is prefaced by the unsuitable appointment of Lord Auckland as Governor General in 1836. He was an amiable Whig MP who had held cabinet office in Whig administration since 1810 but this did not qualify him to rule India of which he was quite innocent and, furthermore, he was bored in his appointment, although he arrived with good intentions. He was enjoined by the British Government to do all he could to counter Russian pressure from the north-west. The Russian Bear had been casting his shadow ever further over Central Asia.

Afghanistan became part of the Moghul Empire in the early sixteenth century following Babur's invasion. Two hundred years later Moghul power was beginning to wane. In 1739 Nadir Shah, ruler of Persia, led his army into India and sacked Delhi, massacring the inhabitants. In 1747 Nadir's Persian officers, sick of his barbarities, murdered him on a hunting trip. One Ahmed Shah, a member of the Abduli clan, had been chief of Nadir's Pathan bodyguard. He now stepped into the power vacuum and was elected King of Afghanistan, assuming the name of Durr-i-Durran or Pearl of Pearls, whence the Abdali clan became known as Durrani and the state of Afghanistan was born.

In 1773 Ahmed Shah died, having failed to nominate one of his twenty-three sons as his heir. As a result there was the customary Central Asian scramble for power, and anarchy reigned for some years. One of the sons, Zaman Shah, seized the throne in Kabul then imprisoned and starved all the other brothers until they acknowledged him. One brother, Mahmud, escaped to Herat, he then had Zaman seized and blinded. A power struggle ensued between him and another brother, Shuja ul Mulk, and resulted in the latter gaining the throne between 1803 and 1819, but he proved unpopular and was driven out, taking refuge with Ranjit Singh in the Punjab, and Mahmud was restored to the throne with the powerful support of Fateh Khan, chief of the Barakzai. The latter was incurring the jealousy of Kamran, Mahmud's son and Governor of Herat. In 1818 Fateh Khan saved Herat from capture by the Persian army, but Kamran refused him money to pay his victorious troops. Fateh was furious and sent Dost Mohammed, his young brother, to take what was necessary from the Palace; he unwisely divested a young woman of her clothing in Kamran's harem, and removed a jewelled girdle from her person. She turned out to be a sister of Kamran who saw his opportunity to remove Fateh, wreaking at the same time, with his father's agreement, a vile and sadistic vengeance – Fateh was seized then he was blinded, scalped, flayed and finally had his limbs amputated.

In the face of such hideous cruelty the Barakzais rose and drove out the Durranis. Mahmoud and Kamran fled and, after some more years of turmoil and plotting and feuding, Dost Mohammed, the most able of the brothers of Fateh Khan, gained the throne.

Lord Auckland had no particular wish to get embroiled in Afghan politics. It seems he was propelled into a situation in which he felt himself bound to act. The motivating force was Palmerstonian gunboat diplomacy, encouraged by his advisers, in particular Sir William Macnaughten, Chief Secretary to the government, who knew nothing of Afghanistan.

Auckland's policy hinged on his unreasoning distrust of the Amir Dost Mohammed and this led inexorably to the folly and frightful carnage of the first Afghan War. He had sent a Scottish traveller and diplomat, Alexander Burnes, to Kabul with a commercial brief. Burnes reported favourably on Dost Mohammed whom he said, wanted an English Alliance in preference to a Russian. Some wise advice was no doubt also passed on by Josiah Harlan, a remarkable American soldier of fortune who had lived as a native, in fact disguised as a dervish, among the ordinary people, and was then a general in Dost

Mohammed's army. Harlan was well aware that his master had no intention of dealing with the Russians and was very disturbed by the British attitude.

Three main factors alarmed Auckland and Macnaughten; the attack on Herat by the Russian trained army, the reception of Vitkevich, the Russian envoy, by Dost Mohammed and the latter's request for support against the Sikhs to re-capture Peshawar. Auckland now resolved, with the help of Ranjit Singh, to place Shah Shuja on the Afghan throne. In a word, a previously unpopular monarch was now to be put back on the throne of a fanatical Muslim country by a Hindu people, part of whose country the Afghans laid claim to. In the event the Sikhs backed out, the Persians retreated and Vitkevich returned to St Petersburg where he shot himself – the danger from Russian intrigues passed away.

The invasion policy was morally unjustifiable, politically inexpedient and was condemned by all whose judgement counted.

In December 1838 the Army of the Indus marched, with a vast number of camels, camp followers, servants and baggage; it was doomed to destruction. The doubtful objective of placing Shah Shuja on the throne was gained and Dost Mohammed fled. The army occupied Kabul and for a short while all seemed quiet, then things deteriorated. Burnes and Macnaughten were murdered. The British garrison, having given up the Bala Hissar (the main fortress) to Shah Shuja and his harem, were placed in a vulnerable position on the plain where, cut off from their stores, they were harried by the Afghans, added to which they were led by the elderly and ailing General Elphinstone who was unable to take effective command. Eventually the order was given to retreat to the Khyber in mid-winter of January 1842. In less than a week the entire force of 700 Europeans, mainly H.M. 44th Foot and Horse Artillery, 3,800 Indian sepoys and sowars, with 12,000 half-starved, frozen and terrified followers had been cut to pieces by the tribes and annihilated – except for General Elphinstone and a few others taken prisoner. There was one survivor, Dr Brydon, who rode, half dead, into Jelalabad on 13 January 1842.

Thus ended the First Afghan War, the worst disaster to befall British arms in the Far East until almost exactly 100 years later when Singapore fell. The Duke of Wellington had prophetically declared that the crossing of the Indus would be 'a perennial march into that country'. For the next century Afghanistan and the North-West Frontier proved to be an Imperial Migraine.

Dost Mohammed was restored to the throne of Afghanistan in 1842. 'I do not understand,' he said. He justified Burnes' assessment of him and proved himself in the next twenty years a loyal friend of Britain.

Much was now stirring across the frontier in the sub-continent. Sind was conquered by a Company Force commanded by General Charles Napier, an eccentric and aggressive man, who believed that the benefits of westernization outweighed all else, but nevertheless sent his famous signal, 'Peccavi' (I have sinned).

In 1839 Ranjit Singh died and for the next decade the Punjab was torn with strife. The Kingdom of the Sikhs, the wide, dusty expanse of plain stretching between the Himalayas, the Sutlej and the Indus, became the scene of revolution, assassination and murder. The Khalsa, the Sikh Army, emerged as the real power in the land, and without the restraining hand of Ranjit they marched across the Sutlej into Company territory in 1846, but they were defeated after hard fighting against some of the toughest soldiers the Company's army had fought. Sir Henry Lawrence was appointed Resident in Lahore and there followed a benevolent regime exemplified by Herbert Edwardes' handling of Bannu, a high mountain region ceded to the Sikhs by the Afghans; previously unruly and harshly treated by the Sikhs, the Bannuchis did not understand an army that did not plunder. Edwardes pacified them by talking to the leaders, and worked a miracle; they dismantled their forts, agreed to pay a reduced rate of revenue and accepted a legal code which Edwardes wrote and turned into Persian. All this was too much for the Sikh dissident barons who mistrusted the leniency shown by conquerors, treating it as weakness – two British political officers were murdered and the army rose.

There was again some hard fighting in the Second Sikh War, in the course of which the British Indian Army suffered a severe reverse at Chillianwallah on 13 January 1849. However, at the Battle of Gujerat in February the Sikh Army was put to flight, and the remnant of the Khalsa laid down their arms on 12 March. This time the Punjab was annexed by Lord Dalhousie, the new, young and energetic Governor General.

The 'doctrine of lapse' first applied in 1834, was vigorously reactivated by Dalhousie. Briefly it stated that in dependent states of those that owed their existence to British power, the sovereignty, when the natural heirs of the Royal line came to an end, passed back or lapsed to the supreme power. In this way seven native states were annexed. Other principles related to Oudh, a large Muslim State astride the Ganges and Jumna bordering on Nepal, where the inhabitants were misgoverned and the King given over to debauchery. The annexation was made in 1856 with a generous pension settled on the deposed King.

British India was now about to experience a great watershed in its history – a cataclysm nobody foresaw. The Indian Mutiny has been seen both as a popular national uprising and a military rebellion; it may have been somewhere between the two, yet only the Bengal Army was involved. Its causes are obscure, and there is no room here to dwell at much length on them, but a few thoughts can be noted down.

A feeling had been growing up among Indians that we had been trying to alter their customs and change their traditional way of life. The railways, the telegraph and other manifestations of western science were opposed to the teaching of the Brahmans. Hindu customs and mythology were being eroded by western materialism. Christianity as preached by the missionaries of the time had become dogmatic and intolerant. Some colonels ruled their regiments with a sword in one hand and a bible in the other. Sepoys felt that their religion was threatened, particularly in the Bengal Army which contained a large number of high caste men, Brahmans and Rajputs, in its ranks. In the early days Englishmen remained in India for long periods, mostly without their womenfolk, and tended to adopt native customs and marry Indian women. As a result, perhaps, there was mutual respect between officers and men in the Company Army. In the nineteenth century communications were faster, more young Englishwomen came to India, officers became increasingly aloof from their men, adopting the elitist and arrogant attitude mentioned earlier, and there was a consequent breakdown of trust between officers and men. The General Service Act of 1856 which made all ranks liable for service overseas, with its implications for caste taboos, added some fuel to the smouldering fire.

'To describe the revolt as a national war for freedom and independence waged by a populace under a sense of injustice and aggression is nothing short of a travesty of history.' This was written, not by a chauvinistic Imperialist, but by an Indian historian, Rustom Pestoni Masani. The East India Company had become smug about the European way of life and had tried to change Indian Society. Dalhousie's annexations had also changed the face of the land with unseemly haste, and alarmed many Indians.

The spark which set off the Mutiny was the notorious affair of the greased cartridges. The Indian Army was being issued with the new Enfield rifle and this required cartridges which were to be greased with animal fats that were exceedingly offensive both to Hindus and to Muslims, particularly as they would be required to bite open the ends of the cartridges before loading, so that the Hindu would taste the fat of the unclean pig. The order was changed, but it was too late.

The Revolt began at Meerut on 10 May 1857, when three native regiments rose on a Sunday evening, shot down their officers, released their comrades from the prison and marched off to Delhi. No action was taken to catch the mutineers and this was seen as a sign that the British had weakened and had been cowed by the hand of heaven. Soon all the British officers in Delhi had been murdered, the magazine went up with the brave defenders and not a man, woman nor child of European origin remained alive in the city. The whole of the Central Provinces went up in flames, the main centres of revolt were Lucknow, Cawnpore and Agra – in which troops of the Bengal Army were stationed.

It was seen as essential to take Delhi, the old Moghul capital and the most important city of India, where the old Emperor, in name only, still sat. The Governor General, Lord Canning, agreed with Sir John Lawrence, now Chief

Commissioner of the Punjab, that troops should be sent from the Punjab, at some risk – for three reasons. It could tempt Afghan aggression, the Sikhs could have risen, and there was the possibility of disaffection in Sepoy regiments. None of this happened and John Nicholson, one of the giants of the Frontier, led a column that stormed and captured Delhi; Nicholson was mortally wounded. While he lay dying, his faithful Sepoys, Pathans, Multani Horse and other ruffians, stood round him with tears in their eyes. This was the beginning of the end of the mutineers in other centres and the Mutiny was finally quelled in June 1858. One of the biggest factors in the success of the operations was the loyalty of Dost Mohammed who had signed a treaty recognizing the Company's trans-Indus provinces, mainly concerning Peshawar; long a bone of contention. Lord Roberts wrote afterwards, 'Had the Amir taken advantage of the Company's peril, I do not see how that part of the country north of Bengal could have been saved'.

The Mutiny was a nightmare from which British India took many years to recover. There had been terrible savagery on both sides, but also great heroism, self-sacrifice and acts of kindness. A number of native regiments stood firm and helped to quell the mutiny. The Madras and Bombay armies were hardly affected.

The detractors of 'John Company' now had their way and the Mutiny was reason enough to bring to an end the East India Company, the largest company the world has ever seen, and transfer the government of India from the Company to the Crown by the India Act of 1858.

On 1 September 1858, the last day of their authority, the Court of Directors of the Honourable East India Company held their final meeting at East India House, Leadenhall Street. In their statement of farewell ran the passage:

'. . . Let Her Majesty's Government appreciate the gift . . . let her take the vast country and teeming millions of India under direct control; but let her not forget the great corporation from which she received them.'

'All...to be mine,' the Queen remarked with satisfaction; nevertheless she had rejected the first draft of the proclamation, requesting that it should 'breathe the feelings of generosity, benevolence and religious toleration'. In its final form the proclamation ended with a promise of measures for the material and moral improvement of the Indian peoples in whose 'prosperity will be our strength, in their contentment our security, and in their gratitude our best reward'.

On 1 November 1858 the new government was proclaimed at Allahabad by Lord Canning who became the first Viceroy and Governor General for the Crown.

India was now under one government for the first time in her history: Indian princes still retained their independence and their inheritance was secure because the 'Doctrine of Lapse' was discontinued. After much bloodshed and fighting many benefits had come to the population: sati, thuggery and corruption had been much reduced. A period of stable government gave the opportunity for building railways, roads and canals.

The tide of Imperialism had washed the frontiers of British India up to the grim bastion of the Khyber Pass, and we must now return to this wild area and watch 'The Great Game' unfolding across the wastes of Central Asia.

Perhaps the modern history of the North-West Frontier could be said to have begun in the time of Napoleon when he suggested in 1807 that he join forces with Russia against 'les possessions de la Compagnie des Indes'. A joint invasion via Constantinople, Asia Minor and Persia was favoured. Constantinople was a long cherished ambition of the Russians, bequeathed from Peter the Great. Napoleon, of course, was seen as the main threat. The frontiers of India and Russia were then about 4,000 miles apart.

At the beginning of the nineteenth century Russia began pushing her eastern boundaries forward into Siberia, the land of her former conquerors, the Tartars, and from 1836 into Central Asia. It was a logical expansion since the peoples of Central Asia shared the same land mass.

By the 1860s they had advanced to the Syr Daria and built a line of forts extending towards Tashkent.

In 1864 Prince Gortschakoff, the Russian Foreign Minister, issued his Dispatch, the first line of which ran: 'It has been judged indispensable that our two lines of frontier, one reaching from China to Lake Issyk Kul, the other from the Sea of Aral along the Syr Daria, should be united by fortified points, so that all our posts may be in a position mutually to support one another.' In the third article he goes on to stress the difficulties of annexation in these lands, and states: 'It is unnecessary for me to call attention to the evident interest Russia has in not extending her territory.'

Gortschakoff and the Russian Government apparently realized the difficulties of expansion in this area which contained the wild and cruel Uzbeks, Tajiks, Khirgiz and Khazak descendants of the hordes of Genghis Khan and Tamerlane. The Central Asian Khanates and the great cities of Khiva, Bokhara, Samarkand, Tashkent and Khokand had all fallen into anarchy since the dissolution of the Timurid Dynasty.

Added to this, the climatic and geographic conditions of this region, which contained the Kara Kum and Kizyl Kum deserts, were among the harshest in the world; searing heat and sand storms in the summer, screaming polar blizzards in the winter. The Russian General Mikhail Skobolev wrote that 'if known to Dante, the Central Asian roads would have served as a corridor to hell'.

In 1839, General Perovski, after careful preparation, marched his force of 5,000 men, 22 guns and 10,000 camels from Orenburg, intending to reach Khiva, a distance of 800 miles. He suffered serious losses in men and camels and had to turn back some 500 miles short of his goal.

In view of the above, there is some doubt whether the Great Game ever really involved the serious threat of a Russian invasion of India.

The Russian Government had a similar problem with their governors and generals in Central Asia, as had the East India Company with their governors and military commanders in India – they were on a long lead with poor communications. Ambitious and aggressive they gradually pushed the frontier forward. In 1865 General Tchernaeff took Tashkent and went on to seize Hodjent, an important crossing point on the Syr Darya, and further surrounding territory. On a series of pretexts and pin pricks, Russian territory, at the expense of Bokhara, was further extended by General Kaufman, Tchernaeff's successor and an unashamed expansionist; Samarkand was taken and a treaty forced on Bokhara. In 1867 the province of Russian Turkestan was set up with General Kaufman as Governor. Khiva fell at last in 1873.

The Russians had reached the Amu Darya (the ancient Oxus) and the British Foreign Office began to sit up and study the map. Only 400 miles now separated the Tsar's dominions from the North-West Frontier. The primary frontier of the British Empire – no formal treaty fixed the line – it possessed length but no breadth and never really presented a serious obstacle to invading hordes. The natural frontier of India was really the Hindu Kush.

At this time Sir John Lawrence was Viceroy and Governor General of India and he favoured the 'Close Border' policy, limiting the boundary of India to the Indus. He wanted no adventures in the un-administered tribal areas. In fact he had even suggested giving Peshawar to Afghanistan.

The expansion of Russia's eastern territories threw the political spotlight on Afghanistan and this mountainous and arid land assumed great importance as a buffer state between the two greatest imperial powers of the nineteenth century.

The frontier of British India had now advanced to the Khyber Pass and we soon discovered that Afghanistan could not be considered in isolation. The joker in the pack was the wild and rugged area around the Khyber inhabited by the Pathan tribes. They were fiercely independent and demanded to be left alone; neither Moghul, Durani nor Sikh had dared to enter their mountain fastnesses – and nor did the British, beyond punitive expeditions following raids. The tribesmen lived in a poor country, a stony and infertile land, and they frequently descended from the mountains to plunder and gain a little extra to *buy* a rifle or other necessities. They were paid a subsidy to stop raiding – 'blackmail payments' the British had inherited from the Sikhs.

The Amirs of Afghanistan often tried to gain suzerainty over the tribes but usually only by proxy through itinerant Mullahs. The Pathans were hard men in a hard school and lived by a strict code. This code was called Pakhtunwali of which Badal, or retaliation, was one of the three main maxims – blood feuds could go on for years. The second was Nanawatia, or obligation to grant protection to those in distress, murderers or whoever. The third was Malmastia, or hospitality – most villages had a guest house, and guests were inviolate while in the care of their hosts. Political officers used to make good use of this.

The riddle of the frontier was closely linked to the enigma of the Russian Bear prowling in the wastes of Central Asia, with a ruggedly independent and largely inscrutable Afghanistan lying in between; a political conundrum which exercised the best minds of successive Conservative and Liberal Governments at home.

Sir John Lawrence's 'Close Border' policy suited the Liberal Government of the time. He insisted that his Deputy Frontier Commissioners must show the solid advantages of British rule. The tribes were not disposed to admire good administration and, although it was not a bad exchange for the rope, knife and bullet of the Sikhs, they continued to enter the settled districts to trade and loot and sometimes to conduct 'jihad'. So we entered the tribal territories to burn villages and exact a fine. It was a 'butcher and bolt' policy.

Sher Ali, Dost Mohammed's son, came to the Afghan throne in 1863. He was much exercised by the Russian drive towards the Afghan border, and was especially apprehensive over the letters General Kaufman was in the habit of writing to him. He, therefore, requested from the British a firm commitment of aid, should Russia attack Afghanistan. This was not forthcoming. However, the period of masterly inactivity was coming to an end.

In 1874 Disraeli became Prime Minister and Lord Lytton was appointed Viceroy. The Russians continued to advance; in 1875 they annexed Khokand and renamed it Ferghana, bringing the Russian boundary up to Afghanistan. Sher Ali was disturbed and started to try to come to an accord with General Kaufman. This move was interpreted as a ruse to try to force concessions from Great Britain. Lytton wrote to the Amir in 1876 and announced that he was sending an envoy, Sir Louis Pelly, 'to discuss matters of common interest'. The proposal was turned down by the Amir and Lytton was furious, suspecting that the Amir was seeking an alliance with the Russians.

The stage was set for a replay of the events of four decades earlier, leading to the First Afghan War. It is easy, perhaps, to blame the hawkish attitude of Lytton and the Conservative Government for the way that events unfolded, but it must be remembered that the fear of Russian intentions in Central Asia at this time was very real. Captain Fred Burnaby of the Royal Horse Guards travelled across Russia to Khiva on a sledge in 1876, meeting many Russian officers on the way; he remarked on their longing for war and, in particular, a war with England about India.

In 1877 as a result of Turkish action in the Balkans, the Russians declared war on the Turks and, in January 1878, the Tsar's army stood before Istanbul. The British, alarmed, sent 5,000 Sepoys to guard the Suez Canal. The Russians countered by mobilizing an army in Russian Turkestan and sent a mission to Kabul headed by General Stolietoff.

A glance at the map will show the Hindu Kush spilling over into Chitral. Lord Lytton considered these mountains the real frontier of India and that effective control of their passes should be secured. For this reason, in 1876, the Mehtar of Chitral had been offered friendship, becoming a vassal of Kashmir and so practically of the Imperial Government.

The viceregal government, in an official dispatch, declared its intention 'through the Ruler of Kashmir the power of making such political and military arrangements as will effectually command the passes of the Hindu Kush' and further, 'If we extend and by degrees consolidate our influence over this country and if we resolve that no foreign interference can be permitted on this side of the mountains or within the drainage system of the Indus, we shall have laid down a natural line of frontier which is distinct intelligible and likely to be respected'.

Dispatch No.49 – 28 February 1879.

The forward movement had begun. The retention of Chitral was a cornerstone of this policy. The tribes regarded it as a threat to their independence. A nineteenth century imperial scenario was unfolding. The holy men and priests would make the most of this and foment a general uprising, but this was nearly twenty years in the future. In the meantime there was the main issue of Afghanistan.

Although Stolietoff's mission left Kabul following the Congress of Berlin, Lytton blamed the Amir, quite unfairly, for instigating the visit and insisted on his accepting a British mission. His ultimatum was not identical to those in which the First Afghan War began. In Parliament Gladstone thundered, 'We made war in error upon Afghanistan in 1838. To err is human and pardonable. But we have erred a second time on the same ground with no better justification.... '

Three British Armies marched through three great passes of Eastern Afghanistan, the Bolan, the Kurram Valley and the Khyber; considerable local fighting followed with tribesmen, and the main cities were captured and occupied. Sher Ali fled, to be succeeded by his son, Yakub Khan, with whom a treaty was signed at Gandamak in May 1879 in accordance with which the British Government's wishes were to be followed in the matter of foreign relations. There was to be a permanent British Resident in Kabul and all British troops were to be withdrawn except those stationed in Kandahar under General Roberts VC, which were to be evacuated in the autumn.

Lytton's satisfaction with his Afghan policy was short lived. He could not appreciate that any Afghan ruler who surrendered sovereignty to a foreign power, forfeited the respect and allegiance of his fellow countrymen. Sir Louis Cavagnari, who was appointed Resident, had a similarly blinkered view. On 2 September he sent a telegram to the Viceroy saying 'All well'. On 3 September he and his escort were all murdered in the Residency by unruly Afghan troops, in the course of which Lieutenant Walter Hamilton of the Guides won a post-humous VC leading the defence against overwhelming odds.

General Roberts was then ordered to advance on Kabul with his Field Force numbering 7,500 men and 22 guns. Harassed by Ghilzai tribesmen, short of food and transport and outnumbered 4 to 1 by the Afghan Army who opposed him, he occupied Kabul on 9 October. Yakub Khan abdicated and Roberts was de facto ruler of Afghanistan.

In early December 1879 an ancient Mullah went on a circuit preaching tour of Afghanistan inciting the people to jihad. He reminded them how their fathers and grandfathers had driven the thrice accursed Feringhi camel entrails from the country. Roberts saw trouble coming and on 8 December telegraphed for the entire Corps of Guides as reinforcements; the same day that the Afghan Army took to the field.

Roberts was heavily outnumbered and was besieged inside the fortified Sherpur cantonment north-east of the city by 100,000 tribesmen. In the spring of 1880 he was relieved by a force commanded by General Stewart.

In June the Battle of Maiwand near Kandahar resulted in one of the biggest defeats of the British Army in the east. Over 1,000 men were killed and the remainder driven back in full retreat. There was one very gallant action when 100 officers and men of the 66th Regiment made a stand; surrounded and hope-lessly outnumbered they inflicted heavy losses on the enemy until the eleven survivors broke cover and charged with their faces to the foe, fighting to the death.

The British garrison in Kandahar was now under siege and Roberts was ordered to relieve it. With 10,000 men, which included the 9th Lancers, 60th Rifles, 72nd and 92nd Highlanders, Sikh, Gurkha and Punjab Infantry, mule borne artillery and scaled down baggage, he made his famous march in searing 110 degrees heat by day and freezing conditions at night. Covering 313 miles in twenty days, he routed Ayub Khan's forces at the Battle of Kandahar outside the city walls. 'Roberts of Kandahar' had become a Victorian military hero.

In the meantime Gladstone and the Liberals were back in power and opposed to the Forward Policy and the situation it had brought about in Afghanistan, with which they were now saddled. But the country was fragmented and disunited and they had no wish to leave it in this state. To the rescue came Abdur Rahman who had been in exile in Russia. A nephew of Dost Mohammed, the Russians sent him back to try his luck in his native land, probably in accordance with Russian wishes. They were right in the former assumption. The British accepted him as Amir and he proved to be one of the best rulers Afghanistan ever had. In the mould of an eastern potentate of that period, he subdued and united his people as never before. Utterly ruthless and cruel – torture and execution were rife – he was, nevertheless, a great administrator and his political acumen, which tilted the balance in favour of Britain, averted war on one occasion and kept the peace in his country during his lifetime.

The Russians were continuing to press forward and consolidate their position on the Afghan border. This time their previously irresolute designs – as Gorchakoff had said ten years before, 'it is difficult to know when to stop' – were advanced by a young aggressive general called Mikhail Skobolev. He told an American journalist that he held it a principle that in Asia the duration of peace was in direct proportion to the slaughter inflicted on the enemy. He talked about hurling masses of Asiatic cavalry into India as a vanguard, recreating the bloody invasion of the Mongols. The Turkmen called him 'Bloody Eyes'. In January 1881 he reduced their capital, Geok Tepe, to rubble, slaughtering 10,000 women and children in the process. At almost the same time the Transcaspian railway reached Geok Tepe.

Geok Tepe was on the caravan route to Merv, an oasis only 130 miles north of the Afghan border. It was considered by British nineteenth century strategists as the best jumping off place from Russian Turkestan to Herat, thence via Kandahar for the easiest invasion route to India, avoiding the Hindu Kush.

The British Imperial watchdogs became alarmed once more. St Petersburg, however, deemed it expedient to reassure London that Russia had no designs on Merv. In fact Russia, since the Second Afghan War, had accepted that Afghanistan lay within the British sphere of influence. Withdrawal of British troops from Kandahar had altered the Russians' view of what was politically expedient and, in 1884, they had annexed Merv.

Gladstone's cabinet met hastily to discuss possible countermeasures. The Duke of Argyll mocked that they were suffering from a case of 'Mervousness'. Then came the panic over a miserable water hole in the desert known as the Panjdeh Oasis, 100 miles south of Merv and very near the Afghan border. The Russians had been edging towards it, and on 30 March 1895 General Komarov attacked and defeated the Afghan forces defending it There was consternation in London and St Petersburg, troops mobilized on both sides, Gladstone was voted a credit of 11 millions, and there was a near panic on the Stock Exchange. The world waited for a conflagration. However the issue was settled by diplomacy, boundary commissions and Abdur Rahman, who agreed to waive his claim to the place in exchange for Zulficar about eighty-five miles to the west; he had no wish to see his country turned into a battle ground. The protocol signed at St Petersburg in July 1887 settled the frontier up to the line of the Oxus and put limits on Russian expansion towards Herat.

In the following years until Indian Independence, the Lion and the Bear would growl and snarl at each other, but each had come to realize the limits of prudent expansion, for both empires lay on the frontiers of Afghanistan. Neither wished to colonize this wild and rugged land which had no exploitable economic or mineral resources. For centuries Afghanistan had been a highway to conquest – now it had become a buffer state resisting conquest; an important pawn in the power politics of the nineteenth century. The tribes continued to loot and plunder as they had always done. In 1863 Hindu fanatics, who included fugitives from the Mutiny, stirred up the Bunerwala and it was necessary to send the largest punitive expedition so far mounted, under General Sir Neville Chamberlain, with 5,000 men comprising 11th Bengal Cavalry and Guides, the 71st Highland Light Infantry, 101st Royal Bengal Fusiliers, Gurkhas, Sikhs and a Mountain battery. There were 238 killed and 670 wounded – the tribes had suffered 3,000 casualties – after a three month campaign in the Ambela area.

'This prickly and untrimmed hedge', Sir Olaf Caroe had termed the North-West Frontier. It was necessary to trim the hedge as far as possible. The tribes acknowledged no man as master, but the Amir of Afghanistan claimed suzerainty over them. The first move in the balancing act between the Amir and the tribes was the Treaty of Gandamak in 1870 which gave the Indian Government control of the Khyber Pass, the Kurram Valley and other immense tracts along the vaguely defined Afghan-Indian frontier.

The main problem was with the trans-Indus tribes occupying the wild, mountainous area about 300 miles by 100 miles broad between Chitral and Baluchistan, of whom the Afridis, Orakzais and Mohmands were probably the most troublesome, with Wazirs and Mahsuds, in the south, beating them by more than a short head. In the extreme south Sir Robert Sandeman extended British control over the Baluchis who were more respectful of authority.

In order to extend the sphere of influence, 'within which,' in the words of one Viceroy, 'we make no attempt to administer the country ourselves, but within which we shall not allow any aggression from without,' Britain increased pressure on tribal territory. The Quetta Railway was pushed forward to the Bolan Pass, to the Amir's annoyance. There was trouble in Gilgit which gave direct access to Chitral that itself commanded the easiest and least elevated passes across the Hindu Kush. Russian activity in the Pamirs and the sighting of Cossack patrols in Chitral hastened the establishment of agencies in both Gilgit and Chitral; the latter under Surgeon Major George Robertson, late of the Indian Medical Service.

In Chitral murder was quite common and most men of importance preferred to sleep in the daytime and to pass the night with a loaded rifle across their knees, while a faithful servant sat on the roof over the central smoke hole to prevent enemies from shooting down it. It was against this dark background that a web of intrigue, stemming from the greed, cruelty and treachery of the Chitralis, set the country alight.

The Mehtar (Heaven Born – Ruler of Chitral) Aman ul Mulk whose tyrannical reign had managed to ensure his survival for thirty years, died in 1892. A number of routine murders followed to establish the succession. His second son, Afzul ul Mulk, murdered three step-brothers and some others, proclaiming himself Mehtar, to be slain in turn by his uncle, Sher Afzul, who seized power, probably with the backing of the Afghan Amir. The British now entered the ring and helped to press the claim of Aman's eldest son, Nizam, who had fled to Gilgit where he was living. The Chitralis rallied to him and Afzul fled to Kabul. Nizam was installed as Mehtar in December 1892 and proved to be feckless and drunken, with no taste for the job. The next move in this lethal game of chess was to all appearances planned by the Afghans with Sher Afzul, who incited Amir ul Mulk, the half-witted brother of the Mehtar, to kill Nizam in January 1895. Robertson refused to recognize Amir ul Mulk as Mehtar and deposed him. In his place he installed his 10 year old brother as Mehtar.

Sher Afzul collected a large body of followers and, supported by Imra Khan of Jandol, a powerful Pathan chief who was not averse to adding Chitral to his dominions, advanced on the fort and demanded that the British leave Chitral. The stage was set for a major epic of Empire to be played out in a vast amphitheatre of silent mountains cloaked in eternal snow. As Sir George Robertson wrote, 'It takes time for the mind to recover from the depression which the stillness and melancholy of the giant landscape at first compel. All colour is purged away by the sun glare; and no birds sing.'

Fort Chitral was set on the banks of the rushing Kunar river, 80 yards square surrounded by 25ft walls of masonry held together by an irregular pattern of wooden beams; the whole ramshackle fortification set off with a tower at each corner. Roberston's garrison consisted of Captain Townshend of the Central India Horse in direct command of the troops, comprising 300 Kashmir Infantry with a leavening of Gurkhas and, the hard core of the defence, ninety-nine rifles of the 14th Sikhs under Lieutenant Harley. The only other British officers were a political officer, Lieutenant Gurdon, and Surgeon Captain Whitchurch. Captain Campbell, the senior Infantry officer, lay badly wounded throughout the siege. There were also about 100 non-combatants, including the little Mehtar, taking refuge in the fort.

The siege began at the beginning of March 1895, the defenders outnumbered 50 to 1 against Sher Afzul's Chitralis and Umra Khan's Pathans. For seven weeks they held out against overwhelming odds; continual sniping, frontal assaults, attempts to burn down the tinder dry walls of the fort doused by chains of battle weary water carriers, an attempt to burn the tower guarding the vital covered passage to the river, and finally a tunnel driven up to the walls to plant mines – this last very bravely and effectively dealt with by Lieutenant Harley who charged out of the gate with a party of picked men, dispatched the diggers and blew up the tunnel. By this time there were eighty-five sick and wounded and rations were low. 'The stenches in this awful fort are simply appalling,' wrote Townshend in his diary. A few days later on 20 April, they were relieved by Colonel Kelly's column of 32nd Punjab Pioneers which, over the previous two months, had fought its way from Gilgit in the face of appalling difficulties, manhandling mountain artillery over the 12,000ft Shandur Pass through deep snow, and overcoming considerable opposition at other places: an outstanding military feat.

An Infantry Division with cavalry, artillery and engineers commanded by Major General Sir Robert Low had also been fighting its way through the mountains from the south in Dir and Swat where the tribes were out, and finally arrived on 15th May. So ended another saga of Empire to brighten Victorian breakfast tables.

Robertson was awarded a knighthood. Surgeon Captain Whitchurch won the Victoria Cross for bringing in a dying man at great risk to himself, Gurdon and Harley were awarded the DSO. Townshend was given the CB and a brevet majority; twenty years later as a major general, commanding the 6th Indian Division at Kut-el-Amara, he found himself besieged again, this time by the Turks. 'I will hold it as I held Chitral,' he said. He held out for 143 days – but no relief came. Colonel Kelly received the CB, although he had been recommended for a KCB and a brevet major-generalship. The importance of his epic march was never fully recognized, most of the acclaim going to General Low and his well known British regiments like the Gordon Highlanders and the King's Royal Rifle Corps.

Morally it was unfortunate for the tribesmen that British spheres of influence clashed with their areas of existence.

There were, indeed, mitigating factors. The fighting was always in wild, mountainous country between foes who respected one another, and furthermore were spoiling for a fight. It was always the British serviceman's wish to get to the North-West Frontier, because that was where the action was; and fighting was the tribesmen's way of life – if they were not fighting outsiders, they were feuding among themselves, or fighting alongside the British. Many of them served in the Indian Army, and Tyndall's Regiment, the 40th Pathans, was recruited entirely from Pathans.

Towards the end of the nineteenth century the Khyber Pass offered safe passage to all for eighteen years; this was entirely due to Sir Robert Warburton who was the Eurasian son of an Irish Army Officer and an Afghan princess, the niece of Dost Mohammed. A 'rag, tag and bobtail' outfit of local tribesmen, mainly Afridis, had been raised to protect traffic moving through the Khyber; it was commanded by an Afghan major, Sardar Mohammed Aslam, and they were later named the Khyber Rifles. Warburton, as the Political Agent, cooperated closely with them and, speaking fluent Pushtu and Persian, was held in high esteem by the tribes among whom he mixed at will entirely unarmed.

In the meantime Abdur Rahman was becoming irritated with British pressure on tribal areas which was increasing in direct proportion to the growing need to maintain law and order with the unfolding of the Forward Policy. British suppression of the Ffunzas and Kajutis, who were carrying on a brisk business looting caravans for booty and slaves, and the annexation of the Pushtoon Turis of the Kurram Valley in 1892, alarmed the Afghans. This, in spite of the fact that the former were not Pushtoons, and the latter had asked to be put under British control and protection, being members of the minority Shia sect of Muslims and with fertile lands subject to raids by Orakzais and others.

There was a stream of visiting agents from Kabul in the tribal areas and the situation began to give cause for alarm. The Indian Government threw up a line of defensive works along the Samana Hills overlooking the Tirah. The tribesmen were acquiring rifles stolen from the Indian Army or smuggled into Afghanistan and British military expeditions were becoming increasingly bloody excursions as a result of the 'Butcher and Bolt Policy'.

Against this uneasy background Lord Lansdowne, the Viceroy, sent Sir Mortimer Durand, his Foreign Secretary, to Kabul to negotiate with Abdur Rahman a new political boundary delineating new tribal areas. The result was the Durand Line which became the new political boundary intended to establish definitive areas of influence over the tribes between Afghanistan and British India – in fact, as Sir Kerr Fraser Tyler wrote, 'It was illogical from the point of view of ethnography, of strategy and of geography – it splits a nation in two, it even divides tribes'.

The wild men of the hills did not care much about such matters. Their lives were of ceaseless labour in a barren land to provide the needs of their families and to buy a Martini Henry rifle. Every man was a soldier and they embarked on war with careless levity; with an absolute lack of reverence for all forms of law and authority. They fought without malice and made friends not infrequently over the corpses of their comrades or suspended operations for a festival or a horse race. Despite his belligerent independence, the Pathan was, by tradition, race and language, an Afghan and not at all suited to becoming a subject of the Queen and he generally wished to avoid attracting the attention of the Frontier Scouts who became the political officers' striking force if needed for a punitive expedition.

Abdur Rahman considered the British had stolen a march on him after the Durand Agreement. It seems doubtful if he fully understood its terms because he was unable to read a map and so found that he had lost suzerainty over an area about 100 miles by 300 miles in length now created between the Administrative and Durand Lines, including tribes over whom he claimed spiritual influence.

Thus, the Durand line created more problems than it solved, and was one of the factors which helped to cause the explosion of 1897 on the frontier.

A spark in a far off country jumped across the trackless wastes of Central Asia to start the conflagration. The war between Greece and Turkey and the massacre of Christians by Turks led to severe condemnation by the British. Although the censure was well deserved, it infuriated the Sunni Muslims and an agent was sent from Constantinople to Kabul to urge jihad against the British.

The Amir, who had recently proclaimed himself a Caliph of Islam, sent for his Mullahs who were only too ready to give ear to the word of the Prophet as preached by this fiery messenger.

Soon after the siege of Chitral fort a new political agency was established for Dir, Swat and Chitral with headquarters at Malakand under Major Harold Deane. The Khan of Dir and Swat was given an increased subsidy to protect and maintain the Chitral Road. For two years the native population of the Swat Valley prospered with the increased trade under British rule. The Chitral road was used without let or hindrance; not a post bag was stolen nor a messenger murdered. Political officers rode freely about among the fierce hill men, settling disputes which would otherwise have been resolved by armed force. The British Government conferred upon the Khan the title of Nawab, and when Major Deane, with his own hands, bound a fine puggaree on the Khan's head, he vowed that he 'valued this honour more than lakhs of rupees'.

The Mullahs recognized the significance of the Chitral Road, both as evidence of a further increase of British influence on the Frontier and also as a threat to their own power and wealth. They needed little encouragement, therefore, to start an extensive but silent agitation among the tribes, urging them to holy war against the infidel. Vast and mysterious forces were set in motion by the chosen Mullah, Sayed Akbar, to raise up the Afridis and Orakzais. A materially minded and rapacious cleric, he'd had a magnificent house built for himself; a contrast to the Malikden Khel Mullah whose life had been spent in prayer and who had been exhorting the Afridis to more peaceable ways. The Haddah Mullah, a God-fearing but persistent and vindictive enemy of the British, raised the Mohmands and Sadullah 'The Mad Fakir' of Swat instigated the attack on the Malakand and Chakdarra; he swore by the beard of the Prophet that British bullets would turn to water and that the stones he would throw into the Swat river would become artillery shells.

The stormy course of Indian history has brought us to the biggest uprising ever known on the North-West Frontier where, at this point, we find Lieutenant Tyndall of the 40th Pathans, attached to the 38th Dogras, facing the wild men of the mountains.

The Malakand Pass is a sparkling contrast to the sombre Khyber. Pine forests cover the flanks of the mountains, and the cold blue waters of the Swat river rumble along below the road. The Pass connects the three princely states of Swat, Dir and Chitral with what is now Pakistan. It was here, where it would have been least expected, that the first action of the uprising was fought. On the night of 26 July 1897, 10,000 Pathans hurled themselves on less than 1,000 Sikhs in the Malakand Position, and another large force attacked the small garrison at Chakdarra. An eyewitness account of the Malakand Campaign is given by Tyndall.

Winston Churchill appears, perhaps for the first time in history, in his own words 'looking for trouble'. The bush fire, as it was thought, became a conflagration and soon the whole frontier was alight. It spread south to the Tirah where the Orakzais and Afridis rose up under the Mullah Sayed Akbar and took over the Khyber Pass.

It fanned west and north into the Mohmand and Bajauer country whence General Sir Bindon Blood took his Malakand Field Force with two brigades; the Mohmand Field Force, also with two brigades, under Brigadier General Elles, came up from Peshawar. Tyndall gives an account of his part in Blood's campaign and describes the Durbar on 16 October 1897 at which the Mohmands made their submission.

The Tirah Field Force was raised under Lieutenant General Sir William Lockhart, a very experienced officer in frontier warfare. The Force comprised 35,000 men with a vast amount of transport; the biggest and most well equipped force ever to campaign against the tribes, who were assailed for the first time in centuries, in their mountain homeland.

One of the most famous actions of frontier warfare took place during this campaign on 20 October 1897 – the storming of the Dargai Heights, held in strength by 12,000 Afridis, well entrenched in stone sangars. Lieutenant Colonel Mathias, commanding the 1st Battalion Gordon Highlanders, formed them up for attack and called, 'Highlanders, the General says the position must be taken at all costs. The Gordons will take it!' With *'Cock o' the North'* skirling out on the bagpipes, the Highlanders surged forward through withering fire from the tribesmen on the heights; many dropped, among them Piper Findlater, shot in both ankles, but he continued to play, cheering his comrades on. When the Afridis saw the dark green kilts coming near they knew it was time to go, and the Gordons captured the heights. Colonel Mathias, also wounded, and Piper Findlater were each awarded the Victoria Cross.

By the spring of 1898 the Tirah Campaign was over. After some protracted guerrilla warfare the tribes finally sent a jirga to negotiate terms and the rising came to an end. It helped that Warburton was Lockhart's political officer; he had been on leave when the rising started and was convinced that he could have stopped it had he been there. He was greatly saddened by the whole affair.

The policy of 'Butcher and Bolt' combined with the 'Forward Movement' had proved ineffective. The campaign had settled nothing except to quieten the tribes and to win back the Khyber Forts; this was necessary and was, perhaps, all that could have been expected. Ironically, when Lockhart left Peshawar on leave, he was seen off by hundreds of cheering Afridis vowing they would fight on the British side next time.

This was, maybe, a not unsurprising facet of life on the frontier. The tribesmen respected a worthy foe and there was nothing they liked better than a fight, particularly if it gained them a rifle and some loot, while the British serviceman was only too glad to get away from a dull and hot Indian cantonment for some action on the Frontier. It became, 'a brotherhood of arms,' as Sir Olaf Caroe said. 'Englishmen and Pathans looked one another in the eyes, and there they found – a man.'

Just as Britain had previously recruited races it had conquered, such as the Gurkhas, Sikhs and Dogras, so the Pathans were found to be extremely useful in units operating on the Frontier, and the 40th Pathans, in which Tyndall served, were no exception.

The Forward Policy was now to be seriously reconsidered and curtailed. The Tirah campaign had cost many lives – about 1,200 British and Indian casualties – and many thousands of pounds, and the tribes had nothing to surrender but their arms.

Lord Curzon arrived as viceroy in January 1899 at the zenith of British power in India. George Nathanial Curzon, in the words of the well known doggerel, 'A most superior person,' was an appropriate man to govern the Indian Empire at this time. He was the youngest, at thirty-nine, ever to hold this high office and had long prepared himself for the task.

He, at once, adopted a modified 'close border' policy involving withdrawal of frontier troops from sensitive areas and concentration in the newly formed North-West Frontier Province. Lord Kitchener, a man of similar character, reorganized the Indian Army.

Russian moves at this time alarmed the Indian Government, particularly as Habibulllah, the new Shah of Afghanistan, behind a bland exterior, was anti-British, and the Russians were seeking to establish a presence in Kabul. The Russo-Japanese War of 1905 and the St Petersburg Convention of 1907 brought the 'Great Game' to an end.

There were new political horizons: the balance of power had shifted in Europe creating new alliances. Germany was now the main threat and pressure on Afghanistan's northern frontier had decreased.

In the First World War Afghanistan remained neutral, thus enabling vast numbers of men to be released to fight on the Western Front and in other theatres of war. It was a war that hastened the end of the British Raj. However, long before this, the more far-seeing administrators foresaw the day when the British would leave India to be governed by Indians. The members of the Indian Civil Service were seen in the role of Plato's Guardians, the district officer as the lynchpin of this system, a father and mother to the people he administered, living in a tent out in villages for months in the year, giving land settlements, dealing out justice and making decisions on all kinds of affairs.

It was a system based on that of Akbar and the Moghuls, administered by not more than about 1,300 officials at any one time, backed by an army of perhaps 60,000, over a population of 350,000,000. If a sceptic, you may, perhaps, aver that it was one of the biggest 'cons' in history; on the other hand it could be said that it was one of the greatest feats of empire building that the world has seen.

The Indian National Congress had been formed by the British Administration at the end of the nineteenth century as a basis for the beginning of Indian self government. The first session was held at Bombay in 1885; the direct offspring of the educational changes of 1854, it was drawn, at first, from only a small section of Indians who spoke English and had acquired a western education, but its scope was very much broadened in later years.

From the end of the First World War the Indianization of the ICS proceeded apace, until, at the beginning of the Second World War, it was nearly half Indian and the role of the district commissioner had changed from a guardian or ruler to that of a committee man or official, subject to the orders of an increasingly active Congress. Just after the Great War there was one of those upheavals in Afghan politics which led indirectly to armed conflict. Habibullah was assassinated in February 1919 on a hunting trip. His brother Nasrullah assumed the title of Amir but was opposed by his nephew Amanullah, the third son of Habibullah, who was supported by the Army. Nasrullah was arrested, tried for the murder of Habibullah and sentenced to life imprisonment.

Amanullah was young, ambitious and, like his father, wanted British influence removed from Afghanistan, particularly in the field of foreign relations. He felt insecure on his throne and there were riots in the Punjab – what better than to march his troops across the border into India, unite his country behind him and, with the British, as he thought, fully occupied, make any demands necessary.

On 3 May the Afghan Army crossed the border at the western end of the Khyber and occupied the village of Bagh, at the same time that an uprising in Peshawar had been planned. At first Afghan intentions were not fully evident, but Sir George Roos-Keppel, the formidable chief commissioner of the North-West Frontier Province urged upon Lord Chelmsford, the viceroy, the necessity of evicting them as soon as possible. At the same time Roos-Keppel took steps to put down the riot in Peshawar. The Third Afghan War had started, but it was a very short affair compared with the first two, although the front stretched from Chitral to Baluchistan. The heaviest fighting took place in the Kurram around Thal which was besieged by Nadir Khan, one of the ablest Afghan generals, and Brigadier General Eustace, commanding the garrison, had to call for assistance. Brigadier General Dyer of Amritsar massacre notoriety, marched in with a mixed force of Punjabis, Dogras and Gurkhas and a battalion of British Territorials, the lst/25th London Regiment and, by consummate generalship, saved the situation – it did not, however, save him from being relieved of his command shortly after as a result of his action in Amritsar, and he died a little later.

The Frontier Corps, comprising recently formed militia troops and scouts, were much involved. Major Russell's withdrawal from Wana on 26–30 May, with remnants of the South Waziristan Militia who had not mutinied, was described in the *Official History* as 'one of the finest exploits recorded in the History of the Indian Frontier'.

For the first time on the frontier, aircraft of the Royal Air Force, BE2Cs, were used in support of army operations.

By 3 June it was all over and an armistice was signed. The peace conference of 8 August gave the Afghans, inter alia, the right to conduct their own affairs as a fully independent state. So Amanullah had gained his main objective after all.

The tribesmen were still treated like tigers in a cage. If they behaved themselves behind the administrative line they received a pat, in the form of the usual subsidy to stay their hand from looting convoys and sacking villages. If they broke out beyond this, punitive measures were taken for which troops on the border were at readiness. This was the 'Modified Forward Policy'. The exception to this was in Waziristan, the home of the Wazirs and Mahsuds, probably two of the fiercest and most treacherous tribes among the Pathans. The war had stirred up unrest and they continued to give trouble until 1939, inflamed during the thirties by the Fakir of Ipi who was a thorn in the flesh for many years. In order to control them a garrison was established at Mazmuk, situated in the centre of Waziristan at 7,200ft; biting cold in winter and burning hot in summer. A brigade was stationed here and roads were constructed to enable troops to move quickly to trouble spots.

Further north, Khan Abdul Ghaffer Khan was agitating for Pathan autonomy. Physically imposing at 6ft 6ins, the Khan was a powerful personality and he dominated the North-West Frontier Province for many years. He was a contradictory figure, a Muslim among a fiercely devout people, he became a disciple of Gandhi, supported the Congress Party, which he saw as an increasingly powerful opposition to the British, and opposed partition. He was nicknamed 'The Frontier Gandhi' and formed a new party called 'Khodai Khidmatgaran (Servants of God)' who wore plum coloured, home dyed garments and became known as the 'Red Shirts'. In spite of these peaceful appellations much trouble was made in the 1920s and 1930s which included riots in Peshawar and uprisings of the Afridis and Mohmands. Ghaffer Khan wanted a separate Pathan State 'Pakhtunistan' and was often in prison both under the British and when the North-West Frontier Province became part of Pakistan. He died only in 1988 aged ninetey-eight years.

The principles of frontier warfare had not altered over a century but some of the techniques had, and so had the rules governing punitive expeditions which were very much restricted in their freedom of action against the tribes. Due to political considerations, the tribes had replaced their old muzzle loading jezails with snyders and Lee Enfields smuggled across the Gulf of Aden through Persia to Afghanistan. By the time Tyndall retired in 1924, aeroplanes were often used to bomb villages instead of burning them, warning leaflets being dropped before-hand. A proposal had been made that the Royal Air Force should take over control of the frontier, as it had successfully controlled Iraq, but this was never fully implemented as the frontier did not lend itself to control from the air. Field Marshal Lord Birdwood, who was C.-in-C. India from 1925 to 1930, was convinced that the personal factor was all important in dealing with the Pathan tribesmen, and he thought that civil and military officers on the border should be able to keep in the closest touch with the tribes. This view was borne out, to some extent, by the tribesmen themselves who thought bombing was unsporting, mainly because it deprived them of a good skirmish with the ground forces. They loved a fight and recognized good soldiering when they saw it. There is a story of a patrol of scouts which was sent out to capture some bandits who had been a nuisance in the countryside. The patrol had the bandits in their sights behind some rocks but were firing low when one of the bandits jumped up to signal the range; he had been in the British Army himself and hated to see good ammu-nition wasted.

At the end of 1928 the Royal Air Force played a distinguished role in a situ-ation which could have led to a Fourth Afghan War. Rioting broke out in Kabul as a result of Amanullah's attempts at reforms, and the legation found itself under fire from both sides. The minister, Sir Francis Humphreys, requested an airlift. Vickers Victoria transport aircraft of No. 70 Squadron, led by Squadron Leader Maxwell, and some DH9As, airlifted 586 people and 41 tons of baggage to safety in India, flying a total of 84 sorties in two months. It was one of the severest winters ever experienced on the frontier and an ordeal for the crews flying in open cockpits at temperatures of minus 20 degrees Centigrade. Nevertheless the first major airlift of the RAF was accomplished without a single casualty, although one or two aircraft were 'bent'.

In India events had long been leading towards independence. The Acts of 1833, confirming certain posts to Indians, and 1853, formally opening the higher and covenanted posts to Indians; the formation of the Indian National Congress and the Muslim League; and the declaration of 1917 setting out the steps to a future self-government. Between the wars Mahatma Gandhi's Civil Disobedience Campaign hit the headlines, national leaders had spells in gaol, delegations went to London for round table conferences and reforms continued gradually. By 1939, amid growing nationalism, it was evident that only a government native to the country would satisfy Indian aspirations, and growing hostility between Hindu and Muslim made partition inevitable.

The Second World War postponed reforms while the largest non-conscript army ever raised was put into the field; 1,300,000 men. Indian troops fought on many fronts. In North Africa the 4th Indian Division was considered second to none. Battle hardened veterans of the North-West Frontier were thrown into the breach against the Japanese on the North-East Frontier which they never dreamt of having to defend.

Gandhi and the Congress Leaders were unsympathetic towards what they considered a European war and they really hoped that Japan, an Asiatic nation, would win. In 1942 Mr Gandhi asked Britain to leave, and Congress prepared to come out against it having fomented insurrection, but the leaders were arrested on the eve of the rebellion. Nevertheless for ten days there was anarchy in the United Provinces and Bihar, and it looked like a repeat of the Mutiny until it was suppressed, and Britain got on with repelling the Japanese.

After the war the end came more quickly and explosively than anyone could have imagined. Earl Mountbatten arrived as the last Viceroy in February 1947 and by August he had handed over his powers to Nehru in India and to Jinnah in Pakistan, the new Muslim partitioned state, accompanied by disturbances and strife between Hindu and Muslim resulting in about 500,000 dead and 2 million injured.

It was over 300 years since Hawkins stepped ashore from the first ship to fly the English flag off the coast of India. The turbulent march of history over this period had given the English the brightest jewel in the Crown, comprising ten Provinces of British India and 562 native states, most of the larger ones with a British Resident, Hyderabad being as large as England and Scotland together.

It was an age of conquest and empire building – conquer or be conquered, and Britain had merely managed to be first in the field. With flag following trade, sometimes reluctantly as we have seen, sometimes out in front leading red coat and sepoy to fresh victories, the British found themselves at the end with an exotic Eastern Empire inhabited by a vast heterogeneous population of volatile, complex and highly intelligent people.

We must stand back now and briefly survey the legacy that was left. Trade and profits were, indeed, the original objectives; like many other conquering nations the British had been lured to the East by the prospect of rich pickings and had done well from it. It would be hypocritical to pretend otherwise. But the Age of Enlightenment, which entailed, to some extent, the application of Christian principles, dawned and British Governments became concerned for the welfare of the people they governed. It might be pretentious to say that 'there was infused into Oriental despotism the spirit of British freedom' but this, in fact, became the aim of successive administrations.

Lord Bentinck 1828–35 was the first Governor General to act on the principle that the welfare of subject peoples was the main duty of the British. He abolished cruelties, effaced humiliating distinctions and gave liberty to the expansion of public opinion. Widows were saved from immolation; Sati or Suttee was forbidden – in 1818 in Bengal alone 839 women were burnt alive on the funeral pyres of their husbands. Children were saved from sacrifice, and the old and sick were no longer disposed of by drowning them in the Ganges. In 1830, the Thugs were broken up. They were a brotherhood of hereditary assassins who worshipped the Goddess Kali and made sacrifice to her by strangling and robbing travellers.

Administrative and educational reforms were made. In rural districts zamindars, rent collectors inherited from the Moghuls, were brought under control and the lot of the oppressed peasant ameliorated. Methods of farming were improved.

The readjustment of the economy into the British dominated system of world trade in the nineteenth century had brought increased prosperity, particularly in regard to the great expansion of cotton exports. By the turn of the century there were eight major railway systems with five different gauges, there were new roads and canals, which helped to alleviate the effects of the terrible famines, and the electric telegraph covered the country.

In the last years, at least, the British had sent out their best men and often generations of the same families had given good service to the Raj. In the all – consuming, debilitating breadth of the landscape of India they had sweated and toiled – at the worst they had been racists and bullies and perhaps there were not many of these; at the best they had high ideals of duty and service, and saw themselves as apostles of western enlightenment.

To the skirl of the pipes the Union Jack was lowered for the last time by the Somerset Light Infantry. It was 28 February 1949 and the farewell parade to the last British troops in India was commanded by Lieutenant Colonel Prithi Pal Singh of the Sikh Regiment. A silver model of the Gateway of India was presented to the Somersets with the inscription 'to commemorate the comradeship of the soldiers of the British and Indian Armies'. The British were leaving India for ever. No Empire had ever been handed over so peaceably. A unified political system was left – and 2,000,000 British graves.

'And at the end of the fight is a tombstone
white with the name of the deceased

And the epitaph drear – 'A fool lies here who
tried to hustle the East.'

Rudyard Kipling, the Naulahtia.

In conclusion, a postscript to the 'Great Game'. The Russians finally crossed the Afghan border in 1979 with 115,000 troops. Tyndall and every British soldier who had fought in Afghanistan and on the North-West Frontier could have told them what to expect. After fierce fighting and horrendous losses on both sides, the occupation came to an end in 1988.

The Mujahideen, who included many of the Pathan tribes of Tyndall's day, had won. As in centuries past, they called no man master.

Tyndall's Diary

1895–1915

1895

Horsham to West Ridge, Rawalpindi.[1] Left Horsham 10.2a.m. 23rd Feb. 1895. Stopped night 'George Hotel' Portsmouth with Father. Sailed morning 24th in HM transport *Malabar* (Capt. Tudor, 8,000 tons) for Bombay. In pandemonium cabin with J. Buckley & Strong. Sailed via Gibraltar, Malta, Alexandria, Port Said and Suez. Arrived Bombay 25th March. Stopped night Great Western Hotel. Left on 26th March by train. Arrived Pindi 31st March and joined 3rd Battln. Rifle Brigade at West Ridge lived in tent.

West Ridge to Rawalpindi. 4th June. Lived with W. Allen K.O.S.B. in Major Montgomery's Bungalow at back of the RA Mess.

Rawalpindi to Murree 16th July on leave at Rowbery's Hotel, drove up in tonga[2] via Barrakow and Tret.

Murree to Natia Gully Abbottabad and back Rode from Murree to Natia Gully 17th August. Stayed with Major and Mrs. Stuart 2nd Punjab Infantry. Rode to Abbottabad[3] 20th. Back to Natia 21st and Murree 21st August.

Murree to Rawalpindi. 23rd August drove down in tonga Rawalpindi to Gharrial (Muree) 1st Sept drove up in tonga with Machlachlan 3rd R.B. On duty with detachment 3rd R.B. under Major Norcott, and detachment Gordon Highlanders.

Gharrial to Attock. 1st Novbr marched down to Pindi with detachment arrived at Pindi 3rd Novbr and on to Attock same day by train to do duty with detachment. Major Winn and Captain Annerley.

Attock to Khyber Pass and back. By train to Peshawar 17th Dec with Annesley, stopped at dak[4] bungalow. Drove up pass next day to Ali Musjid back to Attock by train 19th Dec.

1896

Attock to Pindi. On relief 12th Jany. by train, lived in tent at West Ridge.

Rawalpindi to Quetta for Fort Sandeman. Owing to mistake in warrant. Left Pindi 13th April by train via Lahore, Suceur, Ruck and Sibi, arrived Quetta 16th stopped with Hislop of the Sind Horse/ 5th Bengal Lancers at Mess.

Quetta to Fort Sandeman. Left 24th April by train to Humai (7 hours). Drove in tonga with Captain Hatch 29th Baluchis as far as Lorelai. Finished the journey on riding mule with baggage.[5] 24th to Torkhau 12 miles. 25th through Razgai to Sunjawe 24 miles. 26th to Lorelai 20 miles. Stopped at Dak Bungalow and 29th Baluch Mess. 28th April to Murra Tangi 24 miles. 29th to Zirra 18 miles, 30th to Murgha 15 miles, 31st to Luckaband 24 miles. 1st May to Fort Sandeman 32 miles. Joined 40th Pathans (Colonel S. H. P. Graves) Major Pelham Burne, Captains Dillon, McKay, Rennick, Ridgeway, Lieuts. Bunbury, McLachlan, Preston, Craster, Tyndall, St John.

Fort Sandeman to Quetta. Left Fort S. 6th August and rode to Hurnai, arrived Quetta 15th August, stopped at dak bungalow and 24th Baluch Mess for Staff Corps exam (passed) taken by General Gatacre.

Quetta to Fort Sandeman. Left Quetta 20th August reached Lorelai 24th and Fort S. 28th Augst.

Fort Sandeman to Drug and back with Subedar Azam and escort on duty. 17th Sept to Kashmir Kilah 16 miles, 18th to Adle Kuch 15 miles, 19 to Toi Saw 15 miles, 20th to Muss Khel 12 miles, 21st to Kharrsowan 15 miles, 22nd to Drug 12 miles, stayed in fort, returning 25th Sept by the same route reached Fort S. 1st Oct.

Fort Sandeman to Mir Ali Khel and Moghul Kot on detachment duty, marched 20th Oct. to M.A.K. 45 miles via Brunj and Safi. 100 men 40th Pathans and 40 Sowars Vll Bengal Lancers at M.A.K. and 40 Sepoys and 20 Sowars at Moghul Kot 14 miles further on. Relieved Downes at Vll B.L. shot at Fort S. 28th Oct with Yates R.E.

Mir Ali Khel to Fort Sandeman Left 20th Novbr stopped night at Brunj and reached Fort S. 21st relieved by Craster.

1897

Fort Sandeman to England on three months privilege leave. Rode to Luckbend 2nd January, rode to Murra Tangi by Zhob Levy dak 3rd Jany and drove into Lorelai by tonga. Drove to Razgai on 4th to Hurnai on 5th and missed mail on account of baggage not having arrived. Stopped at dak bungalow till 10th, had an extra week granted on representation Colonel Dyce, leave to commence from 12th January. Reached Karachi after 30 hours in train 10th Jany. going via Sibj and Ruck (no change). Sailed from Karachi in B.I.S.N.Co's S.S. 'Dwarka' on 14th Jany.

After stopping in Reynold's Hotel, 30 hours to Bombay, changed into P& O Co's *Shannon* leaving Bombay 16th Jany. and reached Aden 21st Jany. Changed into S.S. *Rome* and reached Brindisi 29th Jany from there across the Continent by ordinary train, 1st class via Foggia, Bologna (change), Turin (change),

Mendane, Mt. Cenis and Paris. Stopped night in Paris with Wincklers and Merecki at Hotel Magenta near Gare du Nord. Left Paris 1st February via Calais and Dover to Victoria. Stopped night at Alexander Hotel near Victoria and reached Horsham 2nd February. Horsham to Rawalpindi.[6] Left Horsham 9.2a.m. 18th March. Left London 11a.m. via Dover and Calais arriving Paris 7.30p.m. 18th. Stopped night at Paris with Merecki. Left Paris 2.15p.m. 19th via Mendane and Mt Cenis, arriving Brindisi 11 am. 21st March. Sailed 12 midnight same day on P & O S.S. *Himalaya.* Arrived Aden 28th and changed into S.S.*Ganges.* Arrd. Bombay 6a.m. 4th April. Changed into B.I. S.S. *Dunera*, sailing at once arrd. Karachi 6th April 9.48p.m. by train arriving Lahore (no change) 9.25a.m. 8th April. Stopped night at Turton Smiths'. Left by train 4p.m. 9th April, reached Pindi 2.15a.m. 10th April and put up at Flashman's Hotel opposite club.

Rawalpindi to Kohat and back. Left by train 10.57p.m. 11th April arriving Khushalgarh 6.15am on 12th and drove by tonga to Kohat with Major Wallace 27th Punjab Infantry arriving at 10.30a.m. and rejoined 40th Pathans in camp. Left Kohat 5a.m. 13th April and marched with Regiment 16 miles to Gumbat, camped there for night and marched 5a.m. next day to Khushalgarh 15 miles. Regiment left for Pindi in two troops trains, went with second train leaving 4.30a.m. 15th April and arrived Pindi 11.30am same day.

Pindi to Natia Gutty and back on 3 days leave from 20th June to 24th June, walked from Murree to Natia.

With 38th Dogras in Malakand Field Force Left Pindi 2a.m. 30th July, returned 14th December 1897.

The Regiment (40th Pathans) was not eligible for the Malakand Campaign but certain British Officers were attached to other units:

Lt. Tyndall to 38th Dogra (Malakand Campaign)
Lt. Bunbury to 15th Sikhs (Tirah Expeditionary Force)
Lt Craster to 35th Sikhs (Tirah Expeditionary Force)
Lt. Walker to 45th Sikhs (Malakand Garrison then Tirah)

Malakand Field Force – see Appendix D.

29th July 1897

On the afternoon of Thursday, 29th July being very hot weather I was in my bungalow at Pindi with Stockley, No. 4 Coy Punjab S&M. We were very much annoyed at not having got up to the front and at having to sit still and watch other regiments going through Pindi on their way, first during the preceding month to Waziristan after the Maisar[7] affair, and also only a day or two previously to the relief of the Malakand garrison of which place was besieged by the tribesmen who had risen simultaneously and without warning. Only the guides so far had succeeded in reaching the Kotal; other regiments were on the way.

About 5p.m. an orderly brought me a telegram, it was from the Hd.Qtrs Punjab Command to the O.C. 40th Pathans, directing him to send a Wing Officer immediately to do duty with the 38th Dogras proceeding to Malakand. Major Pelham-Burne, the CO., had forwarded it to me with instructions to go over to his bungalow at once. I was the only officer available, so I was detailed by the Major, and having got a railway and tonga warrant I started the same night by the 2a.m. train for Nowshera where I arrived at 7a.m.

30th July

Harington arrived soon afterwards. The centre of the camp was full of carts, animals and baggage, besides there were the 35th Sikhs who lost 21 men from sunstroke that day, 30th P.I. 2 companies Guides[8] and some of the Guides Cavalry and 11th Bengal Lancers. Col. Reid lately commanding at Pindi, was in command of the force. We slept the night, as we were, on the ground, a dust storm blew for some time and then came a thunderstorm with heavy rain. They were not conducive to cleanliness or rest, however we got accustomed to both later on. In the evening we were turned out by a false alarm, but the whole night we saw and heard the firing from the top of the pass.

1st August

There were 3 ways up the Pass –
   (1) A good broad road for wheeled traffic, made by the sappers and pioneers in '95 Chitral Campaign [during the Chitral Campaign]
   (2) The old Buddhist Road cleared and repaired and passable for mules and
   (3 a narrow footpath which is the shortest but steepest.

The next morning, 1st August, the whole force commanded by Col. Reid marched up by No.3 to the Pass, a distance of 7 miles, but owing to the heat and climb it took 4 hours to accomplish. There was very little opposition, the enemy firing from a ridge about a mile to the right without hitting anyone. As we climbed up under the fort we were greeted by the garrison waving their puggaries from the walls.

We halted on a flat piece of ground (Gretna Green) at the lowest point of the pass shut in by wild olive trees, to the right is Castle Rock, further on to the north in a flat bottomed hollow surrounded by rocky hills is Crater Camp, and to the West the Ridge – Maxim Point leading up to the Fort, beyond which are the Guides and Sikh hills. These are all protected by sangars [protective stone walls or breastworks] and small towers the whole being a very straggling and unprotected position for a small force to hold. About a mile down the north side of the pass is the stated position of North Camp which was abandoned on the 26th July[9] the night of the first attack, the tents and a lot of baggage, owing to insufficiency of transport falling into the enemy's hands.

We found the 45th Sikhs, 31st Punjab Infantry, 24th P.I. and Guides up there, the first three Regiments together with a Mountain Battery and a company of Madras Sappers and Miners having held the Pass, fighting day and night for a week. The whole camp was in an indescribable state of confusion the tents having been cut down as they obscured the view. Baggage, as it arrived, was deposited anywhere, there being no proper place to put it, and camels, bullocks, mules, goats, sheep and chickens wandered uncared for through the camp, directed entirely by their own sweet wills.

We spent the first day on Gretna Green on which fell the enemy's bullets which passed over the pickets at Castle Rock, which was the more unpleasant as we could not see the enemy. Two men were wounded, one strange to say being the only Muhamedan in the Regiment, a specially enlisted armourer, who was severely wounded in the ankle. The great object of the enemy was, of course, to hit Englishmen and Hindoos. In the evening we were told off to pickets, and the first night I spent on Maxim Point where we turned out once or twice, but for nothing serious. The garrison had been running short of ammunition but we had brought up with us a convoy of mules with a plentiful fresh supply.

The next day the enemy continued sniping from a ridge above Castle Rock, and once made a determined attack causing a great panic amongst the camp followers and servants. The enemy came very boldly down the hill but were checked by the pickets on Castle Rock and in Col. Sawyer's house and by the two mountain guns. It was a fine sight to see them coming down fearlessly with their flowing garments and [I] found it hard to realize that they were genuine enemy and that I was not looking on at a play. The Buneri contingent were clothed entirely in dark blue.

This day some of my bedding came up with some mules from Darghai, I had had nothing when I marched up but the clothes on my back. It was not till four days after this that my bearer came up with some clothes and I was able to have my first wash and change, when the syce arrived with my pony also.

The garrison at Chakdarrah, a fort about 8 miles to the North, at the bridge over the Swat River, and which consisted of 2 companies of the 45th Sikhs under Rattray and Wheatley were being very hard pressed, and an attempt was made by the 45th, 31st, 24th and some Guides Cavalry during the day to relieve them, but the enemy were still in too great numbers and the force had to retire, on which occasion the Guides Cavalry were nearly cut off and Keyes was wounded.

The next night I was sent in charge of a picket on the South side of the Pass where nothing occurred beyond sniping and false alarms occasioned by stray sheep. There was heavy fighting for about 5 minutes in the middle of the night from Darghai, and looking down I could see the twinkling flashes, but I heard subsequently that it was entirely a false alarm.

3rd August

On the 3rd August the same force, only increased in numbers, was again sent out to relieve Chakdarrah[10]; this time they were successful and completely dispersed the enemy killing about 2,000 of them. The Guides and 11th Bengal Lancers made brilliant charges, the whole action spread out like a panorama could be seen from the walls of the fort.

After this the enemy entirely disappeared, and the next few days were spent in putting the camp and fortifications to rights again, tents were pitched, the baggage and transport were collected in the Crater Camp, sangars were built and strengthened and more troops were brought up. The 1st Brigade consisting of 11th Bengal Lancers, West Kent, 45th, 31st and the 24th Punjab Infantry under General Meiklejohn, were being concentrated at Amandarrah close to Chakdarrah. The Buffs, Guides and Cavalry and Infantry, 35th and ourselves comprising the 2nd Brigade under General Jeffries, were kept on the Malakand together with troops for the line of communications under Col. Reid as it was decided to carry out punitive expeditions. Stockley arrived with his company of Sappers and Fitzgerald from the 26th joined the 38th.

14th August

I accompanied a column about 500 strong which was dispatched to collect grain and fodder from a village called Khar, about 4 miles off, the first time I had been outside the pass since entering it. There was no opposition and the village was empty, the whole country was strewn with the dead bodies of the enemy which could not be buried. The grain is usually kept in cupboards made of mud, but before leaving, the enemy had removed it and buried it under the floor of the huts, I found amongst other things a 9 lb shell, an empty bottle of Worcester sauce and a lance pennant of the 11th B.L. We got several mounds of grain and bhoosa and also recovered many stores and property looted from the North Camp.

15th August

Two or three men of the 40th who presented themselves with leave certificates were kept in our Quarter Guard for some days pending enquiries, they were eventually sent back to the 40th and allowed compensation for damage of property where possible.

We were much surprised to hear about this time of the attack by Mohmands on Shabkaddar [a police post about fifteen miles north of Peshawar] and the consequent retaliation by the Peshawar Garrison under General Elles and Col. Woon. During this time the weather was very bad, there was heavy rain with violent thunder storms day and night for 10 days on end. Pattison, Browne, Harington, Fitzgerald and myself got remarkably wet. A force of Buneris having collected in Upper Swat, the 1st Brigade was dispatched on 15th August with 10 days rations to disperse them. They met the enemy at Landaki and dispersed them without much trouble but in the action McLean of the Guides and Griffiths, a war correspondent, were killed, and Col. Adams of the Guides and Lord Fincastle were awarded the V.C.[11] The 1st Brigade proceeded as far as Mingalora and then returned. The 2nd Brigade moved down to Khar on 15th August to take the place of the 1st Brigade and there made ourselves pretty comfortable in spite of the uncertainty of our future movements. While at Khar Major Cadell and Captain Tomkins rejoined the Regiment from general leave in England. The Swatis had entirely left this end of the valley, only their camp fires were visible on the hills at night.

27th August

Meanwhile arrangements were being made for an expedition in Buner, a 3rd Brigade was concentrating at Rustum with a view to entering Buner from the South through the Ambeyla Pass while, on 27th August, the 2nd Brigade marched to Thana (the chief town of Swat) to be in readiness to enter Buner from the North and effect a junction with the 3rd Brigade from the South. On the march we passed the 1st brigade returning from Upper Swat.

While at Thana I was sent in charge of a fatigue party and escort to collect wood for fuel from the village. It was a large village of mud huts, quite the largest I saw anywhere on the frontier, built as usual in terraces up three sides of the hill, but without the usual number of watch towers. As the 1st Brigade had been through it twice and as we demolished much of what was left in abstracting the beams from the roofs of the huts it was in a fair state of ruin for the second time, it having been burnt before in '95 by the Chitral Expedition.

28th August

Shortly after arriving at Thana, however, these arrangements were countermanded, and we were sent back on 28th August to Julagram, 3 miles to the west of Khar and on the borders of the Utman Khel country.

Our camp at Julagram was on a very pretty spot, on a narrow strip of culti-
vated land between high rocky hills and the Swat River, where it rushes into a
dark rocky gorge at the end of the valley[12]. There was plenty of shade beneath
large clumps of chenar and palm trees, through which green banked irrigation
canals trickled coolly, wild olive and fig trees abounded and there was a profu-
sion of sweet scented wild thyme. The sappers had daily been at work here
making a path along the steep sides of the gorge into Utman Khel country.

29th August

We were not allowed to stop here long however as the Khan of Dir (our ally) was
being threatened by the Haddah Mullah and his following and a flying column
composed of the 2nd Queens, 22nd P.I, 38th, Major Anderson's Field Battery
(No. 10) and a detachment of the 11th B.L. was ordered to concentrate at Uch
at the foot of the Laram Pass to support the Khan of Dir.

Consequently the next day – the 29th August – we left the 2nd Brigade and
marched to Chakdarrah, crossing the river by the suspension bridge, which took
a long time to accomplish as the bridge was only safe for a few men or animals at
a time. It rained hard the whole time and all the following night, when Harington
and I sat in an ambulance wagon which had a covered-in-top. The fort looked
none the worse for the siege, and the enemy had not damaged the bridge. The
next day we marched to Uch and were joined by the rest of the column.

30th August

While we were here we heard the rising of the Afridis and that a force of three
divisions was to enter Tirah, the 38th Dogras being included in the Peshawar
Column under General Hammond, owing to our having plenty to do, however,
where we were, we could not be spared and our place was eventually taken by
the 45th Sikhs. We were employed while here in collecting rifles and fines from
the tribes concerned in the late rising, the guns and jezails they invariably gave
us loaded in the hopes that some harm might arrive to us thereby. One day
General Woodhouse commanding the column ordered all the useless guns to be
burnt, a large bonfire was consequently made outside our quarter guard, and the
guns were all thrown in, we not suspecting that they were loaded, we were soon
made aware of the fact though by loud reports and bullets flying about the camp.
I do not think anyone was hurt however.

It was then determined to operate against the Mohmands and Bajauris, two
tribes under General Elles were to march from Peshawar through the Mohmand
country, and two brigades under General Sir Bindon Blood from Malakand to
march through Bajauer, unite with General Elles and return with him to

Peshawar. The Haddah Mullah[13] in the meanwhile however determined on another raid, and news was received in our camp of his intention to destroy the suspension bridge across the Panjkora River near Sadu, which was erected by the Sappers and Miners in '95.

5th September

At 4a.m. on 5th September the whole column fell in and marched off to hold the bridge, some 15 miles from our present camp. The road was extremely bad the whole way, narrow and winding through rocky hills and ravines, with steep gradients at one point going over a fairly steep pass and next winding along a dry nullah bed. At the time it was uncertain where the Mullah and his gathering were and if attacked we should have been in a very bad way. It subsequently transpired that we reached the bridge only just before he did, the main body arriving about 12 noon and seeing us in possession of the bridge he determined not [to] risk a fight.

I was told off with a company to escort Major Anderson's Field Force Guns on the march and to help them and the hospital wagon over the bad places, the latter should never have been brought and had to be sent back as they could not be taken on, often the patients had to turn out and lend a hand in dragging their own conveyances. We got into camp at 4p.m. having been twelve hours on the road.

Luckily I fell in with a doctor (Capt. Fisher I.M.S.) about half way who was cooking a tin of soup, which he generously shared with me.

We camped on the west bank of the river, between the river and some high cliffs, near the scene of Col. Battys's death in '95[14], in an absolutely indefensible position, and our pickets on top of the cliffs were quite cut off from us in the dark. Luckily the enemy, through ignorance of our condition, did not attack us. While having our dinner on a ruined wall in the camp a scorpion was found under one of the stones, and on turning over the others a scorpion was found under nearly each.

6th September

The next day we moved back to the East bank of the river and took up a more defensible position which I was told off to make a sketch of.

The food obtainable so far had been plentiful and varied, the swat mutton being especially good, but here we had some difficulty in obtaining fresh meat for the mess and lived chiefly on tinned beef served up in various disguises by an ingenious Khausamah. The mess of the 38th under Capt Stainforth was very well managed, his staff consisting of a Khausamah and two Khitmatgars, there was a complete set of folding camp chairs and tables, aluminium cups, plates, etc. and two boxes transferable into tables which carried a day's supply for the whole mess, and went one on each side of a mule.

The 2nd and 3rd Brigades also came up from Malakand the latter camping near the ford at Sadu about 2 miles further down on the West bank of the River, and the former on the site of the first camp opposite us. The river here was very swift and ran between high rocky banks opening out into a valley at Sadu.

General Woodhouse believed in having all troops in an enemy's country under arms at daybreak to repel a possible attack, daybreak being the favourite time all the world over for making attacks, consequently every morning at 4 the 'rouse' was sounded and everyone had to turn out in whatever clothes he liked but fully armed. This was a very sound measure but at the same time a very chilly one.

12th September

So far we had always been with tents, but on 9th Sept. an advance was ordered on light scale, so that tents and heavy baggage had to be left behind, the light scale constituted 40 lbs for officers and 10 lbs for men. We left the flying column, which was now used for the line of communication troops, and rejoined the 2nd Brigade marching 12 miles to Ghansam the 3rd Brigade overtaking us. We marched through Kura Khan's fort at Mudia on the Ghandol River near which we camped, the sangars held by the enemy in '95 were still visible on the hills around us. Our first night here the political officer – Gunter – reported that the enemy intended attacking us, and it certainly looked like it as the enemy's camp fires were very numerous, we consequently took every precaution but passed a peaceful night in spite of it. We halted four days collecting more guns and fines which the enemy were very slow in bringing in. As there seemed a prospect of prolonged campaigning I wrote to the Army and Navy Stores in Bombay for a complete and serviceable field kit, such as I had brought with me from Pindi in my hurry being very insufficient.

I was detailed to make a road report to our next camping ground and accompanied a reconnaissance in force for this purpose. We had a very pleasant halt for lunch in a shady spot called Secunderai, where there was a fort in the Khan of Nawagai's territory, who with his followers were friendly and subsequently behaved very well.

On 13th Sept. we continued our march along the Watelai River and camped about 16 miles from Ghansam on the North bank, there was heavy rain that night – the first we had since bivouacking.

The next day – the 14th we marched along the River Rudd 6 miles to the Rambat Pass which we ascended without opposition, though we expected to find it held in force. The valley at the foot of the pass was very pretty, plenty of cultivation and mud forts, surrounded by clumps of trees, were studded about the plain. On the Pass grew very fine olive tress covered with mistletoe. The Buffs and Guides were left on top of the pass, the 35th and ourselves descended to the plain and encamped on a spot called Markhannai about 5 miles off.

We were very pleased at the prospect of soon reaching Peshawar and joining the Turah force as there seemed nothing to do where we were. Colonel Vivian had, as usual, ordered a trench to be dug as soon as we reached camp, but the 35th had made no defensive arrangements acting on the advice of the political officer who was sure that there would be no opposition.

14th September

About 8p.m. just as we had finished dinner and were sitting round the lights, a volley was fired at us from close outside the camp. There were no pickets out as it was considered safer to have a strong line of sentries round the camp, the ground being very broken outside. The lights were immediately extinguished and the men fell in, the volley being the signal for heavy firing from all sides but chiefly from the opposite side of the camp to our back, so we had to sit and listen to the bullets coming over from behind and from both sides without having much to fire at in front of us. There was a broad nullah running round three sides of the camp, being only fifty yards distant from our Quarter Guard, which was at the S.W. corner of the camp. We held the W. face and the S. Face with the moun-tain battery. The 35th Sikhs held part of the W. face and the N. Face, 2 coys of the Guides and a squadron of the 11th B.L. held the E. face. My company extended from the Quarter Guard along the S. face.

The firing continued for 2 hours during which time the 35th dug a shelter trench, and after which the enemy drew off to the south, and appeared to hold a council of war with much shouting and tom-tomming but just out of range. Then they came on again with considerable reinforcements and began firing from our end of the camp and we could hear them urging each other on, but they knew the game too well apparently or else could not screw up sufficient courage for they would not risk coming out into the open. Star shell did not show us much of the enemy either. It was during this time that Baillie the Adjutant was shot through the heart and died almost immediately while standing by the Colonel's side at the Quarter Guard. He was a colonial and came from New Zealand. Shortly after this Tomkins was ordered to make a counter attack with his company and while on his way to the Colonel for instructions was shot through the head and killed. Harington was also hit in the head by a bullet from behind mortally, while lying in the trench. We had one man killed and two or three wounded. The 35th Sikhs, Guides and 11th B.L. had only two or three casual-ties each. Most of the casualties occurred amongst the transport animals which were very much crowded up in the centre of the camp, nearly 100 were hit. There was a half moon which rose about 8p.m. and it was a clear night so that we could occasionally make out shadowy forms of the enemy, while objects in our camp must have stood out clearly against the sky line. About 3a.m. the firing ceased, and the enemy entirely withdrew. A squadron of the 11th B.L. was sent after them as soon as it was light and catching up the rearguard of the retiring enemy killed 21.

15th September

The next morning I attended the funeral of Tomkins and Baillie, they were two of the very best fellows and excellent officers, liked by everyone, officers and men, and we found it hard to believe that they were gone and had been with us only the evening before. They were buried in the centre of the camp, the spot being well pressed down and covered over with litter so as to be quite unrecognizable. Harington was in a bad way but hope was not then given up. We had nearly the whole of the transport animals of the Brigade and all the cavalry horses and battery mules in our camp which accounts for the heavy casualties among them.

The same day the whole brigade moved 3 miles up the Mahmund Valley where a camp was pitched on a better site, the 38th took part of the North and West Faces.

16th September

On the 16th it was determined to punish the Mahmunds who were found to be the chief offenders in the attack at Markhannai by burning as many villages as possible, and as it was not expected that we should meet with much opposition in the day time, the Brigade was formed into three columns. The Guides were sent to the west side of the valley, the Buffs and 35th Sikhs under Colonel Goldie, were sent straight up the valley to the North, and 5 companies of the 38th with Stockley's Company of sappers were sent to the east side.

We burnt two villages and had a pleasant lunch under some shady trees in the second village without seeing any opposition, and then advanced towards the next village – Dumadillah. I was sent with a company as flank guard and had to advance along the hillside in a direction parallel with the column in the plain, and while thus proceeding came suddenly on the village, which was a large one with great natural defences and held in force by the enemy. No reconnaissance had been made so the position or strength of the villages was unknown.

I took up a position on a ridge and opened fire, and waited for the column to arrive. As soon as the Colonel came up he determined that the village was too strong to be taken by our small force so he took up a position on [a] small hill and ordered me to retire through. Our whole force then retired slowly before the advance of the enemy. Our casualties being rather out of the ordinary, are worth noting. Stockley's helmet was shot through. Two Native officers were slightly wounded in their little fingers. One man's bayonet was smashed by a bullet, the stock of another man's rifle, who was standing beside me was shot through, and the cartridge pouch of another was hit exactly on the muzzle of the barrel and split up to the hands [sic]. We were in the first party back to camp where we arrived at 4p.m. In the evening we heard heavy firing up the valley and some wounded were brought in under escort. A very heavy thunderstorm with drenching rain and lightning came on and we could do nothing in the darkness to relieve the troops up the valley. The whole night long stragglers and wounded came in having lost their way in the dark, about midnight the guides marched in and towards morning most of the 35th were in. Just before daybreak we marched out to the village of Bilot, where we found the General, about 12 men of the Buffs and the remnant of Captain Birch's Mountain Battery – they had spent the whole night in the rain fighting practically hand to hand with the enemy and the casualties were heavy. Captain Crawford R.A. and 9 men killed and Watson R.A. and about 20 wounded, nearly all the Battery mules were shot. Winter R.E. was shot through both legs. We then learnt that the Company of the 35th had got into difficulties on top of a hill and some more of the 35th and Guides had hard fighting to relieve them. Hughes, the Adjutant of the 35th and 20 men had been killed and Ryder, Gunning and Cassels and 40 men wounded.[15]

We buried the dead and burnt the mules and marched back to camp. The same day – the 17th Sept. – I was ordered in charge of 3 companies and Fitzgerald, 3 companies of the Buffs, the whole under the command of Major Moody of the Buffs to march back to the village of Jhar and bring back a convoy with ammunition and rations which was arriving from Malakand.

We bivouacked under the walls of the Khan of Jhar's fort[16] and were able to get helio communication with the outside world, the convoy, however, never turned up and as we had orders not to wait after 9 a.m. the following morning, we marched back to Inayat Killah without it. The convoy was subsequently brought up by a force of the Khan of Jhar's men.

On nearing Inayat Killah we heard the sound of firing and shortly after saw the troops returning after having burnt the village of Dumadollah from which we had returned on 16th.

Soon after reaching the camp we got helio communication with General Elles' two Brigades from Peshawar, they encamped with General Woodhouse's Brigade at Narwagai about 20 miles to the east. General Woodhouse's Brigade was severely attacked on the night of 23rd Sept and the Genl. himself was wounded, they drove off the enemy with heavy loss. Genl. Elles had a small fight on the Badmanai Pass but met with no opposition elsewhere and returned almost immediately with Genl. Woodhouse's Brigade to Peshawar via the Mohmand country. We stopped here till the 12th October burning villages and sending out foraging parties. We used to get grain from the villages and mackai, and when we had eaten that up barley, bhoosa and green rice from the horse and mules. The enemy in their turn used to snipe us at night.

On the 19th Sept as we were passing the village of Bilot the Colonel sent me to see if the graves were all right. I found them all dug up and the bodies mutilated.

On 25th Sept the Buffs and 35th were relieved by the West Kents and 31st Punjab Infantry. On the 26th Sept. a jirgah came in, but as we could not get satisfactory terms from them they were sent back. I saw Harington before he left for the last time, he recognized me but was wandering a good deal. There were a good many casualties on our side in attacking the village of Zeghai and Keene and Power of the Buffs were wounded.

30th September

There was pretty heavy fighting at the villages of Agrah and Gat. It was my turn on the latter occasion to stop in camp. They were two adjoining villages with very strong natural defences. We burnt the first but had to retire under very heavy fire without reaching the second village. Col. O'Brien, 31st P.I. and 2nd Lt. Brown Clayton, West Kents and Peacock 31st P.I. and 40 men wounded. I was told all this by Winston Churchill[17], war correspondent, who was the first man I saw returning. I heard afterwards that Harington died at Panjkora on 29th Sept. and was buried at Malakand.

3rd October

There was some fighting at Badelai; we had about 16 casualties of which 6 were in the 38th. I was looking over a bank once in the course of the morning, a bullet struck the bank and threw dust into my face. I amused myself in my spare time by drawing sketches which I sent home. One of these was taken by the Illustrated London News. More troops were ordered up as the enemy were disinclined to come to terms. On 2nd October Genl. Sir Bindon Blood with half the 24th P.I. and No. 8 M.B.R.A. Genl. Blood had returned to India to take command of a Division for Tirah.[18]

On the 4th October the other half of the 24th P.I. the H.L.I., No. 10 F.B.R.A. and No.7 M.B.R.A. arrived. No.7 M.B.R.A. had been sent back for fresh mules after Bilot, the guns being taken down on camels.

On the 8th October and again on the 11th the jirgah came in bringing the full number of rifles and the rest of the fine, they also implored us most submissively not to burn any more villages, consequently on 12th Octbr. the camp at Inayat Killah was at length evacuated and both brigades marched back 10 miles to Jhar. Col. Vivien was sent back sick from here, we were having very cold nights and in consequence of an insufficiency of clothing I caught a severe chill. The next day – the 13th Octbr. we moved camp a short distance to the North into the Salerzai country to a place called Matta Shah the inhabitants of which had been giving some trouble and from whom some fines were due. No reconnaissance had been made and the site of our next camp appeared rather uncertain. The two Brigades marched separately and the first happening to hit on the right road were soon encamped on a high flat piece of ploughed land fairly free from nullahs. We did not get in until 12 noon after having wandered about in circles vainly trying to avoid the winding river and nullahs which were worse here than anywhere I have ever seen. The sappers were constantly digging the Field Battery out of nullahs and if the enemy had only thought of attacking us they could have given us a repetition of 16th Septr. We took the east face of the camp with the Guides alongside on our right in front of us 600 or 800 yds wide, on the further side of which friendly pickets of the Khan of Jhar's men were posted. We were sniped at every night of the week we spent there but without much damage – one man of the Guides was wounded.

On the 14th Octbr. the Guides Cavalry and Infantry made a reconnaissance to the Eastward and reported that the inhabitants seemed friendly and that a jirgah was assembling.

While here our Doctor, Col. Scott Reid went back to take up an appointment in India (P.M.O. Lahore District) and Surgn. Captain Hayward came up to us instead.

The lower Sakrzai paid up their fines at once, but the inhabitants of the North end being in the hills seemed undecided so on 16th Oct, the two brigades marched up in three columns about 6 miles up the valley & halted in the shade of beautiful trees at the village Tarslarah. The inhabitants seemed very friendly and brought our charpoys for the officers to sit on and great quantities of walnuts by way of hospitality and were much interested in watching the troops and guns. I was trying to air my pushtoo when a wild looking Pathan came up and greeted me with the words, 'Good morning, Boss!' He had been for ten years a coolie on a Demerara sugar plantation.

General Blood invited all the mounted officers to ride up the valley with him, to Salarzai stronghold of Paskat and meet the jirgah, consequently I, and as many as could be spared, went with an escort of cavalry and field guns. We went about two miles further up the valley and halted just outside Pasket where the jirgah met us, as they seemed a rather large body of men and well armed the guns were brought up and ostentatiously trained on them, and no doubt influenced them considerably in agreeing so speedily and swiftly to all our terms.[19]

The valley was very fertile and marshy and we saw a good many snipe and teal. After a short halt we rejoined the column and marched back to camp.

On the 17th October the 35th Sikh again joined us; they brought up a convoy. During the remaining few days here, waiting for the full complement of guns and fines to be paid in, nothing of importance occurred. We amused ourselves with cricket against the HLI with whom was Major Cavendish, late of Horsham.

20th October

Having collected 50 rifles and some guns and swords we marched back to Jhar, demolishing 3 villages on the way. These villages belonged to a man who refused to pay his share of the fine and whose followers had sniped us every night we were in Mutta Shah. I was with the advanced guard on this march and was rather surprised to see, apparently, some well armed enemy in one of the villages, they made no resistance and I took them prisoners, they turned out eventually to be friendlies whom the political had sent on ahead to clear the village of inhabitants. After two days of doubt as to our future movement, we suddenly received orders to return to Malakand.

22nd October

Consequently the 2nd Brigade marched 15 miles and camped on the West Bank of the Panjkoras, the 1st Brigade halting at Kolkai a mile to the West.

The nights now began to get very cold, my usual sleeping costume consisted of my ordinary clothes, plus a 2nd flannel shirt, a coat warm, British, a greatcoat and two blankets and a towel wrapped round my head. Our heavy baggage was sent up to meet us at Panjkora, and I was able to sleep in a tent again.

As an example of the time required for moving troops and transport on a bad road, I may mention that for the march of 15 miles from Jhar to Panjkora, the 38th being the advanced guard left Jhar at 8.30a.m. and reached Panjkora at 1.30p.m. while the rearguard left at 11a.m. and got in at 4p.m. That is to say that a Brigade with transport takes from 2 to 3 hours to pass a given point.

23rd October

The 2nd Brigade marched to Sarai, while the 1st Brigade merely crossed the river. I, with a company, was told off as escort to the guns on this march.

24th October

The 2nd Brigade marched from Sarai to Chakdarrah, the 1st Brigade remaining where they were.

25th October

The 2nd Brigade reached Malakand again and encamped at North Camp, when I slept in a bed again for the first time for over six weeks.

10th November

We moved up onto the Kotal, the HQ of the right wing to the fort, and the Left Wing (with which I was) to Castle Rock, we messed with the 21st P.I.

I went on 10 days leave on 11th Novbr. to look after my kit at Pindi and do a little shooting at Hazaroo with Marden Ali, the shikarri of Attock days.

On 22nd Novbr. an expedition consisting of the Buffs, 21st, 35th and No 8 M.B.R.A. and Madras sappers and miners under Col. Reid, went through the Utman Khel country. They went via the Kot Pass and returned in a fortnight without meeting any opposition.

The Guides returned to Mardan, and the 1st Brigade crossed the Kotal and camped at Jalala.

I met here my Father's old orderly of the 2nd P.I. by name Gul Mahd. then serving in the Swat Levy!

General Jeffries about this time left the Brigade to take up a command in India.

I was chiefly occupied with working parties making defences and platforms for Comst. stores at Rs 1/- for 8 hours work.

I was recalled to join the 40th and went back to Pindi on 14th Dec. 1897.

1898

Rawalpindi to Mian Mir with Regiment on relief by train. Left Pindi 4p.m. 5th Feb. '98 arrived Mian Mir 7a.m. 6th Feb.[20]

Mian Mir to Amritsar. Stayed with Charlie Dallas at Amritsar from 5th to 7th March '98.

Mian Mir to England. Left Mian Mir morning of 1st June 1898 by 2nd class mail train with Major Wallace and Green R.E. Arrvd. Bombay 3rd June, stopped at Watson's Hotel the night and sailed next day 4th in *Caledonia* on board amongst others Col and Mrs Coates 25th P.I. Colonels Stuart, Davidson and Adams also Walker, Pigot-Carlton, Lindsay, Green and Priestley 1st M.L. In cabin with Leslie P.W.D. and American Missionary. Arrived Aden 9th, Brindisi 2p.m. 16th and Marseilles early morning 19th June. Stopped night at Hotel with

Lindsay, reached Paris evening of 20th. Stopped night at Hotel du Nord, reached London 21st stopped night at Alexander Hotel, arrived Horsham 2.7 p.m. 22nd June 1898.

1899

27th April
R.M.S. *Arabia* off Gravesend. Started back to India this morning by 8.23 train from Horsham after a year's leave at home. Father and Mabel[21] saw me off at the docks and were able to walk alongside the ship for a long way, and at one point when we stopped I had a long conversation with them through my cabin port hole and shook hands with the end of Mabel's umbrella. The ship started at noon, got clear of the docks about 2 p.m. and we appear to be just out of the river now 5p.m. Saw fleet of destroyers manoeuvring.

7th May
Off Crete, voyage so far calm, cool, and uneventful. Reached Gibraltar 1st May had just time to run ashore as Montegriffo's shop and dispatch some nougat to Audrey.[22] The Channel Fleet came in just before we sailed, 12 grand ships in line, a splendid sight. We reached Marseilles on the afternoon of 3rd May, the sea and the weather being everything that they should be in the Mediterranean. Went ashore with Arnott, Hincks and Shanks, had dinner at a restaurant and afterwards saw a variety entertainment at the Palais de Crystal. Slept on board, and went over the cathedral next morning with the same party, sailed afternoon of 4th May. Had been in cabin with Hincks so far, but owing to another fellow being put in at Marseilles (Kennedy, Somersets) I went across to cabin with Arnott. Passed through the Straits of Bonifacio on the 5th May, and the Lipari Islands and Masena on the 6th. Last night and this morning the sea was roughish, worse even than the dreaded Bay where it was not very bad. The double revolving flash light in the light house near Cape Finisterre is at a place called Solano.

Arnott told me an interesting fact yesterday: – that in a locomotive the piston has no backwards stroke, i.e. it pushes the wheel round forward and then waits till caught up and taken on by the engine itself when it shoots out forwards again!

Just remembered a story told me by Col. Howell before I left Horsham:– scene Station in Northern India, cavalry 'stables' going on, flight of 'kulon' passing overhead, young orderly officer, new to the country, to his orderly 'What is that noise?' Smart orderly saluting 'flight of Kulon, Sir'. Officer, 'What is a Kulon?' Orderly, saluting, ' On the principle of a goose, Sir.'

14th May

Since my last entry on the 7th May we have got as far as Aden. We arrived at Port Said about 11 a.m. on the 9th and did not start up the Canal till early on the 10th as the *Osiris* bringing the mails was late. HMS *Harrier* was anchored at Port Said, in the Canal we passed HMS *Narcissus* and P&O SS *Sumatra*. We went slightly aground while trying to avoid another ship in the lake off Ismailia and reached Suez early on the 11th only stopping to take on some vegetables. Since leaving Suez it had been hot (84 degrees in the barber's shop) but not unbearably so, or as hot as it ought to be. The *Arabia*'s longest run so far has been 385 miles, the *Caledonia* used to do over 400. I have omitted to mention that the 3rd Officer was put ashore dangerously ill with pneumonia, contracted in the Channel at Marseilles, we heard on arrival at Port Said of his death a few hours after being taken on shore. Two lascars and a fireman have also been buried, two off Suez and one yesterday. I also have not mentioned that when we entered the Palais de Crystal at Marseilles we happened to arrive rather early and were the first people in the stalls, when somebody raised a cry of 'Anglais' which was followed by much hissing from the gallery!

Since coming on board I have read the following books – *The Christian* by Hall Caine which I didn't care for, *My Lady Rotha* by Stanley Weyman, which I didn't think as good as his others. *Roden's Corner* by Henry Seton Merriman, very well written but rather a lot of padding in the beginning. *Tribes on my Frontier* by E.H.A. *The Wonderful Visit* by J.M.Barrie, very amusing. Miss Wheeler also lent me a Pushtoo Testament which I was able to make out with the aid of an English one. I am now reading a book lent to me by Evans, *British Central Africa* by Sir H.H. Johnstone the founder of the Protectorate, he states one very interesting fact, namely that the more enlightened Arabs and Mohamedans recognize the superiority of Christianity and civilization over their own religion and customs. I was also surprised to learn that the country and climate, especially on the high plateau in Nyasa, are among the finest in the world.

A practical joke has been played on a certain couple on board this ship who seemed very pleased with each other's society, their deck chairs have been found tied together!

Lindsay showed me a good puzzle – how to make a Maltese Cross with 3 lucifer matches – also make a figure with 5 matches, take three away 3 and add 2 and leave the same figure.

15th May

We got into Aden yesterday 2 p.m. and left at 5 p.m. There was just time to go ashore for an hour but not time to see anything, so Evans and I just sat in

Dinshaw's shop to avoid the heat and dust, I have never been on shore there before so was very anxious to do so. While there a German boat, the *Prinz Heinrich* came in with the Princess Henry of Prussia on board who was returning from China.

Have just read a very amusing set of verses called *The Modern Traveller* by H.B. and B.T.B. The account of Africa I must send to Mabel.

> 'Oh Africa! Mysterious land,
> Surrounded by a lot of sand
> And full of grass and trees
> And elephants and Africanders
> And politics and salamanders,
> And Germans wishful to annoy
> And horrible rhinoceros,
> And native rum in little kegs
> And savages called Touregs
> (a kind of Sudanese)
> And tons of diamonds and lots
> Of nasty dirty Hottentots'
> Great Island, made to the bane
> Of Mr. Joseph Chamberlain.
> Peninsula, whose smouldering fights
> Keep Salisbury awake at nights
> And gave for quite a year or so
> Such sport to Monsieur Hanotaux.'

Later on the hero is caught by savages and tortured, as follows :-

> 'Then I was pleased to recognize
> Some thumbscrews fitted to my size,
> And I was pleased to see
> That they were going to torture me,
> I find that torture pays me best,
> It simply teems with interest.
> They hung me up above the floor,
> Head downward, by a rope,
> They thrashed me half an hour or more
> And filled my mouth with soap,
> They jabbed me with a pointed pole
> To make me lose my self control
> But they did not succeed.
> Then (though very vulgar to narrate)
> There happened what I simply hate
> My nose began to bleed!'

I read today in Johnstone's book on Central Africa of two English elephant hunters settled there, by name Pettit, wonder if any connection of the Hamilton's African friend. Must find out.

17th May

Weather is very warm and sticky, the breeze, which is pretty stiff, is from behind, so we practically feel none at all. There are signs of the approach of the monsoon, cloudy and South Westerly winds.

Have just finished reading *Rupert of Hentzau* sequel to the *Prisoner of Zenda* by Anthony Hope, an awfully good book and very exciting. There is an ayah on board who is now finishing her 111th trip to England and back, having been in nearly all the different lines. She says she thinks the feeding in P & O the worst. Her husband is the Viceroy's cook. Have been in for half a dozen sweepstakes on the run, never won one but was second the other day, scoring nothing.

Herewith I will describe the usual manner of spending the day in the hot weather on board ship:- Sleep on deck, rise 6 a.m. when the decks are washed, have 'chota Hazri' and smoke a cigarette on deck in pyjamas and bare feet, shave, tub, dress, breakfast 8.30. Smoke a pipe and do a 'quarterdeck' with somebody. Then select a cool spot with a breeze if there is one available and read, smoke, sleep, meditate till dinner at 1.30 (dinner 2nd saloon P & O is a lengthy proceeding and a heavy meal & includes soup, fish, joint, second, legume, curry & sweet courses & cheese, ices, desert & coffee). After this one is in a proper condition for a further period of reading, smoking, sleeping and meditation till 6 p.m. when it is time to dress and wash for tea. Tea at 6.30 comprises cold meat, buns, jam and tea. After this an hour's 'quarterdeck' with somebody on 'spar' deck whilst 1st saloon dinner is going on, then we retire to our premises and have music of an elevating and refined nature till 9 p.m. when a frugal supper of biscuits and cheese is served, after which the time is passed in promenading and conversation till 11 p.m. when comes bed time and lights out. Pastimes of an active nature are not much indulged in after entering the Red Sea, so the day can hardly be said to 'teem with interest'!

18th May

Voyage nearly over, arrive Bombay early tomorrow morning. Played deck quoits with Buttar for cocktails. Little more breeze today. List of passengers who have interested me more or less during the voyage

HW Arnott. Bombay Nagpur railway.

Mr. Beer and son, dentist Mussoorie knows Hamilton.

Mrs. Broome, Ermount Depot Bombay.

Brown, Wood and 2 others, Goldfields Hyderabad.
Butter, Scotchman, going to India for short time on business and pleasure.
Capt. Cartwright, 6th Bo.C. was at Fort S. with 40th.
MG Cole, schoolmaster, Mussoorie.
FT Warre-Cornish, 17th B.C., at Mian Mir.
Mr.D. Elder, Calcutta Jute Mills.
JM Hincks, Goldfields, Mysore (electrical engineer).
Capt. HN Kelly, Royal Irish (met in Pindi).
FM Kennedy, Somersets.
GG Lindsay, 35th Sikhs met at Malakand and went home with him.
Capt PC Elliott-Lockhart, Guides.
Major G.Moore, Malwa-Bhil Corps.
H Playfair, Police Central Provinces.
Miss MA Shacklock, CMS.
AD Shanks, wine merchant, Bombay (very Scotch).
Major GR Westropp, Commissariat.
Miss Wheeler (doctor) CEZMS Quetta.
Mrs. Harvey, Irish Rifles.
Gerald Evans, Coffee Planter, Coorg, Mysore.
QM Sergt. and Mrs Ramsey, RA Roorkie.
Mrs Fink.

20th May

Arrived Bombay after strong head wind and choppy sea at 6 a.m. on 19th May. Went ashore 8.30 after luggage had been cleared. Had to pay duty on gun, because I had no gun pass for previous importation into India. Went to Great Western Hotel, Room No. 1 with Evans. Met NR. Medley who was at Wellington with me, going home today, in Egypt on 3 months leave.

Wired to Vansittarts yesterday to ask them to put me up. Got reply today so proceed to Mussoorie by mail train tonight leaving Victoria Terminus 8.30p.m.

2nd June

Been too busy and unsettled to write up account of my travels, now at an end for some time, I hope – herewith from noted:-

Copy of time table supplied by Medley very kindly.

Victoria Terminus	D.	21.0	Saturday night (20th May).
Bhusawal	A.	6.4	Sunday morning, chota hazri.
	D.	6.14	

Khandwa	A.	8.22	Breakfast
	D.	8.37	
I.M.Ry	A.	12.23	
	D.	12.55	
Bhopal	A.	15.20	Tea.
	D.	15.30	
Bina	A.	18.47	Dinner
	D.	19.19	
Jhansi	A.	22,45	
	D.	23,10	
E.I.Ry.	A.	5.30	Monday morning, chota hazri
Tundla	D.	5.58	
	Passenger		
N.W.Ry.	A.	10.40.	Breakfast
Ghaziabad	D.	11.5	
Saharanpur	A.	15.8	Breakfast
	D.	15.37	
Phillour		A.	21.2. Dinner
	D.	21.27	
Lahore	A.	1.30a.m	Tuesday morning.

The 'Mohurram' was going on the night I left Bombay, there being many tamaskas, & men preaching & all the native streets lit up. 1st class train fare from Bombay to Lahore Rs. 81/127-.

I started by mail train, evening 20th May via Itarsi, Jhansi, Tundla and Ghaziabad. The through carriage to Lahore was occupied by a lady (Lt. & Mrs. Uniacke R.A.) so I was obliged to go by ordinary carriage and change at each of the above places thereby incurring much discomfort having to change twice in the second night and no time for breakfast at Ghaziabad. Arnott travelled with me as far as the other side of the Ghats (Bombay Baroda & Central India Rly.)

The top of the Ghats is a place called 'Icatpuri'. The train was more than an hour late, the whole owing to a strike of signalmen throughout India, a little while before they had been 24 hours late. It was cloudy most of the way, and at Bhopal we had a shower but the heat was frightful the whole way.

Reached Saharanpur 4p.m. 22nd May. Agatha had wired & written to me c/o Stationmaster but I had not been expecting anything so never asked for it. I had a wash and change in the waiting room & then found that a Captain Williamson R.A. who had come up in the train with me from Bombay and had just arrived from England in an Australia Lloyd boat, wanted a tonga as far as Dehra so we agreed to share a special one (Rs 15/- each) and started after some dinner at 5.30p.m. (The price of a special tonga from Saharanpur to Rajpore has since been reduced to Rs 20/-, a seat in a small tonga being Rs. 10/-). Captain Williamson in Frontier Battery, Dehra Ghazi. The first 30 miles were flat and uninteresting except for the trees along the road, which were shady and pretty, and of various kinds. At Saharanpur there is a botanical garden where nearly every known Asiatic tree and plant is grown, but I had no time to go and see it. After driving 30 miles you enter the forest and begin to ascend the Siwalik range by the Mohan Pass, at the top of which you enter the Dun, the other Pass over the Siwaliks is the 'Tinley' on the Chakrata Road.

It got dark as we entered the forest, however it looked very pretty by moon-light & the fact that it was very good big game and tiger country gave an added interest to the drive. We arrived at Dehra about midnight where I dropped Williamson at the dak bungalow and continued the remaining 4 miles to Rajpore. Was much struck with Dehra, it is pretty and green with many and various flowering trees, and not very hot, it had not the usual burnt up and dusty appear-ance of the Punjab cantonment in hot weather. I stopped in the Rajpore dak bungalow for the night and rode up early the next morning to Mussoorie on a bazaar pony sending up my bag by coolie. I fell in with a fellow in the B.B & C.I. Railway, name unknown.

I found Agatha at home at Oak Lodge & then heard for the first time the news of poor Reggie's death. Herbert arrived late in the afternoon from Goodrich. I was not much struck with Mussoorie which Agatha showed me that afternoon, it seemed very big and bare, and I did not care for the set of people there much.

Agatha showed me a letter which I had written thanking her & Bala for some presents on my 6th birthday. It was dated Islington, Devon and stated that it had rained and that I had my birthday party in a barn, all of which I remember well.

Rode with Mrs. Stringfellow, Agatha's great friend, the next day – 24th May – on a pony lent by Mrs. Newcomin to a Gymkhana in the Happy Valley, there I saw Col. Bear V.D. & son, & also made the acquaintance of a Mrs. Malvin.

On the 25th Herbert, Agatha, Mrs. Stringfellow and myself walked to Mossy Falls, taking tea with us. We were caught in a thunderstorm and had tea in a summer house. The scenery was remarkably English looking and very like the valley of 'Watermeet' at Lynton, N. Devon. We went for a stroll afterwards and picked sort of yellow blackberries.

3rd June

Mussoorie, beginning from the south end, consists of Landour (the milty. cantonment), Castle Hill (property of H. Vansittart, Esq.) Club Hill, The Mall, Happy Valley & Vincent's Hill.

Herbert brought from Goodrich some Papitas, the fruit of the tree melon, which I tasted for the first time, they contain pepsins, and are supposed to be great blood purifiers.

My weight at Mussoorie in ordinary summer clothes was 11st. 1lb.

I left Mussoorie early on the 27th going down the 1st 2 miles in a dandy and walked the rest of the way to Rajpore, caught the ten o'clock mail tonga and reached Saharanpur about 5 p.m. Left S. by the 6 p.m. train and reached Lahore early Sunday morning and drove down to Mian Mir found McKay, Leslie and St John present. The latter started for England in my place on Tuesday the 30th May.

Took up quarters in my old bungalow moving into St John's room when he left. Took over Quartermaster and Regimental Wing Commander. Very unsettled as I haven't heard yet whether I am to be sent to Peshawar to relieve Craster on recruiting duty.

Colonel Haig, I.M.S. in medical charge of 1st Punjab Cavalry and temporary Medical Store Keeper here, says he once bought a chest of drawers from Father which he only sold the other day on coming here, they were very strong and serviceable he says, and have Father's name on them to this day.

I read Tennyson's famous lines in *The Man of the World* which struck me as rather incongruous but I must enter them here:-

'Sweet and evening star,
And one clear call for me,
And may there be no moaning of the bar,
When I put out to sea.
Twilight, and evening bell,
And after that the dark,
And may there be no sadness of farewell,
When I embark.'

4th June
Craster's pony which I use, was shod (Rs 1/8).

5th June
English mail arrived.

6th June
Received medal and wore the riband for the first time. I have a bathe in the swimming bath and a practice on the mess piano every morning. Today was held a Station Board to settle a dispute between the 40th and Messrs. E. Spanier & Co

as to who was chargeable with the cost of 571 yds. of puggari cloth which they claim to have sent us, but which we did not receive. The Board, composed of Capt. Lye, 23rd Pioneers, Lieut. Wilson R.A. & Lincoln, R. Inniskilling Fusiliers, decided in our favour.

Theft of clothes from our servants quarters last night. The thief made a hole under the window sill, opened the window from the inside and abstracted a large box containing clothes. Footsteps traced by native police to our lines.

Temperature in my room during daytime, by my thermometer, 92 degrees.

8th June

Sent off by English mail today an application to have my name entered as a candidate for employment in the British Central Africa Protectorate Forces, to the Under Secretary of State for War, War Office.

Met Capt. Hayward, IMS, the other day, who was doctor of the 38th at Malakand. He has since married Miss Kennard.

Reed, pay yesterday (English rate) Rs.303 –5–1. Forgot to mention that for my first week after arriving at Mian Mir, and until my old bearer came back, I employed as bearer one Saddar Bazaar, Mian Mir. My own bearer turned up on the 4th Inst. from Bhamo in Burmah, he commenced work on the 5th.

Temperature at 6 a.m. this morning 90 degrees in my room, getting hot.

9th June

Hired a bicycle from Phelps & Co. yesterday for a month, but they charge Rs. 45/- a month hire so I am going to send it back, & have got another from Rustinyee & Co., the Punjab Cycle Mart, for Rs.30/- a month.

Biked into Lahore yesterday. Had dinner with Lincoln & a Doctor Butt (Major A.M.S.) the sole representative of the 2nd Royal Inniskilling Fusiliers Mess. Drove into Volunteer Alfresco Concert & dance afterwards, got home about 2 a.m. Up this morning at 4 a.m. to take the Left Wing at company training. Met Cook of the Punjab Bank, & Clifford, profession unknown, yesterday.

11th June

Was on Court Martial for 5 hours yesterday at Royal Inniskilling Fusiliers Mess. Capt. Maynard S.S.O. (Devon Regt.) of 'Maiden's Hope' goes home on leave, starting today.

14th June

Had a heavy thunderstorm the night before last and yesterday, temperature gone down to 88 degrees. Quite cool sitting without punkah and doors open. Dined with Clifford, Cook and Lincoln last night at Punjab Club, Lahore. Had no time to come back to Mian Mir for clothes, so borrowed an entire set of clothes, under-clothing etc. from an entire stranger (Keene, Assistant Commissioner). Just remembered that St John told me before he went home that the Vicar of Berinarbour, near Combe Martin, where we stayed last summer at home, is his uncle & goes in a lot for breeding horses.

15th June

Discovered that the Grays came out with Herbert and Agatha Vansittart last October in the same Messagerie boat. Miss Stoppard sang a song which struck me as being very pretty *Spanish Boatman's Song* by Hamilton Aide, must get it for Mabel. I play cricket at the nets in Lahore in the afternoons.

English mail goes out today, wrote home and to Alice.

Temperature in my room, 12 noon, 87 degrees.

16th June

Saw Julian's promotion to Captain in G.O. today dated 9th May. Also that Hunt the son of the haberdasher at Horsham is posted to the medical charge of the Malwa Bhil Corps. Dined with Lincoln at Mess also Grays and Stopfords last night.

18th June

Took over duties of Adjutant from Leslie today, as orders have been received that I am not to relieve Craster at Peshawar.

Discovered that Surgn. Col. Haig, who was in 1st Punjab Cavalry, Graham's Regt., knew Uncle Morrison and Aunt Ju out here and had been to see them at Ealing, also that he had met the Hammers at Lowestoft.

Following are some of the entries for Sandhurst donkey Race at last sports:-

Chucked, by Kitchener out of Khartoum.

Success, by Hard Work, out of Government.

Raised, by Mellins, out of Cradle.

Maddened, by Bagpipe, out of Tune. When I was there one of the Tecks called his donkey 'Texas'.

20th June

Took over Craster's bay pony from this date.

Following riddle I read today:-

Q. Why was Eve Low Church before the fall and High Church afterwards?

A. Because before she was 'Eve-angelical' and afterwards she took to wearing vestments. Following is an extract from the *Sporting Times* by 'Pitcher' re a man who stammered: 'He can hardly be said to speak at all, he opens and closes his hands spasmodically, takes a large bite of climate, and shuts his eyes, then he lets off a low gurgle and a long whistle for a labial, while one of his dentals have been known to knock a quart of growing plums off a tree.'

22nd June

Had lots of rain the last two days and nights, looks almost like the monsoon. Temperature in my room 90 but very sticky.

Lincoln and Cook dined with me last night at Mess.

24th June

There was an eclipse of the moon last night but not quite total as we saw the whole of it, between 8 and 9 p.m. It was full moon.

Learnt the following facts with regard to fever from Col. Haig:- It is best to take quinine overnight with some aperient medicine. If you have regular inter-mittent fever an emetic (20 qrs. of epicac:) half an hour before it is due will cure you.

Herewith Kipling's *Recessional* which I found in T.P. O'Connor's paper *M.A.P.* I write it down because I have not seen it published in any book yet:

> We have had a lot of rain, yesterday morning the maidan by the range
> was entirely under water and the raised firing points stood out like
> islands. This damp heat is the worst I have ever felt, the men do not
> like it either. This morning – 6a.m. – at kit inspection, standing still at
> attention without moving at all, most of the mens' coats and pyjamas
> were wet through front and back.

25th June

War with the Transvaal seems imminent, it has been growing more serious every day since the failure of Sir Alfred Milner to get any concessions which Kruger has made so expensive – a Govt. monopoly – as to seriously affect the gold mines out there, also on account of the fact that Ouitlanders are not allowed to vote till they have been 13 years in the country by which law they are debarred from having any voice in the Government of the country.

It has been 83 degrees in the shade in London lately, about the same temperature that it is here today owing to the amount of rain there is much doubt which of the two places – London or Mian Mir – would be the most comfortable. English mail due this afternoon (Sunday).

2nd July

Last Wednesday the 28th June we had a ladies dinner in the mess, Mrs. Elliott & Mrs. Hayward the only two ladies in Mian Mir came. We have had a lot more rain lately but it doesn't seem to cool the air at all. Yesterday I drove to Mian Mir East Station to see the furlo' men off & was caught in very heavy rain.

Leslie went off on 10 days leave to Dalhousie yesterday so McKay and I are left alone.

The following is a new version:-

'Drink to me only with thine eyes,
Those eyes so bright and frisky,
Leave but a kiss within the cup
And I'll not shout for whisky.'

Field (Cantonment Magistrate) said yesterday that according to English law, if one man saw another drowning at his feet, and by stretching out a hand could save him and yet did not do so, he could not be convicted of any offence, so that a man might escape for doing a cold blooded thing like that and yet be hung for killing a man for striking him under provocation in a fit of temper.

3rd July

Was examining officer on a L.S. Hindustani exam this morning (8 a.m. to 1 p.m.) four candidates, Major Watson R.A.M.C. (A), Miles N.W.Ry.(B), Silvester N.W.Ry.(C), Symon-Scutt, Bank of Bengal (D). I passed the three former, the latter I ploughed.

English mail arrived.

Subedar Major Kutab Dai died last night at 12 o'clock from abscess of the liver and peritonitis. I was woken up at 12 o'clock by Shahibullah (N.O. on duty) who came to report to me, I went down to the lines to make enquiries, it was fearfully hot night, the worst we have had. The Subedar Major had 32 yrs. 6 months and 3 days service. He was an exceedingly nice old man and liked by everyone.

8th July

A few nights ago Bevan, Petman, Stowe and Wilberforce all civilians were attacked in Lahore by a gang of men armed with lathis, while they were driving at night in Lahore. No-one was damaged, but none of the gang were caught.

I dined with Coventry at his bungalow on the 6th. Fairly cool we have had more rain and it is cloudy, but very bad weather for prickly heat. I have got it very bad on my left forearm.

15th July

Ogilivie arrived 10th & S.S.O.Capt. J.L. Rose 2/1 Gurkhas 11th in Maiden's Hope.

Received a book from Mother called *England in Egypt* by Sir Alfred Milner by last mail, very interesting and well written. This is for my birthday tomorrow, it is along time since my birthday has been on a Sunday, English mail also arrives tomorrow.

Had more rain yesterday, fairly cool, but prickly heat very bad going all over my body.

18th July

Got last mail on my birthday.

Not bad for commems: at Oxford when Lord Kitchener and Cecil Rhodes were given their degrees 'Khartoum College, head of the River!'

19th July

Genl. Sir G. de C. Morton K.C.I.E., C.B. commanding Lahore District on his way out from England has been stopping here for a few days, he came to inspect our Hospl. yesterday, when he told me that he had known Father very well and had met him last month at the Frontier dinner. Major N.A.K. Burne arrives this afternoon.

20th July

Heard the following story yesterday:-

At a General's inspection a nervous officer is called out to drill the battalion. When he finds himself in front of the Regiment being thoroughly 'gabion-ed' his last remaining wits vanish away, there is only one thing he can think of to say and he says it 'Gai hai!' Then the band played.

Major Burne said last night that at Marseilles on his way out he saw the very swell funeral of some officer of high rank and the procession passing through the streets, he described the soldiers as an untidy rabble, when a block occurred they stopped of their own free will and went on again without any word of command. The officers never appeared to take any interest in their men or what they were doing, and if any of the men saw their best girl in the crowd they nodded and winked at them and the officers grinned and saluted their friends with their swords. He said he never saw such an unsmart and undrilled looking lot in his life. This is the great l'Armée!

Am reading a book called *A Pink-un and a Pelican* by Arthur Binstead and Ernest Walls. It is very amusing in parts, but as is the case in all books of reminiscences you find the amusing and interesting bits among a lot of padding and uninteresting matter. Forgot to mention that McKay left sick for Murree on Monday the 17th. From the 16th to 19th when Major Burne arrived, the Regt. was left to the tender mercies of myself and Leslie, however it was an uneventful period.

Tried on A & B Companies tunics this morning, the men felt the heat very much in the warm clothing. SA recruit of B Coy had a wet mark about the size of a saucer under each hand when the perspiration trickled down from his finger tips. The N.O. drew my attention to it.

Temperature in my room 91 degrees but very sticky.

27th July

Was shown over the jail this morning by Capt. Evans I.M.S. the Superintendent of the Montgomery Jail and had breakfast with him afterwards. Beautifully cool and nice, had very heavy thunderstorms yesterday and the day before. Read Jacob's book *Sea Urchins* thought it quite up to his usual style and very amusing.

As a sequel to my entry of 3rd Inst, re: the L.S. Hindustani Exam. I received a letter today from the Board of Examiners, Calcutta forwarded through the S.S.O. requesting me to give my reasons in writing as to why I had not passed Mr. Symes Scott and stating that he had done one of the best exercises ever given in at a L.S. Exam. Of course I do not have anything to do with the exercise at all, and can only account for the excellence of it in one way which I do not like to suggest. I am prepared to maintain my opinion as to his qualifications in the Colloquial Exam which were translation of book – indifferent, good and conversation – indifferent.

1st August

Ridgeway returned from privilege leave yesterday and Leslie went on it. Ogilvie goes off home today on privilege leave to be married.

Discovered an instructive fact in Sir. A. Milner's book yesterday with regard to our occupation of Egypt. It is well known that it was brought about by the force of circumstances and not through any desire on our part to annex the country in spite of the fact that foreigners say that we meant to take it all along and question our right to being there at all, yet always, and especially at the time of Riaz Pasha was Prime Minister and quarrelled with all the foreign representatives, did they come to the British Consul to complain of any ill treatment as if they recognized our right of being the paramount power, so that their very actions helped to force us to assume that power which they say we have no right to!

2nd August

Rose said yesterday that someone wanted to send him a telegram once when he was staying with a fellow called Maude. The sender of the telegram was so ashamed of sending a telegram addressed to Rose c/o Maude by the hand of an English orderly that he had to go out of his way to get a native to take the wire to the office.

He also said that in his British Regt. (H.L.I.) there are two fellows called Singe and Whistler, on one occasion they went out calling together and the maid who answered the door, on hearing their names refused to announce them.

Saw in the *Man of the World* today a new name for the coppersmith bird viz. 'Alexander' because 'Alexander the coppersmith did me much evil'. This reminds me of Mr. Young's riddle, 'What is the odour of sanctity?' 'A high priest!' Also the reference to lying found by a small boy in the Bible – 'Lying lips are an abomination to the Lord, but a very present help in time of trouble.'

6th August

Played last Thursday – the 3rd – in a tip and run cricket match in Lahore – great sport, made 3 not out and caught a catch at square leg.

News received yesterday of cholera in the 17th B.E. over 20 cases and 8 deaths in the first two days, this is an abnormal number of cases for a beginning. The 17th went out into camp this morning and so far there have been no cases anywhere else in the station. It was supposed to have come in along the Ferozepore road, there were one or two cases reported in villages along the Ferozepore road and the cavalry lines are also on the Ferozeopore road. Went round this morning 'pinking our wells' i.e. pouring permanganate of potash, 3 or 4ozs. to each well runs the water pink. The Cavalry Lines, Lahore and the Saddr. bazaar placed out of bounds.

The bath which has been emptied for repairs is now in working order again, had a bathe this morning with Major Burne and Ridgeway.

12th August

On the 10th I went out and selected a site for a cholera camp near Shah ki kui on the canal in case of eventualities, which I am glad to say do not seem likely to occur. There have been no more cases in the 40th or Cantonments the last 2 or 3 days. General Morton, Col. Graves and the P.M.O. Col. Miller came down a few days ago, the two former in our Mess, they all three go back tomorrow.

Capt. Lindsay I.M.S. has taken charge of the Regt. and Capt. Wimberley I.M.S. 15th Sikhs has taken up his abode in the Maiden's Hope. On Thursday afternoon we had another tip and run cricket match in Lahore.

Yesterday I was on another Board on tea at the Fort. Sawyer and I had breakfast with Arbuthnot there afterwards, who showed us over some of the underground passages there. Bunbury arrived on the 10th from a garrison class. I drove into Lahore with him last night to the band.

Got a telegram the other day offering me a transfer to the 2nd Sikhs. In consequence of an interview with Col. Graves on the subject I determined not to accept it.

Heard two yarns the other day. One was of a young lady with a notoriously deep low voice who on being asked to sing once after dinner at a house in this country, said that she was very sorry she could not do so as her music was in her tum-tum. The other is a story from Oxford, a lot of fellows 'up' at Oxford amusing themselves at the railway station. Just as a train began to steam out of the station one fellow up at the front of the train began calling out 'Help!' 'Murder!' etc. whereupon all the passengers stuck their heads out of the windows to see what was taking place. An undergraduate got close to the train and smacked all the heads sticking out of the windows as they went past. At first they went past slowly but towards the end of the train he was smacking away as hard as he could finally ending up with the guard whom he caught a beauty on the side of the face.

17th September

The last month has been spent by Major Burne, Capt Wimberley (I.M.S, 15th Sikhs) Bunbury and myself in cholera camp at Shah ki kui 6 miles west along the canal. I have no reminiscences worth making a note of, it was a weary 'soul clogging' month spent in heat and dust beyond description and the sooner forgotten the better. We went out on Monday the middle of August and returned on Friday 15th Septbr. We had in the Regiment 12 cases of cholera and 8 deaths and got rid of it entirely on going into camp.

I have read *The Murder of Delicia* by Marie Corelli a book which made me mad, and *Round the World on a Wheel* by Foster-Fraser who bicycled round the world with Lunn and Lowe. There is not much information contained in the book it being written in a light style, but it has a great deal of quaint humour.

The *C & M Gazette* took a turn over an article/story I wrote entitled 'Last Post' and nobly sent me Rs. 16/- yesterday.

19th September

10 days leave sanctioned, written to Kitty to ask her to put me up on 25th.

Got English mail yesterday, heard from my belongings at Margate whither they have gone for a change of air. Audrey has had a bad gastric attack and Mother been knocked up nursing her. Willie Hamilton got home from Johannesburg on Friday and is staying with them. Maggie Bostock married to Eric Harben.

29th September

On 10 days leave at Simla at 'Cranagh' with Turton and Kitty Graham.

Left Mian Mir East on Saturday the 23rd with Major Burne and Capt. Pearse (Inniskiilings) both proceeding to Dalhousie. Got as far as Amritsar without adventure, when an unfortunate contretemps occurred. We all 3 had dinner there. While Major B's and Capt C's luggage was put into the Panthankot train, on running out after dinner to my train (I had no change) I found my luggage had been removed too and the train was starting. I just had time to explain matters to the Station Master and was carried off in the train. The discomfort of spending a night in the train without bedding, and the impossibility of being able to continue my journey without luggage dawned on me as soon as I had time to reflect, but it was too late to stop the train. I consequently descended at the next station – Jindiala – a long platform in the wilderness with a telegraph babu and a decrepit porter. There I waited for three and a half hours for the next train arriving at 11p.m. The babu said 'the city is 5 miles off and there is our mission station'. He did his best to entertain me and gave me a missionary tract to read. He also said 'if there is anything you want you will ask freely of me. This is only a 3rd class Station and we are not getting much, I can obtain milk.' The next train brought my luggage and I reached Ambala at 9a.m. and Kalka at 10, starting in the ordinary mail tonga at 11 and arrived at Simla at about 8p.m. finding them at dinner.

Fares and routes. Leave Mian Mir East 5.20p.m., dinner at Amritsar, change at Ambala 3a.m. arrive Kalka 5a.m. Fare 1st class Rs. 19/- mail tonga starts at about 6a.m. and takes 8 hours getting up. Single tonga Rs 25/- return tonga Rs 38/- seat in mail Rs 8/- luggage Rs 2/- per pound extra.

While at Simla I accomplished the following:- First I saw Genl. Sir Alfred Gassier and Col. Martin at Hd. Qrtrs. Offices and got my name put down for British Central Africa and Uganda.

I had lunch with Walker once at the A.S. Club and once at the Elysium Hotel.

5th October

I walked to Annandale and back and saw the final of the Durand football tournament the Black Watch v. the Yorks. at the end of time neither side had scored, they played for 20 mins extra and still no score. They played again two days later. I rode down on a pony lent me by the Hamiltons and saw the match, the Yorks then went to pieces and were beaten by *2* goals.

I went to the Gaiety Theatre and saw the Runaway Girl and met Mellis an O.W. who was acting the part of 'Hipper'.

I had a blue suit, a Norfolk jacket, a pair of mess overalls and a pair of Khaki pantaloons made at Rankins.

I walked twice round 'Jacko' on Sunday and made the acquaintance of Mr. and Mrs. Hamilton my future cousins-in-law.

I went to call on the Templars and Miss Lauren, sisters of Mrs. Strettell.

I had finally to leave on Tuesday morning 3rd Octbr. instead of the 5th as all the tongas were booked. I got out and waited for the next train so as to have a bath and dinner, while in the Refreshment Room a native came in and drank large quantities of whisky and lemonade and made the boy whom he addressed as 'ap' butter biscuits for him, which he ate.

I reached here and found Maclachlan and Preston had returned.

English mail arrived, family still at Margate, Mabel and Bill had biked over to a place called Minster and in the church there is one of the two famous Cranmer's Bibles in which the sentence 'there is no more balm in Gilead' is translated 'there is no more any treacle in Gilead.'

6th October

Walker returned today from the 45th Sikhs.

My measurements taken today are 5' 10 and a quarter' in bare feet. Chest contracted 37', expanded 38 and a half'. Left Forearm and biceps 11' and 12' Right Forearm and biceps 11 and a quarter' and 12 and a quarter'. These are probably not very accurate as I took them myself.

My weight in Simla in summer scale was 10st. 10 and three quarters lbs.

I bought a new bicycle today from the Punjab Cycle Coy. (Ryustinyi and Co.). It is a 'Kingsland' make, 26' frame. Geared to 80 so the man said but I think it is more. I paid the man 100/- Rupees down 50/- of which was for the hire of another machine for the last four months. The new bicycle cost 250/- so I have still to pay him 200/- in monthly instalments.

Preston who has been on plague duty, said he rode his bicycle for 2,000 miles for which he was receiving T.A. at the rate of -/8/- annas a mile.

15th October

Very nice and cool, about 70 degrees at night and about 77 degrees in my room in the day time.

Am going to bicycle into Lahore to the Cathedral.

Have been playing polo and rackets and am sorry that I did not start the latter game before.

Engage syce Bola today for my new grey Arab pony I bought from Dunlop for Rs. 200/-. The syce is to get Rs. 7/- a month Rs. 1/- bedding and Rs. -/8/ cleaning.

1st November

Have all the satisfactory feeling of having performed a great and noble deed and am much relieved in mind and body having just bicycled down to Jones the dentist and had a tooth out.

Yesterday and the day before I was up for H.S. Pustoo exam, the result I am very doubtful of but think it just possible that I may have passed.

Leslie and Preston returned last Sunday the 29th Octbr.

Kitty returned on the 27th. The L.G. is down here and Lahore and Mian Mir are full up. I have done two days calling in Lahore and one day in Mian Mir.

Last Thursday the 25th Octbr. I played in a cricket match Mian Mir v. Lahore, after fielding all day I did not get an innings. I am playing tomorrow in Married v. Single. Went to Lahore Cathedral last Sunday to hear the Bishop of Calcutta (Weldon) preach; was not so much struck with his sermon as I was before, he advocates Christianizing India.

On Thursday the 19th Octbr. Graham came and had lunch here on his way back to Kohat from Simla. Col. O'Malley command. 1st Punjab Cavalry was also in the mess the other day, he said he used to know Father.

12th November

Today being Sunday am going to have tea with Kitty, and dine with the Ridgeways.

Riley returned with the 21st P.I. about ten days ago.

I went to the first subscription dance of the season last Wednesday the 9th. The dance was a great success.

Must enter a story of Rose's. One Scotchman went to dinner with another

Scotchman, after a pleasant evening when the guest rose to go, the host put his arm familiarly on his guest's shoulder and said

''Afore ye go, there is a guid auld Hieland custom I should like ye to indulge in.' 'Na, na mon,' said the guest, 'Ah never touch whisky.'

'Ah was nae refurring tae whisky, I was refurring tae washup.'

Mrs. Ridgeway told me that her small son frequently by way of saying his prayers at night, sits down with a flop, clasps his hands, and shuts his eyes convulsively, and says 'bus' after which he rushes off and cannot be induced to say anything further. The baby is looked after by a strange but honest old Gurkha nurse who has only the vaguest idea of dressing him, putting his inside clothes on top of his outside ones, and the other day Ridgeway found his son with both legs stuck through one side of his trousers, with the other flopping about empty.

16th November

Gerard Howell arrived last night, he wired yesterday to say he was coming and I went down to Mian Mir East station at 11.20a.m. and met him; being in uniform he mistook me for the ticket collector. I brought him back and he stopped with me till today (20th) when he left for Sialkot by the 4.10p.m. train from Lahore. He had come out on board ship with his young lady and future Father-in-Law, who are going on a trip to New Zealand. Gerard was awfully fit and just as jolly and amusing as ever.

Craster arrived on the 16th from leave, the last time I saw him was at the E.I.U.S. Club. I went yesterday (19) with Gerard to a picnic at Shahdrah given by the Beechers.

I received an intimation today that my name had been registered at the War Office for services in B.C. Africa, but I think it will be extremely doubtful if I ever get it.

28th November

Last Saturday the 26th I rode in a paperchase for the first time and thought it rather fun. Afterwards we had a great ladies dinner party in the mess, and sat down 26 I think. I was between Col. Hepburn and Miss Morton. I drew name cards for the dinner.

The other day Col. Bamber came to call on the mess, while I was there. He was much surprised when I reminded him that we had met at dinner in '95 at the Beckets in Pindi, and also before that in about '82 or '83 when he was the 2nd P.I. doctor.

Heard the following yesterday from Preston. 'Why is Heaven like an empty room?' 'Because there is not a damned soul in the place'.

Was vaccinated today by Ogilvie.

Col Hepburn took photos of us the other day. Col. Grave, Major Burne, Capts. Mackay and Ridgeway, Lieuts. MacLachlan, Preston, Craster, Tyndall, Walker, Leslie and Riley. Ogilvie, who is here, was not present.

Heard this also from Preston. 'A knight had a pain, when and where?' 'In the middle of the (k)night.'

1st December

Played polo last Wednesday had dinner with Stewarts and went with them to subscription dance, played cricket on Thursday – Inniskillings and R.A. v. rest of station – unfortunately we declared our innings just before I went in. Played polo today, and am going to play cricket and tennis with Beechers tomorrow.[23] Riley left last night with advanced part (C Coy) of detachment for Dera Ghazi. Lawson of the 26th P.I. arrived the day before yesterday for transport class. Turton and Kitty went into camp on the 25th of last month.

6th December

Left Wing under Mckay with Craster and Walker leave this evening for Dera Ghazi.

The C.O. received a letter the other day from the Medical Officer at Ladysmith about our two Havilders – Hazrat Shah and Abbas – who are there. I expect they little knew when they left us at cholera camp what a time they were going to have especially as the Boers have been shelling the hospital.

9th December

Garrett arrived with his wife yesterday.

16th December

Last Wednesday the 13th I went to Lady Morton's at home and to dinner at the Massons. I met Capt. Armstrong I.M.S. Medical Officer to the Residency at Nepaul, he gave me some account of the shooting there.

On Thursday I went to the Massons' at home, and on my way there I met Katie and Charlie who had arrived that day from Australia. Charlie is posted to Sialkot, but is staying over Xmas here. Owing to the Left Wing being at Dera Ghazi, and having a detachment at the fort, and a fatigue party at the Station & various other causes and a parade the other day consisted of 4 B.O.s 3 N.O.s, 1 Havildar, and 7 Lee Naicks.

1900

6th January

Gerard has been staying with us for the Xmas week. He came on 23rd Decbr. and left on New Year's Day, we had a very jolly time, except for two days when he was seedy. We had the Regtl. Xmas dinner the night he came, there was a Cinderella dance a few days before, and during the week the L.G.'s ball, the Punjab Club dance, Communion Ball and on New Year's Day the R.A. Fancy Dress ball my kit for which was black knee breeches and stockings, long yellow waistcoat, sky blue tail coat and court wig. There was also during the week a horse show (at Mian Mir) dog show, polo tournament and cricket. The 23rd Pioneers and ourselves were at home on Lahore Race Course for the final of the Polo – Patiala v. the Guides won by the former.

Gerard and I sat up for the New Year in the Mess with Forster I./M.S. (in Maiden's Hope) and amused ourselves by singing songs which became patriotic as midnight approached.

Before the R.A. Fancy Dress ball we had a ladies dinner in the mess in full dress. I asked Mrs. Douglas Gordon.

Mabel mentioned some good characters at a 'Book Tea' given by Ethel. Father went with sticking plaster and gashes painted over his face as 'The Woman who did', others wore a pair of butterfly wings as 'A Fleet', in being a visiting card of Ethel's for 'Our Mutual Friend' a photo of a baby as 'Nevermore' and a clergyman as 'The Little Minister'.

I wish to record my aversion to the custom [of] offering one another drinks by way of hospitality. I am not in the least in favour of the temperance movement but I do object to having to swallow drinks at all times of the day and night when not inclined for it. If one were only allowed by etiquette to refuse a drink sometimes when offered one I should not object, but this is out of the question, the matter has become a duty and has to be observed as such. Some individuals and some messes carry it altogether too far. The practice in vogue in our mess of sitting up till 2 a.m. on quiet nights when all you want to do is to go to bed is one I shall discountenance when I am C.O.

I have started today a collection of notes, taken from experience and otherwise, on the interior economy of a Regiment, for use and guidance.

After having started on this practical and useful work and recorded the above manifesto I feel particularly good.

There are in Mian Mir in our mess at the present time – Lawson 26th Punjab Infantry for a transport class and McQueen 20th P.I., Tucker 21st P.I. and Gray 26th P.I. with recruits.

13th January

At Malakand. On 8th Inst. an order was sent to the Regiment to send one Wing Officer to do duty with the 38th Dogras. I was detailed. On the evening of the 9th I dined with the Garratts (also a Miss Garratt a cousin staying with the Butts) and went with them, afterwards to Lahore to see Miss Ada Delroy's Company some of it was rather amusing. I heard one new joke there concerning a blacksmith and his assistant who both stammer. The blacksmith (taking a piece of red hot iron out of the fire) to his assistant, 'H...h..hi, hi, h..hi hit it!' The assistant, 'Wh...wh, wh, wh...where... shall I hit it?' The Blacksmith, 'N, n..n..., n,n..,ne..,never mind it's cold now!'

I left Lahore station at 4.10 p.m. on the 10th Inst. and reached Nowshera at 8 the next morning. I went on at once in a special tonga and stopped at Hoti Mardan for a wash and breakfast. I felt too dirty to go to the mess, so went to the dak bungalow which is quite the filthiest place I have ever been to. I have never been so badly fed in my life. I reached Malakand at about 5 p.m. and found the 38th on the same dreary unattractive spot, living the same monotonous life and generally cheerless and depressed by two years of it. With the Regt. were Capts. Burne (K.P. the brother of N.A.K.) and Tribe, Barstow, Hay, Hugo (I.M.S) the Colonel returns in a few days from 10 days leave.

The place has been cleared and fortified and made ship shape and tidy, but nothing can alter the uninviting aspect of it. There is a fortified barrack on Castle Rock – isolated, another on Maxim Point, the Ridge is enclosed by a high wall in which space is most of the Regt. and personnel of the place. The politicals' house has been built below the fort and commanding the Crater (evacuated) and two isolated picket towers on Gibraltar, the corner where the Khar road comes in is held by the Levies. The tribesmen could never take the fortified barracks or Fort, but it seems to me that they could do a lot of damage to Followers, Mules and Property and cause confusion generally by rushing the wall on a dark night.

The *C and M Gazette* had another story of mine in today – 'Love's Labour Lost'. Its literary value is very small, if not absolutely nil, but intrinsically it is worth Rs 16/- of the best to me, so I shall continue to write them; it isn't as if people had to read them.

15th January

There was a fairly heavy fall of snow last night.

Recipe for cleaning straw hats received from Migs last mail:- a tablespoon of oxalic acid in warm water to be applied with a tooth brush, it is very poisonous.

I saw a thing in a magazine the other day which sounds interesting and which I will try some time, the cultivation of ink blots:- place a wick in a bottle of ink and put the whole in a basin, over the basin spread a sheet of blotting paper just

Major General Henry
Tyndall, father of Henry
Stuart Tyndall.

Major General Tyndall's
wife, mother of Henry
Tyndall.

Studio portrait of Captain H.S. Tyndall, Umballa, India, 1910.

Group photograph of the officers of the 40th Pathans, Jhelum, 1905. Captain Tyndall is sitting on the left, Colonel Campbell, the commandant, is sitting second from the right.

Tyndall with fellow officers of the 40th Pathans and their wives photographed in fancy dress before a dance, Jhansi, 1903. H.S (not H.F.) Tyndall is seated on the left.

The Tyndall-Hildersley wedding at Lawrence Military Asylum, Sanawar, 8 July 1903..

NCOs and Indian officers of the 40th Pathans.

40th Pathan Regiment formed up with British and Indian officers in the front rank, Jhelum, 23 November 1905.

Two photographs showing the more peaceful aspects of the East African campaign in the First World War. Above, South African gunners pose with a zebra and, below, a group photograph of troops in front of a waterfall.

A graphic photograph of the dense malarial bush in which the 40th Pathans operated during the East African campaign.

Gharwal to Attock: 1st Nov 1895 marched down to Pindi
with detachment, arrived at Pindi 3rd Nov and on to
Attock same day by train to do duty with detachment
Major Wann, & Capt. Annesley.

Attock to Khyber Pass and back By train to Peshawur
17th Decr 1895 with Annesley, stopped at dak bungalow. Drove
up pass next day to Ali Musjid, back to Attock by train
19th Decr.

Attock to Pindi on relief 12th Janry 1896 by train, lived in
tent at West Ridge –

Rawul Pindi to Quetta, [Fort Sandeman] owing to mistake in warrant. Left
Pindi 13th April 1896 by train via Lahore, Succur, Ruck &
Sibi, arrived Quetta 16th stopped with His lop of the Sind
Horse (5th Bo L.) at Mess.

Quetta to Fort Sandeman Left 24th April 1896 by train
to Hurnai (7 hours) Drove in tonga with Capt. Hatch
29th Baluchis as far as Loralai. Finished the journey
on riding mule with baggage. 24th to Torkhan 12 miles.
25th through Raggai to Sunjawi 24 miles. 26th to Loralai
20 miles. Stopped at dak bungalow and 29th Baluch men.
28th April to Murra Taugi 24 miles, 29th to Zirra 18 miles
30th to Murgha 15 miles, 31st to Luchaband 24 miles.
1st May to Fort Sandeman 32 miles. Joined 40th Pathans
(Col. S. H. P. Graves) Major Pelham Burne, Capts. Dillon, McKay, Rennick
Ridgway. Lieuts Bunbury, McLachlan, Preston, Craster, Tyndall
S. John

An early page of Tyndall's diary dating from shortly after his arrival in India on his way to join the 40th Pathans.

A second page of Tyndall's diary recording the death of Queen Victoria in 1901.

1901

We heard the day before yesterday that the Queen
was ill, & yesterday that she was very ill & in
extremis

We were to have had a ladies' dinner party of 32
tomorrow, but this has been put off of course –
Today is the "Id-el-fitr"

24th Jan Queen Victoria died on the night of Jan: 22–23.

28th Jan Went to the proclamation ceremony at the town hall
in Lahore yesterday, driving in with Olso & Will Bean
There were Royal Guards of Honour from the Inniskillings,
P. V. Rs & ourselves forming 3 sides of a square the XI. B.L.
& P. L. H. were also represented. The ladies dressed in
black were sitting in the windows & balconies above,
on one side of the platform below were English Officers
Civil & Military, townsfolk & shopkeepers, & on the
other side were Native Gentlemen & natives,
As Mr Clarke. Commissioner stepped on the platform
Capt. Hudge S.S.O. hoisted the Royal Ensign & the troops
presented arms. Mr Casson, Secretary to Govt. read
the proclamation in English, followed by a native in
Hindustani. The Band then played God save the
King & Mr Clarke proposed three cheers for the King,
while the guns at the Fort fired a royal salute.

touching the wick, you can use different coloured inks or water the ink. The blots usually take from 20 to 30 minutes to develop and should be pressed afterwards between sheets of clean blotting paper.

24th January

Nothing but rain, sleet and snow this last week.

The Mehtar of Chitral; and Chiefs of Hunze and Naga left yesterday with Gurdon[24] the Political and Cullen 32nd Pioneers for Chitral.

Col. Vivian, yesterday, speaking of some particularly annoying incident said he believed it was one of the cases mentioned in the Bible in which you were allowed to swear.

From Mabel:– 'Why is a goat nearby?'

'Because it is all but(t).'

31st January

Last Thursday – the 25th – Ghazi Khan left, he said he could not stand the cold. I was glad of the chance of getting rid of him, he was not a first class bearer and had been annoying me a good deal of late by his extremely deliberate way of doing things. The same day Lyall of the 32nd Pioneers arrived for temporary duty with the 38th.

On the 29th, 30th and today Col. Abbott late 15th Sikhs has been inspecting the Regiment. I am left behind today on duty.

The other day at the 25th P.I. sports at Khar I saw novel event:– two men are tied by one wrist to a peg fastened into the ground with a rope about 10 feet long. One man, blindfolded, has a tin in which are some pebbles to rattle, the other man also blindfolded has a rope's end to hit the first man with.

10th February

Last Monday the 5th, I took over the duties of Treasure Chest Officer, Malakand Force from Cruddas who left to take up the appointment of Asst. Inspector of Army Signalling. My hours for work are 10.30a.m. and 3.30p.m. sometimes there is a lot of work and sometimes none. The name of the babu is Lachman Das and the amount today in the chest is roughly Rs 150,000/-.

I also occupied Cruddas' quarter in the fort.

A few days ago Forster turned up here to join a N.F.H. and is in the quarter next to me. I made a great shooting excursion with him last Sunday and we are going again tomorrow. I have had several most amusing and interesting talks with him during our evening pipes together. He said once, 'You can always tell a lazy chap by the quickness with which he dresses,' which I thought was a truth which ought not to be lost.

I have heard two stories lately, old ones but worth remembering. First – A Babu goes to England and is determined to do everything properly, even to the wearing of the latest fashion in clothes. He went one day to a very fashionable gathering in evening clothes, only unfortunately at the top of the stairs was a large mirror in which he saw himself reflected. He could not make out what was wrong with him. Suddenly it dawned on him and throwing up his hands in amazement, he exclaimed 'Arre! Pantaloon boolgya!'

Second – A fair American was asked if she suffered from sea sickness. 'No,' she replied, 'I have never used a storm pan in my life.'

Colonel Vivian said he would ask to have me transferred to the 38th if I liked. He asked me if I had seen an order directing me to return to the 40th, and if I would like to stop on instead. I said I had seen the order but should like to stop on very much, so he said he would apply very kindly.

19th February

Last Thursday Forster went down to Khar with No. 50 N.F.H. mobilized. I went down to Khar camp on Saturday evening returned this morning (Monday) stopping with Forster for a day's shooting. Forster and twin (I.M.S.) 26th P.I.) and I had a very jolly outing together yesterday and fairly good sport for the Swat Valley viz. – 6 and a half brace snipe, 1 and a half brace quail, 1 teal and 1 pigeon in swampy places and ditches by the river. I shot abominably at first but improved later on.

Today is the assault at arms at Khar, but no holiday for the Field Paymaster. Amount in T.C. today Rs 133,792–5–2.

25th February

Went out shooting with Irwin and Forster. Rode down to Khar evening of 24th and back to Malakand morning of 26th. I enjoyed the day very much though the bag was not extraordinary consisting of 1 mallard, 7 teal, 6 couple snipe, 1 and a half quail, 2 pigeon and 2 plover. The night before I went to Khar a Sikh sentry of 26th was shot in the thigh by a rifle thief[25], and the two nights I spent there the sentries fired a good deal.

We leave Malakand on 27th May and I am almost sorry to go as I am making a nice addition to my pay through the treasure chest billet and our weekly shoots at Khar are great fun.

People of note, or in whom I was particularly interested in those parts are:-

General Reid, Comdr. moveable column Col. Abbott C.B. Cmdr, Malakand
Capt. Griffiths 18th Bengal Lancers S.S.O.
Major Kerr I.M.S. No.50 N.F.H.
Capt. Brown I.M.S. No.50 N.F.H.
Lieut.Forster I.M.S. No.50 N.F.H.
26th P.I. Col. Dillon and Lawson and Irwin I.M.S.
29th Bo. I (2nd Baluch. Bn.) Col. Sinclair
Lt. Hannington (to whom I handed over the treasure chest)
Hay (married Miss Cowdell, brother in 38th.)
Hamer 25th P.I. Col. Coates, Capt. Hamilton, H.T. Reed,
Magniac, Bauerman 18th B.L. Provost Marshal.
Capt. Brooke, Commissariat and Carter, Oxfords.

8th March
At Mian Mir. Following is detail of march down:-
    27th Febry. Malakand to Darghai by zig zags 7 miles
    28th Darghai to Jalala 14 miles
    1st March Jalala to Mardan 11 miles
    2nd March Mardan to Nowshera 16 miles
    Entrained with 38th in first troop train leaving Nowshera at 8.13 a.m. on 3rd
March reached Lahore on 4th at 4 a.m.
    Border line lies between Jalala and Mardan.
    Lunched and dined with Guides at Mardan and was introduced to our future
C.O., Col. Campbell. Dined with 14th Sikhs at Nowshera.
    Col. Vivian's application for me was refused and though I like the Regiment
both officers and men, I think it is as well that I have not got it as I would be so
badly placed. Col. Vivian kindly forwarded to me yesterday Medley's reply
which runs as follows:- 'I am afraid we cannot manage to bring Tyndall into the
Regiment, as he would be passing over Barstow who is only a year junior to him
and has been in the Regiment a good deal longer.'

10th March
Col. Campbell from 2nd in Command of the Guides arrived yesterday to take
over command of the Regiment.
    I dismissed a temporary servant – Kuram Din whom I took over after Ghazi
Khan left, and engaged a new bearer, Cheri Ram, today.

25th March
Have returned from a most excellent 10 days' leave of which the following is
some account:-

Left Lahore station at 4.10 p.m. on Wednesday 14th and reached Sialkot at 8.30, changing at Wazirabad. Met by Gerard and had dinner with Dallas. Stopped at Sialkot on 15th, Phil Howell arrived from D.Ishmail. We went shopping and in the evening at the Club I was introduced to Col. Duke I.M.S. Medical Officer to Resident, Kashmir, he seemed very glad to see me for my people's sake and said he would look after me in Kashmir.

Gerard, Phil and self drove to Pokhlian on 16th crossing Chenah by ferry at Sidapur, baggage went on the day before. Shot small jheel same evening.

On the 17th as we were going out to the river we met Hynes of the Sussex coming out to stay the night with us, we took him out with us, and as we were driving back in an ekka[26] the 4 of us were upset into a 7ft watercut by Phil making a bad shot at the bridge in the dark. The ekka turned completely over and was jammed across the top of the water cut, the Sussex fellow and I fell through the roof into the muddy water at the bottom of the cut and G. and P. fell under the pony on the bank, just as we got out of the way the pony fell into the cut and was jammed in the bottom, we had some difficulty in getting him out but no-one was hurt.

On the 19th we rode out to a place called Seulke Jattam about 8 miles off taking bedding and a tent, we had excellent duck shooting in the early morning and by moonlight in the jheels, 7 in a boat on the river by day, unfortunately the first night out we had a gale and rain and the next day a violent thunderstorm so that everything was soaked and we could not get at all dry for two days so that I lost my voice and have now got a cold the like of which I never had before.

We returned to bungalow on 21st. and found Charlie there. That same night we walked out to the jheel at Ajwal, we got very wet and tired and saw nothing to shoot but were much amused by the behaviour of a native who was scared by our sudden appearance in the moonlight; as we crept up to the top of a bank close to the jheel we came upon him and asked if he had seen any duck. He was absolutely petrified with fright and stepping back fell into a ditch of water; when he had recovered we asked him again whereupon he turned round and fled into the jheel looking neither to the right hand nor to the left. The last I saw of him in the darkness he was very nearly stuck up to his waist in mud and water, struggling madly forward fear lending him wings, till he disappeared in the night.

We had a glorious time the whole ten days I was out, shooting and riding the whole day, we tried shooting off horseback, it is an exciting sport and a bit dangerous but not much use for hitting game. My new bearer, Cherry, cooked for us and very well, too. N.B. Light green 'matchless' cartridges from Murray and Co. Karachi, very bad, they all burst. I returned to Sialkot leaving the others still there, on 22nd riding as far as Sidapur and on in a tum tum. I put up with Katie and found Alex and Freddie and the children (2 boys and 1 girl) there and left for Mian Mir on 23rd at 10.30 a.m.

Capt. and Mrs. Rennick returned from England while I was away.
My weight is 11st. 8.

1st April

Leslie left yesterday on 8 months general leave. I took over his pony from today.
Started polo again yesterday.

10th April

Rennick[27] left for Dera Ghazi Khan yesterday.

Bought two Bull Terrier pups, 3 weeks old from the postmaster here, by name Rehill, for Rs 30/- I have lately read two delightfully funny books one *Dolly Dialogues* by Anthony Hope, and the other, *The Babe, B.A.* by E.F.Benson, the latter I thought particularly good. The Babe's sayings are very quaint, one in particular I remember, 'I ate lobster salad the other day and drank port. It did not give me indigestion but acute remorse, remorse for all the foolish things I had done, and all the foolish things I meant to do and for being what I was. Food doesn't affect your body it affects your soul. Conversely sermons which are supposed to affect your soul make you hungry.'

He also says 'I am very fond of devilled kidneys because they are so comfortable, as the psalmist says.'

15th April

It is cloudy and cool (77 degrees) in spite of the fact that today the official hot weather begins.

Heard from Robert Howell a couple of days ago, he has just come out. He ends up his letter 'so long, and short may it be'. I didn't know there was any more of that familiar form of farewell.

I went out on the 13th to inspect cholera camps, 10 miles by bicycle down the Ferozepore road to Parana Khana where there is a very pretty canal bungalow, then I rode 5 miles across the put to Hulloke and 10 miles home.

Riley has been staying here a couple of days, and left last night for temporary duty with the 2nd P.I. at Parachniar.

Craster arrived this morning from Dera Ghazi Khan to take over duties of Qr. Mr.

This is Easter Sunday.

25th April

I began putting A Coy. through the annual course in the 16th.

McKay, the Ridgeways and Garratts left for Kashmir on the 21st.

I am reading a book which Bob Howell brought out from Father, *Modern Weapons and Modern War* by I.S. Bloch. He tries to prove that war is now impossible owing to the size of modern armies and the destructiveness of modern weapons. I have found several mistakes in it, and also think all his arguments are too exaggerated, but still it is interesting.

I can just hear the guns in Lahore Fort booming a salute to His Excellency, the Viceroy Lord Curzon[28] who is stopping for the afternoon with L.G.

3rd May

Finished musketry of A Coy this morning, 1st, 2nd & 3rd periods in 16 days – the percentage for the Coy was 62.

Began punkahs on 2nd I sat under a punkah for the first time this hot weather at dinner with the Campbells on the 2nd, there I met a Miss Geddes, cousin of the Geddes, I came out with in the *Malabar*. I went to an 'At Home' at Govt. House yesterday.

Mother sent me the following cutting out of the Globe:- The old riddle. Why did the Fly fly? Because the Spider spied her, has inspired one of our readers to send us a few variants:- Why did the Whale wail? Because the Smelt smell. Why did the Quail quail? Because the Adder had her. Why did the Owl Howl? Because the Woodpecker would peck her.

Temperature 85 degrees in my room.

20th May

Weather described in the *C & M Gazette* as 'unseasonable but delightful'.

Have not used punkah for a week and slept indoors last night without one.

Temperature about 82 degrees at noon.

B Coy begin 2nd period tomorrow.

Heard of the relief of Mafeking yesterday.

31st May

The 17th Bengal Lancers went out into cholera camp with 4 cases on the 28th. I believe they have had no more cases.

St John arrived from England on 29th. I heard from Gerald Evans the other day in reply to my letter from Malakand. He has joined the Imperial Light Horse and when he wrote was starting off to the relief of Mafeking.

B Coy finished musketry yesterday.

I started work with our scouts this week.

10th June

Heard of our entry into Pretoria on 6th Inst.

I was summoned as a junior for the trial of two men of the 16th Lancers at the Chief Court Lahore on 6th. There were 6 officers of whom only four were chosen. I was one of the two who escaped.

In consequence of the above I was unfortunately able to play polo on the 8th and received a severe ton on the head. I was riding after Wikely of the 17th B.L. to prevent him hitting a backhander. I got almost alongside him but as he was hitting my pony funked and swerved into his pony's hindlegs and came down. I remember no more till I found myself sitting in a trap with Col., Miller the S.M.O. who was trying to find my bungalow. I felt all right then but have subsequently felt very stiff and have had a bad head. I have also been suffering, since about two days before that from choleric symptoms of a mild nature.

It has been very hot the last fortnight with a dust haze; the temp at present in my room is about 94 degrees.

17th June

On the 15th June I got rid of 'Cheri' my bearer and took on Abdul whom I had known in the 38th mess at Malakand.

MacLachlan is away on 10 days leave and I am doing his work from 13th Inst.

I had a go of fever on the evening of Thursday 14th.

We had a very heavy dust storm on Friday and some rain yesterday it is a littler cooler in consequence.

18th June

Waterloo and O.W. (Old Wellingtonians) day.

20th June

Overheard by Col. Campbell an argument between a Tommy and a gharry-wallah.

Tommy, 'Look 'ere. I don't want to 'wit yer, but if you say much more, I'll knock yer bloomin' 'ead off!'

The Colonel also told a story of Native Troops on board a transport. One of the ship's officers caught a Subedar spitting on the deck and, knowing nothing about natives, cuffed his head. The Subedar thereupon drew himself up and said in broken English, 'I am Subedar'. 'I don't care whether you are Subedar or Khubbardar or who you are, I won't have you doing that on my ship.'

Memo: Get Audrey '95 medal ribbon for hat band.

28th June

Everyone off to China[29]. Why don't they employ the 40th Pathans I should so like to go, but I have given up all hope. I don't think I have ever had the blues so badly as I have got them now, such an awfully dreary prospect, we are not even down in the reliefs, however it is darkest before the dawn and perhaps there is a good time coming.

'C' and 'D' Coys, finished musketry yesterday.

30th June

Abnormal heat. 98 degrees in my room.

A Mrs Bigger had a son, who was the biggest? The son, because he was a 'little bigger'. When Mrs Bigger came home who was the biggest? Mr Bigger, because he was 'Far the Bigger'. When Mr Bigger died, who was the biggest? Mrs. Bigger, because the son was 'Far the less'. Next Please.

5th July

Yesterday and the day before the temp. in my room was 100 degrees and several degrees warmer outside at night. Capt. Perry I.M.S. arrived two days ago to take over medical charge of the Regiment vice Ogilvie proceeding to China. I knew him before as doctor of the Guides in the Malakand show.

We had a guest night of 14 last night mostly Doctors mobilizing for China. Turnbull, our former Dr., was there.

Others proceeding to China – McKechney and Dredge I.M.S. Bodham Gurkhas. Goldthorp 3rd P.I. collects curios.

I wish there was an instrument for measuring keenness. I think I should register twice as much as anyone else for China, then if the authorities would only select officers by keenness, I should go other things being equal.

10th July

Had rain yesterday and today, went for route march and got very wet. Temperature 89 degrees.

Rennick off to China on special service. Leslie ordered to join 31st. P.I. and

Riley 25th P.I. Was on H.S.Urdu exam yesterday with Col. Garbett 2nd B.L. President and Dunlop. Candidates were Waller, Gordon, Harvey, Hutchinson and Dyce.

20th July

Since last writing I have moved here to Fort Munro on 2 months leave, but first of all I must mention that in a letter from Punjab Hd. Qrs. w.e.f. 5–7–00 Craster, Walker, myself and St John were appointed to the 40th Pathans the first 3 augmentation and St John vice Ridgeway appointed Recruiting Staff Officer for the Pathans.

After a journey fraught with many trials I have come here on 2 months leave commencing 15–7–00. I dispatched my luggage under Rahminullah from Mian Mir on Friday the 13th Inst by Passenger Train. I left myself on Sunday the 15th at 7.12 p.m. accompanied by the faithful Abdul. It was cool and fairly free from dust as far as Multan where I changed at 3 a.m. From Multan to Ghazi Ghat the train was slow, the waits were long and the dust was an experience. I changed again at Mahmund Kotand; might have changed at Sher Shaf if I had liked. The pups behaved very well in the carriage. The method of crossing varies from day to day at this time of year according to the state of the Indus[30] from Ghazi Ghat to Dera Ghazi Khan.

I had to proceed first of all, starting about 7.30 a.m. a few hundred yards in a tum tum, then we embarked tum tum and all in a large native boat which was rowed and punted across a broad but slow running stream, We were somewhat delayed by Scroggins taking a violent dislike to the boatman working a pole near us in the stern, every time Scroggins broke from my grasp and went for the boatman we missed stays and lost much ground. On landing we started off again in the tum tum and did about three miles to the main stream over swampy ground, on the bank were waiting the dak boat and a large stern wheel steamer, we went in the dak boat which was a six oared sailing boat apparently made of galvanized iron. The crew of seven worked so jolly well that I subsequently gave them Rs 1–8–0 backsheesh, their novel way of rowing by standing on the seat in front of them and falling over backward in places where the stream was very strong, especially took my fancy. The stream was very strong indeed in two places with quite a high sea running. I saw a large 'mugger' [a large crocodile- Hindi 'magar' from Sanskrit 'makara', a crocodile, from Dravidia] waiting on a sand bank at the moment when I thought we should certainly be upset.

We landed amongst some flooded out ruins and after having driven in a tum tum some distance on top of a bank, proceeded about two miles to Cantonments. I spent the day in the mess with St John and had lengthy interviews with the N.O.s.

At 5 p.m. I started on the mail tonga for Sakhi Sarwar 30 miles across the most depressing desert, no food could be obtained so I started the next morning at 6 a.m. after some tea and a chupatti. I rode 20 miles on levy ponies and Baluchi saddles getting a change at Rakhiman and one other place. A Baluchi saddle is a section of a beer barrel with a wall in front and behind and very uncomfortable at that. At Girdoo I found Walker's pony and saddle and some chota hazri, the first meal I had had since 11 a.m. the day before. I reached Fort Munro at about 3 p.m. Walker and McDonald an extra Asst. Commr. in the bungalow. I found Walker had been recalled owing to Rennick[31] going to China.

1st August

People up here. Mr and Mrs Mark and children (2) he is Commissioner of Derajat. The Revd. and Mrs Lee-Mayer and 2 daughters. They used to know us all in Bannu in '81 at the time of Ettie's death. Mr and Mrs Broadway and 1 baby. He commands the frontier levy and is generally responsible for the welfare of the community. Dr and Mrs Adams and one or two babies in charge of the C.M.S. Hospital. Burton a young Commissioner, and Saville of the 1st. Bo. Lancers taking a census of transported animals. There have also been up here Spencer the Depy. Commissioner and a Dr. Smit.

I was to have started on a shoot yesterday, but there is a tennis tournament on yesterday and today and an 'at home' tomorrow with racing in bath tubs on Dawes Lake so I have postponed my trip till the day afterwards and I am glad I did as the weather is very stormy.

This morning I cut Saville's hair and he cut mine there being no barber, afterwards we had trial trips in bath tubs on a small tank, I foundered twice.

I work at Pushtoo every morning with Gulab the chowkidar[32] of the P.W.D. bungalow he is a most enlightened young Eusafsai, I also have 2 men per day to talk Pushtoo to me from the small detachment of our men at Khar.

There is tennis here three times a week and on the other days golf at Khar, on off days I take my orderly for walks and talk more Pushtoo.

3rd August

I have again postponed my shooting trip owing to a very bad accident which occurred yesterday. The Adams gave an 'at home' at Dawes Lake which was followed by racing and fooling about in bath tubs on the water. It was a silly sort of amusement, but one gets up [to] silly amusements at a place like this & gets lots of fun out of them sometimes too. We had been paddling about on the tank for some time, it was rather hard work & I was sitting in my tub near the bank thoroughly blown. No one could blame themselves in any way for what occurred subsequently. Spencer & Smit, of their own accord, jumped out of their tubs and went for a swim, and had been in the water for two or three minutes. Smit I noticed was in the very centre of the tank, in the deepest part, when I heard Smit say, quite quietly, 'Help me' & at the same time I saw him stretch out his hand towards an empty tub floating about two feet from where he was swimming – he said it so quietly there was nothing in his voice to suggest that he was in difficulties, that I thought he was asking somebody to help him bring the tub ashore. He seemed to be treading water, & again he said, 'Help me' very quietly, but I caught something in his voice which warned me at once that something was wrong, I just heard him say something about cramp, when I jumped out of my tub, almost the same time as Broadway did & Savile began began paddling uo to him, Spencer, who was already in the water, also went after him. When I came up I saw Smit slowly sinking without any splashing. I was already very blown from padlding, and the weight of my clothes also prevented me from diving too much, & I presently got so tired I had to swim ashore, which the others also had to do. He never once came up and must have sunk straight to the bottom, as several natives, good swimmers, stripped and went in but could do nothing. The tank was at that time as full as it could be from rain and very deep, just there probably 20 feet. They were using drag nets this morning when I went down to the tank, but had not yet recovered the body. He only came up here last Sunday, he belonged to the C.M.S. The poor fellow was engaged to be married to Adams' sister. The Adams and all the ladies and children were looking on at the fun at the time he was drowned.

5th August
Smit's body was found in the afternoon of the next day, the 3rd August, by one of the men from Khar, a Mohmand called Nagerai, they had been dragging for it with tennis nets all day and had eventually to cut the bund and let out several feet of water. Smit was buried the same evening. I start out shooting tomorrow.

13th August
I returned from shooting on 11th having had continual rain and clouds, I only saw two herds of markhor the 6 days I was out and never got a shot this was probably owing to a number of flocks grazing with their shepherds. I took a local shikharri. orderly, bearer and 6 coolies. I lived in a small 'tent d'abri' and took the inner fly of my 80lb. tent for servants and kit. The camp was pitched by two muddy puddles of water on a hill called Jingar, close to which is Jhari. I had to send about five miles daily for what was called spring water, but which nevertheless I took the precaution to have boiled. Everywhere there were flocks and

shepherds except on the rocky hills and cliffs where the markhor ought to have been.

There was a thunderstorm as soon as I arrived on the 6th it rained every night and the whole of the last day, I managed to keep pretty dry till the last day when everything got washed out. I was out at the time on a particularly bad bit of hill with the shikharri – by name Kaim – when the rain came down solid for three hours – the whole hillside ran with water and I had a very nasty climb to get home. I came back here on the 11th, however , feeling all the better and fitter for my climbing and outing. The coolies I took were simple people with no requirements they slept contentedly in the rain, they had no bedding or cooking pots, they mix their dough on a flat stone, wrap it round a small stone and throw it into the fire to cook. I gave them their atta for the time they were out, a sheep, and a rupee each, and the shikarri two rupees.

The day after I arrived back home I received a letter recalling me to do duty at Dhera Ghazi vice St John proceeded with the 20th P.I. to China. I shall probably start on 15th or as soon as I can get camels.

14th August

I put down the following notes as possibly useful on a future occasion – I pay my bearer weekly, my messing coming to an anna more or less than a rupee a day. Mutton is 3 seers [a unit of weight equivalent to one kilogram –2.2 lbs. – a Hindi ser] a rupee, and beef, when available, four seers. Charcoal is a rupee a maund (1 sack), Milk -/2/- a seer, and bread -/2/- a loaf. Fowls are expensive here and vary from -/5/- to -/7/- each. Potatoes are very expensive -/8/- a seer. Eggs expensive two for -/1/-. I gave my bearer -/3/- for soup dairy, and -/2/- for fat for cooking. I paid Rs.4/-/- for sheep I gave to coolies out shooting.

26th August

I am now settled down at Dera Ghazi, but since writing I have come from Fort Munro to Dera Ghazi, and been to Mian Mir and back. In consequence of being recalled I started from Fort Munro on the 16th Inst walking as far as Girdoo. My luggage also left on the same day by camels. I took the tonga from Girdoo, but owing to untrained ponies and the road being washed away in several places, I had a very uncomfortable journey and instead of getting a sleep at Sakhi Sarwar I only got an hours rest there and was travelling the whole night. I reached Dera Ghazi the next day, Friday the 17th, my luggage arrived on the 19th and I proceeded to Mian Mir on the 20th to get some kit. I left about 5 p.m. in the dak boat the train leaving Ghazi Ghat at 9 p.m. There is only one change at Sher Sha so I was able to get a good sleep but the dust was awful. I reached Mian Mir at

9.20 a.m., on the 21st and found Preston and Garratt alone in the Mess with a gramophone to amuse them. I got my kit and left on the 22nd at 6.55 p.m. and after changing at Multan and Muhd. Kot I reached Ghazi Ghat on the morning of the 23rd and crossed the river by steamer. My pony arrived yesterday.

A curious state of things exists at present between Walker and me, he commands the Regt., being senior to me in Regtl. rank and I am commanding the Station as I am senior in Army rank.

8th September
Walker went on 10 days leave last Thursday evening the 4th Inst to Fort Munro and Rowercroft of the 9th Bombay Lancers came back on Thursday morning. Last Wednesday morning we had Regtl. sports.

22nd September
Walker came back on the 20th

I wrote and asked for the loan of the gramophone from the Mess at Mian Mir, it arrived the other day with the ebonite records wrinkled and spoilt by heat. Have written for some more records today.

I dismissed my servant Abdul on the 15th, inst. for intriguing with a buniah, I also turned the buniah out of the regiment. I received orders on 20th inst. to proceed to Bukloh with 50 men (30 from here and 20 from Mian Mir) for a months course of scouting[33] It ought to be very interesting and I am very keen about it. We leave here on 24th.

6th October
Let me see I have rather a lot to put in. I left D.G.K. on 24th Sept. with 30 men, crossing the river by steamer and arrived at Mian Mir at 9 a.m. the next day. I found Lumsden our Doctor, Preston and Stanley Clarke (30th P.I.) in the bungalow and Garrett, the latter subsequently relieved me at D.G.K. I stopped at Mian Mir on 26th and proceeded early on 27th by special train with 50 men together with a similar detachment of 23rd Pioneers to Pathnakot. I had a bhustie[34] with my lot, Keene had a banian, cook and sweeper as well, we found on arrival there that a Hospital Assistant with a hospital (a bag containing a few medicines) had turned up from somewhere for us.

He had no orders and no carriage so we had to get him along as best we could, shortly afterwards he went sick and I never saw him again. On the 28th we marched to Nurpur, a pretty place off the main road, 17 miles, the next day we marched about 15 miles through very pretty country (Kangar) to Dunera on the main Pathenkoy – Dalhousie road. We made a detour into Kangar instead of going along the main road by mistake really, but it was a good thing as we left the road open to the Viceroy who was returning from a shoot in Chamba. On the 29th we marched in here to Bakloh, we made it about 8 miles taking short cuts. We found here, besides Keene's lot, a detachment of the 30th under Thomson, the 33rd under Harrison, and 38th under Rowlanson. I was given quarters in a small mess annexe. The 1st/4th Ghurkas at present are in China, the 2nd 4th consist of Major Mowbray Thomson, Capt. Ducat and Travers and Lieuts. Sealy, Money and Hogg also Capt. Milne I.M.S.

The last week has been spent chiefly in getting the men physically fit – a run, walk, climb in the morning and lectures or practical work in the afternoons. It is rather hard work, but I like it, the men and myself are all thoroughly fit now, one or two men have had fever, and one or two sore feet, but only two in hospital.

19th November

At Datra Ghazi Khan – rather a lot to enter. First of all I will enter a few names. At Bakloh, Mrs and Miss Brown, Mrs Carnegie and Miss Rawlins. Mrs Travers, Mrs Lee and Mrs Battye, Mrs Ryall (met at Pritchards) and Mrs Colomb, Mrs Lindsay and Mrs Couper. Miss Thomson also joined 4th Goorkhas afterwards Birdwood and Burne and Hay also came up with 250 of the 38th. On the 27th October I marched down to Nurpur to join 'A' Force under Col. Robinson for the manoeuvres with half Oxfords, E. Lanes and Inniskilling Fusiliers, and 1/1st Goorkhas. Of the 1st. Goorkhas I met Col. Robinson, Majors Hatch and Ommaney, Capt Campagne, Evans, Johnston and Yung of the Oxfords I met Major Peter Clarke, Darrel Brown (came out in Malabar) and Chichester (met at Horsham) of E. Lanes. Capt. Pierce, Luddington, Baker, Melville (attach) and Webb Bowen of Bedford Scouts.

On 28th was sent up to reconnoitre Hathi Dar, the mule with food and bedding did not arrive, so I spent uncomfortable night in native hut and signalling party of Goorkhas. Darrel Brown as umpire, we bivouacked up there till 3rd Novbr, keeping connection between columns and scouting generally, on 3rd Novbr. I came down and joined in fighting and marched back to Bakloh on 4th Novbr.

On the 7th I walked to Bassoli with Hay. On the 9th we left Bakloh marching to Dunera, on the 10th to Dhar, 11th to Sharpur, halted there 12th, and 13th to Pathenkot and on the same day by train spending the night at Amritsar. We reached Mian Mir on the 14th on the 15th I started for D.G.K. arriving on 16th.

While I was away Craster left to take over duties as Adjutant and Walker as Qr. Mstr of the new Regt., the 41st Dogras, whereby I become Qr. Mstr. of the 40th.

We reconstituted as follows 2 Coys Oraksais, 1 Coy Afridis, 1 Coy Eusefsais, 2 Coys P.M.s and 2 Coys Dogras.

5th December

Intimation today by wire that a wing 1st BO Grenadiers from Bhuj would arrive here on 10th Inst. to relieve us. I am sorry to go as D.G. Khan suits me very well.

We have done a little mild entertaining here. We had a ladies dinner party in the mess about a fortnight ago, a sing song dance and fireworks in the lines, and subsequently sports, the 40th represented by Bunbury, self and 6 N.O.s pulled the world in a tug-of-war, the world consisting of 7 sahibs and a cavalry N.O. won.

I have had several days shooting, the days were most enjoyable and the lunch plentiful but no large bags have been made. One day with Bunbury and McDonald we got 13 and a half brace blacks, another day with Bunbury 5 blacks. One day in a boat on the river 1 duck (shoveller) and last Sunday on the river we got nothing all day, but as we were rowing home, we saw some geese, which Bunbury stalked, he got 10 with 2 barrels.

People I have met at D.G. Khan, Mr and Mrs Bowden P.W.D., the Broadway, Mayers, Adams, Plowden D.S.P., McDonalds, Spencer, Dist Judge Mills, Immigration, Smith Vet, and Capt. Reed 4th Punjab Infantry, the Gwithers, (Irrigation) arrive today I believe.

16th December

I forgot to mention in the above list Cowin I.M.S. our Doctor who was living in the Mess with us. Subsequently I met Col. Bates I.M.S. Inspector General of Jails.

We went out shooting again on Thursday but didn't get anything.

We were relieved on Monday the 10th by a Wing of the 1st Grenadiers from Bhuj with Capt. Doveton and White and a Dr Dickinson. We left ourselves the next day being seen off by the whole station, we marched to Ghazi Ghat and proceeded by special train 5 p.m. arriving at Mian Mir 8 a.m. the 12th Decbr. On arrival at Mian Mir I engaged a new servant, a Persian by name Shakurullah. On the 14th Decbr. I attended a lecture by Capt. Jennings Bramley on 'marching'. On the 13th Webb Bowen of the Bedfordshires, and on 14th Eliot of the 41st Dogras arrived as Honry. members in our mess for a transport class. Yesterday I drove into Lahore with Bunbury and called on Hutchinsons, Perrys, W.O.Clarkes, Kitty, the Lamonts, Hendleys and Jackson and Dennys. Capt Boxer of the 29th, Punjab Infantry is attached to us at present.

30th December

The Xmas week is just over and I have enjoyed myself fairly on the whole. I had dinner on Xmas day with Kitty and Turton who are living with the W.O.Clarkes. Leslie said he would call for me at 11 p.m. in a gharry (small horse–drawn carriage – Hindi gari) we were sharing and he didn't turn up till 12.30. Leslie and Bruce both of the 31st. PI. are staying in the bungalow with us, the latter is a most amusing fellow and we have had a good deal of enjoyment together. They are both recalled today as their Regt. is marching from Sialkot to Nowsherea.

Bob Howell came to stay for a day and a night on the 23rd inst. I also saw Phil who is staying in Lahore, they had both come to look for the 'Brethren' who appeared to be at Sialkot though nothing was known for certain.

Many O.W.s (Old Wellingtonians) have turned up for Christmas week, viz, Melville of the SW Borderers, Paton of the same Regt, formerly of Anglesea Burrows of the E. Lanes, Brind a gunner, Maude of the Somersets, Dundas 3rd Goorkhas, Lloyd 4th D.Gs, Bill I.C.S.

I have made the acquaintance of Miss Lovett, Graham's young woman, she is staying with the Grants, financial commissioner.

I have got a complete rig out for the 40th from Rankens.

I am dining with the Colonel tonight. The Colonel told me the other day that on the evening of the 12th September 1897, when we were at Markhannai, he went round to inspect the defences of the Guides part of the camp when he saw some coolies and cattle belonging to the Buffs coffee shop and outside the camp, he wrote a note to the F.O. of the day, Major Worledge 35th Sikhs – asking if he had noticed it, the reply came while the Guides were sitting at dinner, to the effect that Major Worledge had noticed them, but did not think it was any use bringing them into camp as he did not think there would be any firing that night. Col. Campbell was reading the reply to Major Hodgson and just as he got to the words, 'I do not think there will be any firing tonight.' 'Bang! Phit! came the first volley that caused us all to jump so.

1901

6th January

Anthony Hope has written a book called *Quisante*, this is being acted and amongst the actresses is Mrs Campbell Praed. The following is from Migs:-

Why did Anthony Hope?

Because Mrs Campbell prayed (Praed).

What did Anthony hope?

To kiss Auntie(Quisante).

On the 3rd inst. the Dorsets marched in on their way to Ferozepore, also the

2nd Patiala Regt. to relieve the 23rd Pioneers off to the Wuzeeri blockade. The Dorsets were Boxer's old Regt. so most of them came to dine that night, also the 23rd The Dorsets and the 23rd both left next day.

I don't think I mentioned that Ogilvie returned from China on the 23rd December.

Capt. Coles of the 37th Dogras is staying in the mess for reservists training, also Capt. Dunlop left with the depot of the 23rd Pioneers. Two companies, composed of Bajaueries, Bunerwals, and Swatrs were taken to Ferozepore yesterday to join the 33rd P.I. Boxer returned this morning, Suhedar Mahmad, Jemadars Bahram and Babozai, went with the 2 companies to Ferozepore.

17th January

The Regt was inspected by General Sir G. de C. Morton K.C.UI.E., C.B. on Monday and Tuesday last the 14th and 15th insts. On Monday we had books and lines, owing to the rain on Sunday, the parade ground was too wet for parade. On Tuesday we had outposts in the morning and ceremonial in the afternoon. The reservists were also out and we had brigade parade. Last night I went to a subscription dance in the Lawrence Hall and didn't care for it much as I did not know anyone.

22nd January

On the 19th I met Charlie and Kitty driving and afterwards went to see Charlie. He is just recovering from enteric and looked pretty weak. On the evening of the 19th we went to dinner with the 11th Bengal Lancers. We heard the day before yesterday that the Queen was ill and yesterday that she was very ill and in extremis.

We were to have had a ladies dinner party of 32 tomorrow, but this has been put off, I believe.

Today is the 'Id d fitr.'

24th Jan. QUEEN VICTORIA DIED ON THE NIGHT OF JAN 22–23.

28th January

I went to the proclamation ceremony at the town hall in Lahore yesterday, driving in with Coles and Webb Bowen. There were Royal Guards of Honour from the Inniskillings, P.V.Rs and ourselves forming three sides of a square, the

XI B.L. and P.L.H. were also represented. Ladies dressed in black were sitting in the windows and balconies above, on one side of the platform below were English officers Civil and Military, townsfolk and shop keepers, and on the other side were Native Gentlemen and natives. As Mr Clarke, Commissioner stepped on the platform Capt Madge S.S.O. hoisted the Royal Ensign and the troops presented arms. Mr Casson, Secretary to the government, read the proclamation in English, followed, by a native in Hindustani, the band then played *God Save the King* and Mr Clarke proposed three cheers for the King, while the guns at the Fort fired a royal salute.

I bicycled into Lahore with Preston for the Cathedral morning service today. It is strange hearing the King prayed for in Church.

I met Godfrey Steward yesterday, he arrived a few days ago with a draft of the Inniskillings.

5th February

Ranken agreed to take back my uniform after many explanations as it was made of the wrong shade of drab.

A fellow called Langton has been staying in the mess, he is the civil surgeon of Dera Dun. Coles, Williamson and Hutchinson left on the 1st after the reservists had broken up, and Webb-Bowen and Eliot on the 2nd.

On the 2nd there were memorial services at Lahore and M. Mir, but I did not go not having any uniform. On the evening of the 2nd I went to dinner at Sykes (Walkers' brother-in-law) it was a terrible affair, there was a Mr and Mrs Bell (Educational Department) a Mr & Mrs Anthony and a Lady Dr Church, the conversation was chiefly about analytical jurisprudence and the Land Alienation Bill.

On Sunday I went to the Cathedral with Preston to a Thanksgiving Service & afterwards to lunch at Mr Maude's where were Lady & Miss Elles[35] & Col. Dillon (the latter two to be married the day after tomorrow) & Miss Ruddock.

Yesterday I went to lunch at General Morton's, the Genl. was away, the company included Miss Morton & Miss Fairweather, Major & Mrs Delamain. Rennick, and Mrs Casson & Ogilvie.

I am just off to meet Gerard at the station on his way to Bombay to be married, 6th February.

I went to Lahore station yesterday but didn't meet Gerard because he had given me the time of departure of the train instead of arrival at the station. His train had just gone.

We have been doing field firing today – in a violent thunderstorm and got very wet.

Bunbury left today with 100 men this morning to join Sir M. Young's camp at Pak Patten as escort, I have taken over one of his ponies today, which formerly used to belong to me.

'Why was Rider Haggard?' 'Because he had to marry Corelli.'

'What did Robert Barr?' 'Seeing Flora Annie Steel.'

7th February

I dined last night at the Joubert's.

I was reading *How we escaped from Pretoria* by Capt. Aylmer Haldane. The following method of making biltong which he mentions as succulent and sustaining. I copy from it :- 'It is made from the flesh of the buck or ox cut from the choicest parts, strips of this meat are steeped in vinegar or pepper for two hours, then covered with salt which it sucks in all night. Next day the strips are hung up in a shady place till their exterior is dry, when they are put in the sun, which soon makes them as hard as wood. This is now fit for eating, and as much as is required for a meal can be cut from it as one slices a cucumber.'

10th February

I went to the wedding of Col. Dillon and Miss Elles at Lahore Cathedral on Thursday the 7th inst. Hodgson of the 34th Pioneers is in charge of the 2nd Patiala Infantry here, he is staying in the mess with Dunlop 23rd Pioneers.

'Have you seen the cuckoo?' 'No, what cuckoo?'

'The cook who cooked the dinner.'

I commenced doing Pushtoo again about a week ago.

'What gave Henry Pain? Mrs Harriet Beecher Stowe.'

15th February

I sold the grey pony I bought from Dunlop at an auction for Rs. 95/- he was very old. I only have Bunbury's now.

18th February

On Saturday the 16th inst. Lieut. G.D.Campbell from the Bedfordshires at Luton joined the Regt on appointment. Yesterday Preston started on 10 days leave to take his fiancee, Miss Willis, to Peshawar to stay with her sister, Mrs Ridgeway. I am doing Preston's work.

On the night of the 16th – 17th Febr. a daring robbery was committed in the following lines, a gang of thieves shut all the doors of the houses in the row by putting up the door chains on the outside, they then made a hole through one of the dhobie's houses and carried off the entire washing of G Company. They took what they wanted and left the rest outside, all this while the dhobie, his wife and 4 children were asleep in the room about the size of a bathroom.

From Dunlop, 'Why does Kruger wear goloshes?'

'To keep De Wet from defeat.'

20th February

I attended another lecture by Capt. Jennings Bramley of the Black Watch this evening, both he and the General agreed that the drill book was a misleading anachronism. Genl. Hildegard when asked what formation he was attacking replied the formation best suited for taking advantage of ant heaps. This was at Colenso.

24th February

The Colonel left for Ferozepore on duty on the 21st. and returned today.

Fitzgibbon, a young Australian, who came out to join the 51st Battery, is staying in our mess while his battery is in camp.

Hughes (OW) of the 1/1st. Goorkhas is also staying in the mess.

I dined with Hodgson at the Punjab Club last night and today, after biking into Lahore for the service at the Cathedral with Hughes, I went to lunch with Turton and Kitty, who are much exercised about the new Frontier Province.[36]

Ogilvie is responsible for the following:-

Three Englishmen drinking beer at a restaurant in France –1st Englishman, 'I wonder what this is, it isn't Laager.'

2nd, 'Well, whatever it is its very good.'

3rd, 'C'est magnifique, mais ce n'est pas Laager.'

28th February

On Monday 25th I went to Lahore Station and saw Gerard and Mrs Howell on their way back from Bombay to Jhelum after being married.

On the 26th I went to an 'At Home' at the Lamonts and yesterday to Kitty's 'At Home'.

Keene of the 23rd on his way to rejoin the 27th is staying in the mess, also Yates of the 4th Ghoorkhas who has come with a footer team, last night Gurdon of the 32nd Pioneers was dining at Mess.

Yesterday I discovered that by putting my finger nail on one of the gramophone records while it was revolving, I could faintly reproduce the tune.

6th March

There was a field day today including all the volunteers who are in camp. I was umpire in an armoured train manned by the N.W.R. Volunteers. We had a railway bicycle manned by scouts and a maxim. I learnt that the easiest way to destroy a line is to get a spanner and take off 2 fishplates (4 screws in each) in some lines there may be wooden wedges fixed in at intervals which can be easily knocked out, there are gangmen in huts at intervals of 3 or 4 miles along the line, where all necessary tools can be procured. I went to Kitty's 'At Home' today and saw Graham. Capt. Montague of the 21st. P.I. and Mackenzie of the 35th Sikhs, both asst. officers of I.S. troops are in the mess today.

10th March

Leslie is staying in the bungalow and Peacock 31st. P./I. in the mess, both with their hockey team.

On Friday Lt. General Egerton, Comdt. Punjab with Genel. Whitby and Major Stannel arrived. We had a brigade parade, and after the General and all C.O.s and heads of departments came to lunch, we had the pipes and drums, lately worked up by Colonel Campbell. It was represented to Genl. Egerton by the P.M.O. that the health of the Regt. suffered very much at M. Mir. The Genl. said he would see what could be done.

17th March

The last week the Punjab Infantry Hockey Tournament has been going on and resulted in a win for the 38th Dogras, the 15th Sikhs being in the final, and 32nd Pioneers in the semi-final. Fellows staying in the mess are as follows – 15th Sikhs, Capt. Hill, D.S.O.(organizer of tournament), Capt. Gordon, McMullen and Muir 32nd Pioneers (besides Hodgson), Capt. Peterson, Cooke, 23rd Pioneers, Kelly and Otley, 31st P.I. Capt Watson, Peacock and Leslie. The 38th Dogras (living with the Hutchinsons), Col. Vivian, Browns and Barstow. Ireland of the 36th Sikhs was also here.

Last night was held the first of an annual Punjab Infantry dinner, I was prevented from going at the last moment by an attack of the collywobbles. On Wednesday the 13th the Regt. was 'at Home' at the Murray Club.

The Colonel and Preston are away for a few days recruiting and Boxer and I are carrying on the reconstitution here, 50 Mohmands left this morning on discharge with gratuity and about 30 Gaduns and Gundiaris leave in a couple of days.

My weight in khaki uniform is 11st. 7lbs.

19th March

Yesterday evening I saw Freddie and the children off at Lahore station, they are going to Delhi for a fortnight and then home in the same steamer with Kitty. Turton hopes to go about June.

I saw off a pay of 30 Gurduns and Gundiparis who were discharged with gratuity on elimination this morning. I afterwards rode into Lahore and said goodbye to Charlie and Katie who were staying for a day with Kitty and sail from Bombay on 23rd.

The Col. and Preston returned from recruiting today.

23rd March

On Thursday the 21st. we had a Regiment 'At Home' in the mess with all kinds of music after dinner, we had the 23rd Band, our pipes and a select programme of songs, Miss Joubert singing in great form. About 150 people came. The mess was illuminated with dewas and the drives and garden were lit up with Chinese lamps. I think people enjoyed it very much . Last night Gwynne Bird of the 47th Sikhs stopped at the mess on his way [to] raising recruits for the new Regiment.

27th March

Last Sunday I went to the Cathedral and afterwards to lunch with Kitty and Turton.

Last night we had a large dinner in the mess consisting of 32 all told, the guests comprised the Reids and Miss Beadon, Col. and Mrs Heath, Major and Mrs Mckenzie R.I.F., Major, Mrs and Misses Holloway, Mr and Mrs Bunbury, Col. and Mrs Dillon, Col. Bates, Mrs Bate and Miss Moroney, Mrs Campbell, Mrs Ogilvie, Mrs Boxer. I took Miss Deane.

Today the Iniskillings had a bicycle gymkhana. Kitty also held her last 'At Home' which I did not attend.

3rd April

This morning Kitty left for Bombay on her way home. Lady Young gave an 'At Home' yesterday for her friends to say goodbye to Kitty. I attended. Kitty received a very fine set of silver plate as a parting gift.

Yesterday and today I have been examined in Pushtoo by the H.S. the board consisting of Col. Dillon, Boxer and Preston, other candidates were Gibb 32nd Pioneers and Watts 41st Dogras, also Bunbury and one or two others.

On Saturday and Sunday I had a slight go of fever.

We began kammerbands for mess and ice about a week ago.

Foster is down here in our mess for a week, he is now with the 23rd Pioneers on the Wazeeri Blockade.

7th April

Easter Sunday. I went to church here this morning. We began white uniform at mess last night. Yesterday I shot 'Doodles'. She had been very ill for about a week with sores, St Vitas' dance and convulsions, there were symptoms of rabies too and she was unable to drink water, so I thought it advisable to shoot her. She was quite quiet.

14th April

Yesterday Cochrane joined the Regiment from the S. Staffords unattached list. Preston left yesterday for Peshawar on 3 months 'leave'. He is to be married tomorrow, I am doing his work. Boxer has gone away on 10 days leave to take Mrs B. to Dalhousie today. We had rain yesterday.

21st April

Some of the Bedfords have been spending the day in our mess on their way from Multan to Ghora Dacca.

The temperature is 74 and a half, it has been very cool last week.

26th April

I dined with Turton. There were also there Graham and Col. Deane.

Bob Howell lately posted to the 15th B.L. on his way to a riding class at Pindi, stopped here for the night of the 24th – 25th.

On the night of the 24th, the two new batteries – 51st and 54th dined with the Regiment.

Do you know how to catch a squirrel? No? Go up a tree and make a noise like a nut!

From the Horsham Advertiser. Mother (in new silk dress), 'Do you know, Tommy, this beautiful new dress was made for me by one little, tiny, tiny worm!'

Tommy, 'And was that worm Papa?'

28th April

Yesterday we had Regimental Sports.

I have gathered the following facts about Mohammadanism :- The Sayeds are descendants of the prophet. The Sheahs(Shias) and Sunnis are two different sects. The former recognize Hassan and Husein the sons of the prophet, the latter do not recognize them, moreover Hassan and Husein were murdered by Sunnis. On this account, during the Muhurram festival (which is now going on) the Sheahs mourn and the Sunnis rejoice as it is the anniversary of the death of the sons of the prophet. Sunnis pray with their hands folded and Shias with their hands open. The majority of Muhammadans in India are Sunnis, in Persia they are nearly all Shias.[37]

The temperature today, 12 noon, is 78 degrees.

5th May

We began punkahs in the mess on 1st May.

On the 30th April I went to a dance at the railway theatre with Boxer and Hodgson.

On the 1st. May we all drove into an evening 'At Home' at Government House.

On the 2nd Boxer, Campbell, Cochran and I went to a concert and dance at the Roberts Volunteer Club.

On the 3rd Bunbury and I drove into the Laurence Gardens after dinner with the C.O. and Mrs Campbell to listen to the band. There was a dust storm and rain yesterday and it has been raining and blowing every since. It is very pleasant and cool in consequence.

7th May

Smiler died yesterday. Exactly a month after 'Doodles'.

The Colonel and Mrs Ogilvie left yesterday on 3 days recruiting for Pindi after which Ogilvie proceeds on 10 days leave to take Mrs O to the hills.

Campbell left today on 2 months leave to stay with his people at Mussoorie.

12th May

Boxer left to take up his appointment as 4th D.C. Commander in the 49th Garhwalis on the 9th. Temperature today 83 degrees.

19th May

The Regimental Hockey Club is started and we have joined the P.N.A.H.T. We played the 1st Regimental Games yesterday and the day before.

There was heavy rain on the 16th and 17th and Bunbury and I were nearly drowned coming back from a hockey match against the Railway.

We heard a few days ago that the question of moving the Regt. to Umballa on account of bad health was under consideration of the C. in C. and that we should probably move soon, but we have since heard that we are not likely to go yet on account of the possibility of plague riots here.

25th May
I dined last night with Major MacKenzie at the Inniskilling mess and discovered that he was a great friend and admirer of Major Collins and was much interested in the G.B.H. and had met Father there and knew most of the notables in connection with the place.

Temperature 83 degrees, not bad at all, and nights cool.

31st May
Lots of work. Regt. moving to Umballa. Cochran with advanced party, left for Umballa on 29th. There has been no hot weather so far but now it is getting hot. Temperature 91 degrees.

16th June
Umballa. Left Mian Mir on relief by depot 20th P.I. and Wing 38th Dogras in special train on evening of Sunday 2nd June. Entrained in dust storm, very cool journey took about 14 hours getting here. Sharing lines with depot 34th Pioneers. Green and extensive cantonment, clean looking, the thing that struck me most were the thatched bungalows to stand the rains.

It has been very cool since we arrived with the exception of 2 days rain in the day before yesterday.

Temperature in my room 87 and a half degrees.

9th July
Rains broke here today.

My weight is 10st. 6 lbs.

I engaged a fresh servant, Kudral Ali.

22nd July
Chambra [In the foothills of the Himalayas about 140 miles NE of Lahore]. I have arrived here on one months general leave. I left Umballa at 9.30p.m. on the 19th reached Amritsar 6 a.m. on 20th, having a 3 hours wait I went over the

Golden Temple there, a priest hung garlands over me and I felt awfully foolish walking about like that in carpet slippers several sizes too big for me, but I tried to look as if it was the sort of thing I did every day. I went on at 9.23 a.m. and reached Pathankot at 2.30p.m. I left at once and arrived at Duneera the same evening 30 miles by tonga and ekka and went on to Dalhousie the next morning 21st 30 miles. I stopped the night at the Springfield Hotel. I walked out here 18 miles the 22nd stopping a few hours half way at the dak bungalow at Khujear which is a lovely place. Here I met Cochran who left Umballa a few days before me. We are stopping here today making arrangements and hope to go on shooting tomorrow the 24th. I append a rough account of expenses so far:-

1st class ticket Umballa to Pathankot	Rs. 14-0-0
Two third class　do　do　do	6-0-0
Surplus luggage to Pathankot	6-0-0
Food Gharries, coolies etc en route	8-0-0
One seat mail tonga Pathankot to Duneera	7–8-0
Two ekkas Pathankot to Dalhousie	15-0-0
Dak Bungalow bill to Duneera	5-0-0
Rickshaw Duneera to Dalhousie	7–8-0
Hotel bill Dalhousie	7-0-0
12 Coolies Dalhousie to Chamba	7–8-0
Tips, tolls, coolies, doolies etc	10-0-0
Total	93–8-0

Besides this my stores, including some camp plates, came to Rs 80/ about.

Memo for future guidance. I have brought a great deal too many clothes and stores, and an 80lb. tent is unnecessary.

16th August

Kujear. Expedition continued. The following is a list of marches, with length. It is no use stating miles as it is mostly climbing work:-

24th　Chamba to Musroond, long, half flat, half severe.
25th　Halt at Musroond, rain.
26th　Musroond to Kabul, short.
27th　Kaleel to Tisa, medium.
28th　Halt at Tisa, washed clothes. Flask and binoculars stolen.
29th　Tisa to Sai. Short. Cochran had fever.
30th　Sai to Jajera. Short. Fleas.
31st　Jajera to Camp Makhan Nullah. Medium.

7th   Camp to Jajera, rain whole way. Cochran at Makhan.

8th   Jajeera to Tisa. Long, rain.

9th   Tisa to Kaleel, medium.

10th   Kaleel to Chamba. 2 marches, beer!

13th   Chamba to Kujear, short, rain.

Before leaving Chamba on our way out we called on Burri Singh, the Rajah's brother, a very decent chap. The Mukhan Nullah I am convinced is a good place for sport but owing to the continuous rain and mist besides being uncomfortable we were never able to see a hundred yards when we went shooting. One day I stalked a thar, but the mist came down while I was loading and was not able to get my shot, this was trying. I only once got a shot – 3 shots rather at one thar. They were close but very hard shots and I did not hit it. Owing to the ceaseless rain I left for Chamba on 7th August making 7 marches. Cochran having another month's leave stopped behind but he arrived in Chamba the day after I did having been offered a vacancy at Pachmarri by urgent wire. We slacked for a couple of days in Chamba and then came on here, where we proceeded to slack again. Yesterday we saw Burri Singh again on his way back from Dalhousie, he kindly placed his bungalow at our disposal, which was just as well as we had slept the night and spent an uncomfortable day of mist and rain in the veranda thereof. I am going on tomorrow the 17th August and Cochran is stopping here as he cannot get his musketry class.

Notes on stores, kit etc. I have affixed to this page a list of the stores I took with me from Umballa. Everything in that line can, however, be obtained from Salig Ram at Dalhousie and it would be better to get the stores there if coming this way and save carriage. The stores I got were the right sort and quantity with the following exceptions and additions:- Keatings insect powder absolutely necessary. [ref: entry on 16th August re 30th July march Sai to Jajera. Short. 'Fleas'.] Army and Navy Belgravian rations brought by Cochran, most excellent and portable. I should have liked more bacon. Milk biscuits are good, also luncheon biscuits. A tin of sweet biscuits would make a pleasant variety. Several small tins of any commodity are better than one large one. Do not forget corned beef curry, plenty of rice necessary. Treacle would be a good thing with chuppaties. A folding candle lantern, procurables at Saig Ram's. Dalhousie indispensable, chocolate. Caster oil for boots.

An 80 lb. tent and camp bed are necessary no other furniture required. A tin bath is not required. Permission should be obtained to use the forest bungalows. The question of shikarris is a difficult one, we were badly let in over ours by name Lalla (Chota Shikarri Kablia), a money grubbing scoundrel. I fancy they are all much alike.

All that is required is (1) a man that knows the country (2) a man to make grass shoes (3) a couple of sensible men to help you over difficult places. I fancy the best way would be to take an intelligent tiffin coolie and see if you could make an arrangement with the authorities at your base of operations for the requisite number of coolies to accompany you the whole time, without charge, at a fixed daily wage. I took too many clothes, the following general principles should be applied: – all clothes should be of the very oldest. 4 shirts, 4 vests, 2 shorts, several socks, handchfs. cashmere hat, sweater, waistcoat, 1 warm coat, 1 pr. flannel trousers, 1 large towel, 1 gt. coat, 1 Ryai, 3 blankets, 1 pr. boots, chaplies, several leather socks, 2 puttees (1 to wind round waist if cold) slippers. The experiment of a ruck sack was a great success. Pack writing material uppermost.

16th October

I have been very slack in writing up this book lately. I arrived here Chunglah Gully, after much trouble in getting my uniform from Dalhousie on the 23rd August, to find the class really began the day before, however it did not seem to matter. The course here is really very sound and practical most of the theoretical subjects having been done away with. I won the officers' handicap shooting with 17 points, the greatest number of points given being 30. I won about Rs. 150/– in the lottery.

I have seen the Ridgeways and Ogilvies at Nuthia and Dunga respectively and walked to the top of Mirjham with Major Hodgson, Ridgeway and Ogilvie.

I have been into Murree staying at the Club 3 times from Friday to Sunday. The first time I met Brind an O.W., the second time Hay. On my second visit the latter dined with me and after the club dance we had supper with Miss Sheen and Forest. I also went to tea with Miss Hastings and met Phil and Toolie Howell.

Last Saturday Marsh and I had a dinner party at the club consisting of Genl. Joubert, Miss Joubert and Miss Sheen. The officers of this class are the following:-

Major	Buchanan	Chief Instr.	Lieut.	Ryan	Essex
Capt.	Skinner	Ass. "	"	Deane	XII B.C.
Capt.	Tarte	Junior Instr.	Lieut.	Duhan	19th P.I.
"	Kaye	30th P.I.	"	Brown	3rd Sikhs
"	Watson	31st. P.I.	"	Champain	5th Gurkhas
"	Rice	4th Sikhs	"	Alexander	1st P.I.
"	Hutchinson	41st Dogras	"	Tyndall	40th P.I.
"	Warburton	Hampshires	"	Dunsford	33rd P.I.
"	Williams	Hampshires	"	D'Oyley	19th B.O.I.
	Mitchell	R.I.F.	"	Marsh	21st. Pioneers.

Lieut.	Heath	Queens	2nd Lieut. Watson	Somersets
"	Lyons	Sussex	" Denny	Wiltshires
"	Ogg	Dorset	" Beaumonth	K.R.R.
"	Webb–Bowen	Bedfords		
"	Kelly	K.R.R		
"	Abadie	K.R.R.		

1902

7th January

Jhansi arrived 28th October from Chunglah Gully after stopping a few days in Lahore at Nedous' Hotel. I left Chunglah 21st. October.

This is not a bad place in the cold weather the country being undulating with kopjes and covered with rocks and scrub and nulllahs and pretty in places, there are a great quantity of ruins everywhere, some of which must have been fine buildings once.

I have had several very good days game shooting, the following game being plentiful:

Quail (brush)

Grey and painted partridge

Sandgrouse

Peafowl

Snipe

Duck, Gadwell, Pochard, grey, spot billed and cotton and whistling teal, shoveller, comb duck, blue winged teal.

At present with the Regt. Col. Campbell, Cochran, Ogilvie.

I stopped for a month first in Ogilvie's bungalow and then took this bungalow where I am trying to make [a] garden.

On the 23rd Decbr. the Camp of Exercise began at which the following Regts. are present-

South Lancashire, York and Lanes, East Surrey, 21st, P.I., 6th M.I.,

1st Brahmins, Bhopal Bn., 6th B.C., 13th B.L., Bhopal Lancers, and also 6 Batteries, also Gwalior Lancers.

We attended with 200 men at first but were ordered back on 28th Decbr. Christmas was an uneventful period which I spent in Camp.

6th February

Savage enemy camp 15th to 22nd January. Col. Campbell, Major Moggeridge (South Lanes), Major Hamilton (Norfolks), Col. Daniell (RA), Maclachlan,

Campbell, Cochran and self with 10 native officers and 246 men. We had 3 days with the 1st Brigade and 2 days with the 2nd Brigade with a night attack on each.

I am struck off Qr. Mrs, work to do signalling, my name having been sent in for the class at Kassauli commencing 1st April. I have obtained the following list showing the number of fighting men of each tribe :-

Bajaur	18,500	Nawagai	6,000
		Khar	4,500
		Jandol	8,000
Dir	13,800	Malizai	3,000
		Talash Valley	2,500
		Maidan Bajaur	2,000
		Jaubatai	1,000
		Rabat	1,000
		Bibiar	700
		Dir	1,500
		Pauakot	600
		Khauluus	1,500
Chitral	10,000		
Utman Khel	5,000		
Buner	17,300	Nasosai	4,000
		Gadaizai	2,500
		Ikassai Jalarzai	1,800
		Ashajai	2,000
		Daolatzai	2,000
		Milazai Chagarzai	2,500
		Nurazai	2,500
Swat	18,000	Khawjozai	8,000
		Raizai	6,000
		Ranizai	1,000
		others	3,000
Mahmands	17,400	Tarakzai	2,800
		Halunizai	2,600
		Baizai	9,000
		Khwaizai	1,800
		Utmanjai	400
		Dawerzai	800

Afridis	26,500	Kuki Kheyl	4,000
		Malikdin Kheyl	4,000
		Kambar Kheyl	4,000
		Kanar Kheyl	1,100
		Zakha Kheyl	4,500
		Sipah	1,200
		Aka	1,800
		Adam Kheyl	5,900
Orakzais	24,800		

14th February

Last Saturday the 8th Maclachlan, Preston and I went by the 8.10 p.m. train to Babina, 3 stations towards Lalitpur, I having arranged previously the Saturday before for a beat of 50 coolies. We slept the night at Babina bungalow and early the next morning proceeded to the beat, one Chink only however was turned out which I shot, eleven and a half inches, the head is in the Mess. We did some bird shooting during the rest of the day and returned by the 7.60p.m.[sic] train from Babina.

On the 12th Sir Arthur Power-Palmer, C.in C., arrived in the Station and inspected the Brigade in review order. We were afterwards introduced to him.

24th February

On Saturday and Sunday the 16th and 17th Insts. I went with the Col's shooting party to Dinera, also went Preston and Farmer, a Gunner, Mrs Campbell, Mrs Preston and Mrs Farmer. I slept in the new bungalow and Mrs Campbell arranged the Commissariat, we got about 8 geese and 60 duck.

Saturday and yesterday Ogilvie, Cochran and I went to Garhman, slept under a tree, we got 30 duck and a few snipe.

24th March

Macpherson arrived out from sick leave at home to join the Regiment on the 15th. We started white at the Mess on the 17th I have just returned last night from 3 days leave shooting. I went to Duvangunj about 8 hours by slow train in the Bombay direction. I left at 8.10p.m. on the 19th and arrived about 5 a.m. the next morning. I sent my orderly on with my shooting pass and letter to the thanadar asking to be supplied with a shikarri and 8 coolies. These men met me, but after having tried a beat in which nothing turned up, the man said he wasn't a shikarri and knew nothing about the place. I went to the thana and saw the moonshie who promised to let me have a man the next day. On the next day as no man came I went out alone, in the evening another man came, however and said he had been sent on the thanadar's orders but that he wasn't a shikarri and knew nothing about the place. On the 3rd day I went out alone and came back early having seen nothing. I determined to pack up and try for buck at Gulabgang, as I was leaving a man came and said he had been sent by the thanadar, he seemed to know about the shooting but there wasn't time to do anything then, so I went to Gulabgang and shot one buck the same evening 21' and two yesterday morning both 22'.

I was using Rennick's Lee-Speed rifle and ordinary L.M. cartridges which I prepared myself by filing off the nose and scooping out a little lead, a method which proved most efficacious as they broke up well and dropped the buck pretty quickly. I shot two through the heart, and one, standing with his tail towards me, through the body lengthways.

Memo. for next shoot – Basoda, Pubai and Gulubgung good for buck, the best plan would be to get out at Basoda and make a chukkar round to Gulubgung. keeping some miles from the railway.

Also Daura and station this side are good places for Sambhur, Cheetah and buck.

26th March
Rennick arrived yesterday from training reservists. I've been one day on the sick list for chill contracted when out shooting.

29th March
I have ordered today from the Kashmir Manufacturing Coy. as part of Mig's wedding present 6 Kang salt cellars with chenar spoons. I hope to get a Jeypore Table as well.

9th April
I bought from Colonel Campbell a Lee-Speed Rifle for Rs 180/- before leaving Jhansi. I am now at Kassauli.

I left Jhansi at 11 p.m. on the 31st March, that being the Lahore mail. I met in the train Alex and Freddie on their way out from England. Alex handed over to me a large box of cream caramels sent by Mother. I travelled as far as Delhi with them the next morning, there I got out and at Alex's suggestion went to

Laurie's Hotel. The food was good and it was clean and cheap in fact the best hotel I have ever been to in India. I drove round and saw Nicholson's Tomb, the Kashmir Gate, the Magazine, the Lahore and Delhi gates, the Makal and the Jumna Musjid.

I continued my journey at 11.30 a.m. the next day (2nd April) and without changing at Umballa reached Kalka the same evening. Three of us (Alexander, Perkins and myself) slept in the carriage and rode up the morning of the 3rd inst. I am staying at the club.

At present we work from about 9 a.m. to 2 p.m. and 7 p.m. to 8 p.m. book work and extra practice being extra.

19th April

I passed my preliminary tests on arrival here all right failing only in helio the first time but qualified subsequently.

In the first written exam on bookwork I was bracketed 11th – not good.

In the first reading exam my total percentage brought me to 6th the separate percentages being as follows:-

Sounder	8's	nil(12)	100%
Flag	8's	99%	99.50%
Lamp	10's	nil(17)	nil(16)
Semaphore	10's	nil	
Helio	8'2	98%	nil(29)

I was woken up by a slight shock of earthquake on the night of the 17th–18th Insts.

26th April

Mabel should have sailed for Durban in the S.S. *Johannesburg* Bucknall Line yesterday, due to arrive 23rd May and she will be married on 25th May [His sister – see notices below in *West Sussex Gazette* May 29th 1902, *The Times* Friday May 30th 1902 and Photo and report in the *Natal Mercury* Friday, May 30th 1902.]

The second reading exam brought me to 3rd my total percentages being 641 (Turnbull 1st. 644, Spencer 2nd 643

Sounder	8's	100	nil(28)
Semaphore	10's	100	
Small Flag	8's	97.50(5)	98.50(3)
Helio	8's	100	99.00(2)
Lamp	8's	99.00(2)	99.00(2)

3rd May

In the written exam I was 4th with 60 marks. Following is the result of reading exams. Total percentage Turnbull 655, Spencer 654, Tyndall 650. I read 10's in all except Sounder:-

Helio	10's	98.80	99.60
Sounder	8's	nil(16)	100.00
Lamp	10's	98.80	96.00(10)
Semaphore	10's	98.80	
S. Flag	10's	98.40	98.40

10th May

On Monday I spent the day signalling with Sargent in Pine Woods. In practical work for the month of April I was 2nd with 16 marks, Spencer 1st. 20 marks. Results of weekly reading exam:-

Helio	10's	99.20	98.80
Lamp	10's	100	99.20
Sounder	10's	95.60	96.80
Semaphore 1	0's	100	100
S.Flag	10's	100 (one message)	

I was 1st in the above with percentage 547.

I received a telegram on the 6th from the Regt. asking me if I would take appointment of Comdt. Lakhimpur Milty. police for about 7 months. I am waiting the result of a telegram enquiring particulars from the present Comdt.

14th June

Result of next exam (6th).

Helio	12's	95.34	98.34
Semaphore	12's	99.00	95.34
Sounder	12's	100.00	nil (fudge)
Lamp	12's	95.00	97.34
S.Flag	12's	nil	nil

There have been one other and last exam of a similar kind in which I was 6th, but I have not got back the papers.

We are now reading for rates, and doing exam work.

The Col. sent me a copy of the report on the Jhansi Manoeuvres the other day in which my birds eye sketches appear.

We had a week in Kassauli consisting of the Sirkind District Hockey tournament, the signallers played the Welsh the first round and after playing 20 mins. extra were beaten by 3 to 1. The team of the Northampton Regt. Dagshai won.

There was a concert in which Mrs Sandamore and Capt. Poole were the best performers.

The signallers dance took place on the 11th, June. I ran the programme (copy of signalling manual) and cut out a large illuminated one for the fire place. Last night was a torchlight tattoo, the first I have seen.

The signalling' class is now over, we had a 3 hours written exam on the 1st. and ditto on the 2nd. I have got a special in my practical work it remains to be seen what happened in the exam.

Last night Pratab Singh gave a fancy dress coronation dance. I attended in a borrowed domino. Tonight is the signallers' dinner to the Signalling Staff. I have drawn a menu for it. I have got 3 months privilege leave from 7.7.02 to 3.10.02.

People of interest I have met up here:-

Revd, Mrs and Misses Hildesley, Sanawar Mily Asylum, Mrs and Miss Barlow, two Miss Warburtons, Mrs Wimberley, Mrs Martineau, Surgn. Col. Mrs and 3 Miss Barrows, Genl. and Mrs Creagh, Caot and Mrs Graham, Northampton Regt., Col and Mrs Llanyon-Penns A.A.G. District, Major and Mrs Scudamor S.Fus. Supt. Army Signalling Punjab and Bengal. Capt and Mrs Stuart, Inspector Gymnasia, Major and Mrs Cripps S and T.C. Mrs Hawkes S and T.C. Mrs Maloney with Hildesleys – with Depot Smart R.A. Harman RA Reeves R.A. Allington E. Lancs. With Garrison class, Harrison 33rd PI, Goodene [Illegible] Horse, Gunter RE.

The following comprise the Signalling Class:-

	Major Scudamore	S.Fus.	Supt. Punjab and Bengal	
	Hobart G & L (84th)		Asst. Instructor	
Capt.	Hardon	1st P.I.		
"	Carvert	20thBOI	Instr.	
"	Marshall	1st B.I.		
"	Perkins	42nd Goorkhas	Instr	
Lt.	D'Oyley	19th BOI	Instr	
"	Sargent	23rd BO Rifles		
"	Turnbull	26th PI		
"	Spencer	3rd RB		
"	Gool	S.Staffords	Instr	
"	Fraser	9th B.L.		
"	Crombie	3rdP.C.		
"	Morris	2nd Sikhs	Instr	
"	Allen	37th Dogras	Instr	
"	Alexander	Somersts		
"	Rideout	R.A.		
"	Blundell	Yorks		

18th July

Sanawar. On the 7th July 1902 proposed to Miss Hildesley and was accepted.

On the 9th July I went up to Simla and stayed with the Rennicks for two days, there I met Gerard and Phil and the Lorne Campbells also Bob Rennick whom I used to know in the Inniskillings at Mian Mir. I went to the Military Offices and tried to get my name put down as a signaller at Delhi Camp. I am afraid the list was made out.

I left Simla on the morning of the 12th and on my way to Kasauli I interviewed Mr and Mrs. Hildesley and obtained their consent to my engagement with Audrey who was over here though at the time staying with the Barlows in Kasauli. On Sunday Audrey and I came over and spent the day here, and on Monday she returned to her family and I came over to stay, so here we all are including Mrs Maloney, Miss Barlow and Mr Smith (Mrs Maloney's Father) who came over today.

'Statement of a Bengali Pleader at Barisal'.

'My learned friend with more wind from a teapot thinks to brow beat me from my legs. But this is mere Gorilla warfare. I stand under the shoes of my client, and only seek to place my bone of contention clearly in your honour's eye. My learned friend clearly runs amuck upon the sheet anchors of my case. Your honour will be pleased enough to observe that my client is a widow, a poor chap with one post mortem son. A widow of this country, your honour will be pleased enough to observe, is not like a widow in your honour's country. A widow of this country is not able to eat more than one meal a day, or to wear clean clothes, or to look after a man. So my poor client had not such physic or mind as to be able to assault the lusty complainant. Yet she has been deprived of some of her more valuable leather, the leather of her nose. My learned friend has thrown only an argument 'ad hominy' upon my teeth, that my clients witnesses are all her own relations. But they are not near relations. Their relationship is only homoeopathetic. So the misty arguments of my learned friend will not hold water. At least they will not hold good water. Then my learned friend has said that there is on the side of his client a respectable witness viz. a pleader and since this witness is independent so he should be believed. But your honour, with your honour's vast experience, is pleased enough to observe that truthfulness is not so plentiful as blackberries are in my profession. I am sorry to say though this witness is a man of my own feathers, that there are in my profession black sheep of every complexion, and some of them do not always speak gospel truth. Until the witness explains what has become of my chee chee client's nose leather he cannot be believed. He cannot be allowed to raise a castle in the air by beating upon a bush. So, misting in that administration of British justice on which the sun never sits, I close my case.'

6th October

At Jubbulpore. I went up to Simla and stayed at the Métropole Hotel on the 4th Septr. Audrey came up with Mr Bell and Mr. Orange on the 6th and stayed with Major and Mrs. Russell R.A.M.C. at Woodbine Lodge just above Annandale.

I tried for Transport and Burmah Police, but owing to my applications not being recommended by Col. Campbell I had to chuck them and am now trying for Political without much chance of success I am afraid. Audrey and I went to the Masonic Ball at Simla and then Audrey went to stay with Capt. and Mrs Brazeley R.E. at Kerston Hall Chota Simla. We also went for a picnic at Mascobra and got very wet. We came down from Simla together on 16th Septr. in 2 tongas (one supplied by Mr Bell) and had a jolly picnic on the way.

On the 17th I went to a Masonic dinner with Mr Hildesley in Kassauli.

As my leave was up on the 3rd October I left Sanawar on the 1st., rode as far as Kassauli with Freda, and walked down to Kalka. Left Kalka by the 1st accelerated Bombay mail at 9 p.m. and reached Jhansi at 1 p.m. on the 2nd October and shared a small bungalow with Macpherson. Macpherson and I left Jhansi at 12.54 yesterday with the hockey team and after changing at Itarsi at 9 p.m. reached here at 5 a.m. this morning.

My weight at Sanawar varied from 10 stone 11 to 10 stone 7 lbs.

15th October

Jhansi. Returned from Jubbulpore on 9th Inst. after having been beaten at hockey by 33rd P.I. by 4 goals to one.

Col. and Mrs Campbell returned from Thandiana yesterday. The Prestons returned today.

3rd November

Jhansi. Just returned from 10 days leave. I left here on the 25th October and stayed with Alex and Freddy in Lahore for 26th, 27th and part of the 28th driving to Mian Mir on 27th and 28th for the H.S.Pushtoo exams. I met Dunlop and Kelly of the 23rd Pioneers, Bob Howell, the Lamonts, Elliott, 41st Dogras. On the 28th Octr. I left Sanawar and met Phil Howell at Umballa on his way home. I got up to Sanawar at lunch on 29th and found Mr Saunders and Brett there. I left yesterday after a very jolly 4 days and got back here today, at Kalka last night I met Gerrard and Mrs Howell and Mrs Brown.

27th November
Brigade Signalling Officer 5th Brigade Northern Army Delhi Manoeuvres Bdr. Genl Abbitt till 20th Decr. 1902.

20th December
Bde. Signalling Officer Viceroy's Escort Delhi Durbar till 9th January 1903. Retd. to Jhansi. I saw Audrey with the Maloneys at No.3 Visitors' Camp.

1903

1st March
Audrey came to Jhansi and stayed with the Ogilvies till 15th March.
   I passed H.S.Pushtoo.

4th June
Reached Sanawar on 2 months privilege leave from 5th June.
   Got appointed Asst. Inspector Signalling (Northern Circuit).

8th July
Married, went to P.W.D. Bungalow Dharampur and to Mashobra Gables Hotel on 10th July.

22nd July
Returned to Sanawar.

1st August
Commenced work with signalling class as asst. Instructor.

25th October
Started signalling inspections till end of March 1904.

1904 – 1905

With 67th Punjabis as D.C.O. and Adjutant from 22nd April 1904 till 15th March 1905. No leave during this period. [He was now a Captain.]

D.C.O. and Adjutant 40th Pathans from 16th March 1905.

Training scouts 40th Pathans, 25th and 31st Punjabis and 58th Rifles from 4.8.05 till 27.8.05 at Karor, Murree Hills.

[During this period a Wing and HQ of the Regiment were sent with an expedition to relieve Major Younghusband in Tibet.

TIBET EXPEDITION 1904

Major Younghusband of the Indian Political Service (later Sir Francis Younghusband) had been held up with a small escort by Tibetans in some small buildings outside Gyantse village. The Tibetans were having intimate dealings with the Russians through the Burist Dorjieff and would have nothing to do with us. It was all part of the 'Great Game' and the purpose of the expedition, besides rescuing Younghusband, was to get things on a friendly footing.

The Tibet Mission Force consisted of five and half battalions of infantry and 12 guns under the command of Brigadier General J.R.C. Macdonald CBE RE. It was not unusual for the force to be marching and fighting at 14,000' to 16,000' at one stage at nearly 19,000', probably unique in military history. The wind chill factor was the worst and temperature was often 50 degrees below freezing. It was difficult to bring water to the boil and a hot drink had to be swallowed at once or it would quickly freeze, a loaf of bread was sometimes unbreakable.

The expedition was essentially a transport achievement: coolies, bullock carts, mules, donkeys, the ekka and yak, were all used and were strictly allocated to certain sections of the route, both by climate and by nature of the road or footpath.

Tibetan arms consisted largely of Lhasa made Martini action rifles and various old fashioned jezails, prong guns and muskets – artillery was comprised of jungals. They could wield swords with some effect.

On 5th July Gyantse Jong, 13,120 feet above sea level the walls having been breached by artillery, was assaulted and captured by the 40th Pathans commanded by Lt. Colonel F. Campbell.[38] Lieutenant Grant leading the Gurkhas was awarded the VC.

This action ended Tibetan resistance. Lhasa was reached on 3rd August and the Peace Treaty was signed on 7th September in the Potala Palace. The Tibetan verdict on the British character vis a vis the Chinese, 'When one had know the scorpion, one looks on the frog as divine.'

On the return of the Mission Force, the Ti Rimpoche (Regent) caught up with the column at Gyantse and presented General Macdonald with a small golden image of the Master, in recognition of his 'tolerant occupation' of Lhasa.

As a result of the expedition we have been on friendly terms with the Tibetans ever since and have received permission for Everest expeditions to climb on the Tibetan side. This is partly due to the good behaviour of the troops in 1904.

1906

90 days privilege leave in Kashmir from 1st June to 31st August 1906. Marched in with Thompson's trap, dunn pony carrying my bedding. I bought a bullock cart and hired bullocks. We lived in a dunga and drove back to India in a Bareilly cart and 2 ekkas.

1907

60 days privilege leave from 1st May 1907. Walked up to Pir Punjal alone and back 3 weeks and spent remainder of leave at Sanawar.

1908

8 months leave from 8th March 1908. Embarked at Bombay on P & O SS *Arabia* 14th March, crowded ship, all the way to London by sea, arrived London 4th April. Worked for Staff College exam; military subjects with Major W. Redway, 90a, Gloucester Road, South Kensington and mathematics with Mr D. Major of Collyers School, Horsham (Wellington Road).

Visits to York Hotel, Woodgates, Hurst Leigh, Southampton, Ealing with Turton Smiths, Yately with Selbys. To Mr. Charles Cottle's farm, Stanbury, Morwenstow, Cornwall. Saw cousin Meg only on return journey and Agatha and Herbert.

13th August

Kenneth Dible arrived on visit. Audrey went to London for the day.

16th August

Heard for certain that Mabel and Robert had started for England on the 9th August. Willie stays behind for a few weeks to settle up affairs.

30th August (Sunday)

Mabel and Robert arrived today in White Star line SS *Africa*. I went to Tilbury Docks from Guildford (staying with Mrs Blair) to Waterloo, Waterloo to Fenchurch Street by tube, Fench. St to Tilbury Docks. Met Father and Audrey at Docks.

With Mr Blair, Mrs Blair (Mother), Miss Cloete (Aunt) Motor, tennis. Sandy Lane walk to Smugglers Caves, Laddie the collie, met Chiltons (old man hunts) address L.F.D.Blair, the Lodge, Sandy Lane, Guildford. Mr Blair stayed one night at Horsham with us first and took us in motor to Guildford next day. Picnic at Petworth en route.

4th September

3rd Sept. went to Hanmers at Gedding. Horsham to London Bridge. Liverpool Street to Cockfield (change at Marks Tey) four and a half miles drive to Gedding. Saw Uncle G., Aunt M. Alice and Edith. Helen away with Graham at Lowestoft. Stayed one night. Dogs Peter and Piper (Alice's toy Pomeranian) Met Mr Bevan other friend Charters. Got photographs of Uncle G., Helen and Edith, promised one of Aunt M, none of Alice. Drove next morning to Stowmarket (7 miles), had lunch with Aunts at 165, Norwich Road, returned afternoon via Liverpool Street and London Bridge (change at Horley).

There has been a correspondence in the *Standard* on 'The decay of Ideals'. The following is my reply to the question 'Is the English Nation deteriorating?'

Our forefathers, by land and sea,
Have kept the flag of England free
From blot or stain; and so will we
Hand down to our posterity
The emblem of our dear country.
So listen all
To duty's call
That no mishap our flag befall.
While gladly for our land we die
And in the lists of honour try
To keep our flag unfurled on high;
Rises the traitor's evil cry,
The vile, despiteful, selfish lie,
So Listen all etc.

Here pseudo-politicians gain
Their votes by statements false and vain,
There men are found, yet scarcely sane,
Unworthy of their fair domain,
Who with our foes to side will deign.
So listen all etc.

And voices ignorantly rise,
In foolish clamour to the skies;
Our arms decry in selfish wise.
Men, whose own ends before their eyes,
Are greater than the Empire's ties,
So listen all; etc.

For partisans of narrow mind,
No pledge within our State we'd find
To clip our wings, our talons grind,
To suit the measure of their kind.
So listen all etc.

But Britain's sons her name uphold,
In spite of black sheep in the fold,
With Statesman wise, and sailors bold,
The Empire in one cause enrolled,
Well win our way through as of old,
And listen all etc.

With army strong to keep our doors,
And navy free to guard our shores.
Our commerce and our Empire's stores;
As strong men armed invite no wars,
We'll keep the peace that strength secures.
And listen all etc.

Then give us strength to guard aright.
Lord of all Nations! In thy sight,
Thy charge o'er peoples, black and white,
That England's rule, and England's might
Reflect on earth Thy Heav'nly light,
And grant that all
When comes the call.
May do their duty, great or small. (see p 118)

7th September
Mabel's American friends – Mr and Mrs Raby came to lunch.

8th September
Heard Father's wishes.

22nd September
Went to Town with Mabel last Thursday and saw battlefield models at the R.U.S.I. in Whitehall. Mabel ill, has been in bed for 3 days. The Youngs came to a farewell lunch today. Revd. AS.F. Young is about to leave for the vicarage of Rudgewick.

24th September
To London with Father and both Audreys. Stores, Teagues (Jermyn Street) Mr. F. Todd, dentist. Old Burlington Street. To lunch with Father at the club, calls on Redway and Mrs Goodenough at Cranley Mansions, S. Kensington. Audrey went on to Ealing to the Turton Smiths for a couple of nights.

In talking of the qualities which go to make a good C.O. Major Redway said he must be a man with sufficient knowledge and character to be able to quietly resist pressure from above (and pressure from below!)

26th September
Tyndall's poem is written in a 'Kiplingesque' style which accorded with the spirit and style of the Imperial Armed Forces guarding the frontiers of the World's greatest Empire. This spirit of chauvinism was not confined to Victorian Britain, and soldiers of most armies of that period had a simple faith in God and bore unswerving loyalty through their Regiment to the Head of State.

It is interesting to compare the poem with this old Russian soldier's song.

Song of Ivan Ivanov Barrack room ballad sung by Russian troopers described by J.A. MacGahan correspondent of the NewYork Herald, *as the 'officer's ideal of the soldier and, everything considered, the best soldier inthe world'.*

Translated by Robert Michell

Campaigning on the Oxus – 1868

For God and the Tsar,
I've served in peace and war
These five and twenty years

I left, when young, my home and kin
My wife and child; theirs the sin
Who sold me for a bribe and parted us in tears
I'm not so old, though wrinkled, scarred and worn,
I've bearded the Turk;
I've snatched the threatening dirk,
And stuck the mountaineer;
I've toiled and marched and bled,
Nor rested under shed,
Nor broken bread for days; and born all these woes
To spread the faith and lay the Emperor's foes
   For God and for the Tsar
   I've served in peace and war
   These five and twenty years

   My term at last expired
   Bleeding infirm and tired,
   I drained a parting cup;
   Embraced my comrades well;
   Brushed off the tears that fell,
   Then gave my bayonet up,
   I took my pass and pay
   Due at three groats a day
   A pipe and hardened crust
   Within my bosom thrust;
   The money safely placed
   Within my boots, I faced
   The road and went
   To Holy Kief bent,
   An ashen staff my rest,
   And all my pride – my medals on my breast.

   For God and the Tsar
   I've served in peace and war
   These five and twenty years

To London for the day by cheap excursion, train full. To Teague, and English in opera arcade (in Pall Mall close to King & Co's) To Ealing and saw Turton Smiths and a hurried visit to Uncle and Aunt (also saw Aunt Edith) to say goodbye.

To Franco-British Exhibition with Audrey and Miss Halliday, pictures charming but was much oppressed by throng, wandered about and saw illuminations. Left London Bridge 11.35 p.m., home about 12 a.m.

29th September
I saw Uncle Alfred Bates for the first time in my life, he turned up unexpectedly from his married daughter at Aldershot and stayed to lunch. Aunt Kitty (Miss Cooke) died this morning.

1st October
Mildred Willis married to Revd. Henry Moseley, vicar of Poplar. Bishop of Lond, Canon Masters and Revd. A.F. Young officiated. Afterwards at Arun Lodge, all Horsham and half of Poplar. Mabel convalescent, able to attend. Robert was page. A.C.T. in London.

3rd October
Audrey went to Selbys at Yately till 7th.

5th October
To Brighton with Father and J. A.T [39]. Royal Fusilliers band on pier.

My impressions of Home and England after an absence of 9 years

(1)   The deterioration of the British Nation and decay of ideals etc. much talked of is not apparent, but radical and Labour Government not worthy of the English nation and unable to grasp imperial problems.

(2)   No apparent change due to motor cars, improved communications, scientific inventions, spread of education etc. there is still some rural life left, but difficulties will arise 50 years hence from over crowding, unemployment and the spirit of aggrandisement due to education. England seems remarkably unaltered so far.

(3)   I have had intense pleasure in watching the gradual change from winter to summer, the relays of flowers and fruit, and the gradual unfolding of nature, and especially from the sense of rest which the peaceful beauty of English country gives Nature, and especially English nature, is a miracle more convincing than any recorded in the Bible. It is always there for those who have eyes to see it.

(4)   My friends and relations have not changed.

(5)   I am sorry to leave it again, but (1), (2) (3) and (4) should prove a consolation to me till I come back.

9th October
Went to Town yesterday with Audrey. Long and painful interview with F. Todd Esqre, (dentist) 23, Old Burlington Street. To Franco-British Exhibition till 11 p.m. scenic railway, pictures etc. Was to have met Macpherson but it failed. Home by crowded excursion.

12th October
Audrey's birthday. Gave a small contribution to Mabel towards a joint present of a gold bracelet. Audrey left for London. I am to meet her tomorrow at Victoria for start to Bombay.

The following people have called on us or become acquainted with us during our stay at home:-

Stirling-Hamilton. Woodgates, Southwater.
Miss Allcard, Mrs von Hartmann. Wimblehurst.
Misses Hodgson, Causeway, Horsham.
Mr and Mrs Portyer (Miss P. came home with us on Arabia).
Miss Williamson (sister of Mrs. P above).
Revd. A.F., and Mrs Young.
The Misses Daniel Mr and Mrs Butler (Valeria, Alex, Buz etc).
Revd. and Misses Rosseter.
Mrs Umpeville (Molly and Joan) South Lodge, Horsham.
Dr and Mrs Kinneir (Eva, Gwen, Giug etc.)
Bostocks.
Mrs Wills, Miss Spens.
Col. and Mrs Jackson and Evelyn.
Dumbells.
Mrs Hurst and Bee, Horsham Park.
Esme Pigott, Bourne Hill.
Revd. and Mrs Bond – Vicar.
Revd. and Mrs Goff.
Vernons, Helen, Madge and Evelyn, Bow and Mark.
Padwicks, Sir Eustace and the Misses Piers.
Frys.
Drummond.
Willis.

Revd. and Mrs Bowcott Warnham.
Godmans (Muntham).

Audrey's birthday – Picnic to Leith Hill. Besides the family, Ethel Hodgeson, Lizzie Hamilton, Eva Kinneir, Valerie Butler, Miss Rosseter, Miss Le Strange and Robert.

18th October

Mediterranean. Left Horsham 7.53 a.m. Met Audrey at Victoria. Left Victoria (S.E. and Chatham Platform) at 11 a.m. Dover 1 p.m. Calais 3 p.m. Arrd. Paris 6.45 p.m. Father saw us off at Victoria. Stayed at St Petersburg Hotel, Rue Caumartin, Paris, went to Sevres by steamer up the Seine, on to Versailles by electric train – beautiful weather. Versailles charming, the whole day most satisfactory. Also saw Madeleine, Place de la Concorde, Le Grand Palais, Trocadero, St Clow, Sèvres China Museum. Versailles, Champs Elysees, Place Vendôme.

Hotel St Petersburg, English and expensive.

Arrived at Gare du Nord, Paris.

Left from Gare P.L.M. (Gare de Lyons) 2.25 p.m. on the 15th arrived Marseilles 4.50 a.m. 16th had coffee and wandered about, embarked on P & O S.S. *Himalaya*, sailed from Marseilles 11 a.m. 16th October, 2nd class cabin No 314/15. Beautiful weather. Through Bonifacio and Messina by night.

6th November

Voyage satisfactory but hot after Suez. Had slight accident with another ship in the canal, one of our boats knocked her bridge down. Transhipped at Aden into S.S. *Arcadia*, old but comfortable, saw Col. Fowle of Bedfords (he had just got command) at Aden.

We met a cyclone in the Arabian sea and had to change our course and were 12 hours late at Bombay.

People on board:-
Bow Vernon. Major Roche, Bedfords.
Major and Mrs Bradon and 'Nora'.
Mrs Phillips wife of Col. P. 28th Punjabis.
Mrs Down, old lady.
Capt. Harding, accounts dept.
Gwatkin 18th L. Squires 23rd P.Ogg.
Sinclair E.T.C. Britain, Mrs and Miss Rundle.
Mr and Mrs Sachse (Ted Dallas Smiths young woman's sister).
Miss Fiennes (travelled up in train).

Landed Bombay 6 p.m. We went to room No. 64 G. W.Hotel. Visited Baldock's stables in Bombay and bought Bay Waler horse, black points 4 white feet and white forehead, 15 hands, 5 years old, price including stable commission Rs 567/- Saw Tom Harrison and Harvey. Wetherall running stable for Boldock away.

We left Bombay by Punjab mail 6 p.m. 1st November. Audrey changed at Delhi for Sanawar and I arrived here Jelhum 2.10 p.m. 3rd. Novbr.

No quarters, went to dak bungalow for 2 days, then moved into bungalow where we were first when Col. Campbell was here. Also in the bungalow Major Maclachlan, Lee and Dalmahoy.

14th November
Bay Waler, Gelding, 15 hands 4 white feet and white 'blaze', brand 'Won' on near shoulder, black mane and tail, arrived from Bombay. R.G. Baldock's bill for horse Rs 574–15-0. J. Anderson's bill for rly. fare etc Rs 110–5–8. Total Rs 685–4–8.

29th November
Staff College Exam. Left Jelhan Sunday 15th November in train with Graham Hanmer by arrangement. Stayed at Imperial Hotel; R. Pindi. Exam begun 16th November till Thursday 26th November. Said to be 65 candidates in India, there were 13 at Pindi including,

Capt.	Little 6. G.R.	)
"	Govan 5.G.R	) Imperial Hotel.
"	Carter V.C. 101st Grendrs. (Somali contingent))
"	Wagstaff R.E.
"	Fitzgerald 18th B.L.
"	Brain
"	Stoney 26th P
"	Crombie 23rd Cavy.

President Major O'Meaghert, R.I.F.

Can't say at all how I did, but expect failure in Tactics, engineering, French and Pushtoo, my best papers were history, strategy, organization and topography.

In the exam it was necessary to work very quickly, cut down questions about which one could write at length, leave doubtful questions to the end, and write something on *all* questions. Obvious questions were not asked but lessons on all campaigns in syllabus required.

Saw Mr Barratt, and met Major and Mrs Dyer at Rileys at dinner.

17th December
Jhelum – Sialkot Inter Brigade 9th–17th Decembr.

9th Decbr.	to Khaian. (Q. Exams) Major O'Mleagher. Tizzard Glasfurd and Kelly.
10th "	Lala Musa.
11th "	Concentration at Lala Musa.
12th "	To Gujrat – night outposts.
13th "	Night march to Dariwalla by 40th and 13th Battery.
	R.F.A. feint on Kauki canal has works early 14th, 15th Concentration on Brigade at Dariwalla and night march & assault on Canal works.
16th "	To Lala Musa 20 miles
17th "	To Jhelum 22 miles.

Red (Jhelum) Force:– 10th Hussars, 13th Lancers, Brigade R.F.A., 21st, 22nd Pioneers, 'V' R.H.A. & R.F.A.

21st December
The following are the marks I consider I have obtained in the S.C. Exam.

Obligatory Math. 225 out of 400

French 180 out of 400

Engineering 190 out of 400

Topography 1st Paper 200 out of 300

      "   2nd Paper 170 out of 300

Tactics 1st Paper 150 out of 300

   "   2nd Paper 175 out of 300

Law 170 out of 300

Administration 250 out of 400

History and Strategy (obligatory) 160 out of 300 1st. paper

    "   "   "   170 out of 300 2nd paper.

Geography 205 out of 400

History and Strategy, voluntary 1st paper 190 out of 300

    "   "   "   2nd paper 190 out of 300

1909

3rd January
Have had sore foot and boil since manoeuvres. Went to Lahore on 27th Decbr. stayed with H. Knowlton Esq. I.E.S. Principal, Central Training College (wife

and 2 sons at home) Also there Freda, Mr and Mrs Clark S & T Corps (late 67th P) and Dodd of 31st Lancers. I did not go out anywhere on account of sore foot. Returned yesterday.

7th January

Marched from Jhelum 7th January. Syce ran away, at Sangoi picked up a P.M. – Mudh, AIki, a P&O stoker, who stayed with me for some time as syce and accompanied me to Wana. March via Pind Dadan Khan, Khushahm Mitha Twanam arrived Der Ismail Khan 25th January. In 'Gudur Kothi' bungalow with Napier, I/NM/S/ and young Campbell. No shooting on march, last 5 marches through heavy sand.[40]

31st January

Staff ride to Wanba., rendezvous by tonga at Murtaza on 31st January. Straight up to Wana and back. Genl Anderson, Capt. Molloy, Bde. Major, Capt. O'Brien (Australian Forces), Capt. Hill, 16th Cavalry, Geoghegan S & T Corps, Major Paul, S.W. Militia, Lt. Col. Davids 1st. B.L. Lt Col. Crawford 40th Pathans, Major Evans 19th Punjabis, Major Hall 47th Sikhs, Captain Ferguson 21st. Kohat M.B.A. Capt. Kelley IM.S. Capts. Buster Brown 47th Sikhs, and self. At Wana, Shea S.W.A. and Lethbridge I.M.S. Returned D.I.K. on 10th January and February.

10th February

The following are the marks obtained by me at the S.C. Exam:-

Obligatory Math	175	out of	400
Mily. Engineering	110	"	400
Topography 1st	209	"	300
" 2nd	111	"	300
Tactics 1st	107	"	300
" 2nd	182	"	300
Military Law	170	"	300
Mily. Administration	200	"	400
Mily History & Strategy 1st	186	"	300
" " " 2nd	163	"	300
Geography	128	"	400
French	174	"	400
History Voluntary 1st	172	"	300
" " 2nd	184	"	300
Pushtoo	150	""	400

15th February

Brigade Training to Paniala. followed by Battalion training at Pezu. Returned in a hurry to D.I.K. on 3rd March for immediate start on reconnaissance.

7th March

Reconnaissance to Wana. Left D.I.K. on 7th March by tonga to Murtaza.

At Nile Kach 8th to 13th March, met Shea S.W.M. and Major Paul S.W.M. travelled with Major Paul to Kajuri Kach (14th to 19th March) Met Bull S.W.M. at Kajuri (transferred to Tochi)

Tanai 20th to 25th Match met Burrows S.W.M. and Lethbridge.

To Khula 26th – 29th March.

Wana 30th March to 7th April (Paul, Brown, Burrows, Lethbridge S.W.M. and Major Elsmie and Capt Lock R.E. D.A.A.G.'s at headquarters).

Brown Lethbridge, Elsmie and Lock and self climbed Kotkum hill overlooking Mahaud country (Waziristan). Discovered that Lethbridge was one of the large family of Lethbridges who were at D.I.K. when I was born. Mrs Lethbridge is still alive and lives with two of her sons at Leicester. To Tanai (8th and 9th April) with Brown and Lethbridge. To Sarwekai (10th to 15th April) with Brown and Lethbridge, had a long day with Brown to Ziarat Zai. To Kajuri Kach via Sui Nullah with Brown and Lethbridge (16th and 17th) To Nili Kach 18th April.

To Murtaza 19th April. Met Mr Donald and Major McNeil S.W.M. en route to Wana. Met Sandeman at Murtaza going to join S.W.M.

To D.I.K. by tonga on 20th April.

5th April

On 12th May the Regt went out partly to outposts and partly to Tank to act against raiders. I remained at D.I.K. in charge of the Depot till young Campbell came back from treatment at Pasteur Institute at Kassauli.

On 31st May I joined Maclachlan at Tank. At Jandola with our detachment are Perkins and Lee, at Jatta Chamberlain (1st B.L.) and Heath (19thP) at Zanu Gillies (lst.B.L.) and Paske (47th).

22nd July

On 13th June I rode with Capt. Barker R.E. to Jandola stopping the night at Kirghi B.M.P. Post. At Jandola[41] & on detachment with Lee till 15th July. Relieved by Cochrane and Boyle. Stopped the night of 15th July at Tank, reached D.I.K. 12 noon 18th July. Six and a half hours crossing the Indus by boat and tonga to Darys Khan.

Left Darys Khan 3 a.m. by train reached Dharmpore midday 20th July went up to Sanwar and on to Simla on 21st July.

At Central Hotel, Simla from 21st. July.

30th July
My weight in ordinary clothes 10 stone 12 lbs.

22nd September
Audrey and Freda came to Central Hotel till 25th.

A method was devised for lighting up the foreground in case of a night attack at the fort. [Major Waters, the author of the *Regimental History*, interviewed Lieutenant Colonel Tyndall after his retirement and quotes him as saying;' I remember going out on the parade ground at night with Colonel Campbell and trying various experiments. The best was some combustible material packed into 'chiragha' by local firework merchant in Jhelum. One of these was put inside a bundle of straw and shavings and by pulling a string it would be ignited. I think method of ignition was by friction tube.']

1910

17th March
Weight in ordinary clothes 10 stone 12 lbs.

While at Central Hotel I walked to Sanawar one Friday (about 33 miles by the old road through Subathu, took 11 hours) and returned by train next Monday. Acted in the chorus of the *Gondoliers*.

I took the Champain's house 'Forest Lodge' Simla E. on Jakko. Audrey came up from Sanawar and we moved in on 9th November 1909 and stayed there till 16th March 1910.

Rent of Forest Lodge, furnished, including everything except linen and silver, Rs 60/-p.m. Expenses, 60/- rent, 120/- servants. 80/- cook, 150/- bills. Total including sundries, about 450/-p.m. Pay as D.C.C. 599–13-0 (Extra, coal 70/-, charcoal 50/-).

Mrs Hildesley and Freda stayed with us there about a fortnight, and Mr Sanderson from Sanwar a week. It was a mild winter for Simla. Joined the choir till Easter. Archdeacon Nicholls, assistant Chaplain, Mr Barne. Choir, Messrs. Hughes, Wyatt, Rogers, Wilkinson, Capt. Moberley and boys, Audrey, Mrs Wyatt, Mrs Barne, Miss Powell.

I applied for combined leave from 15th March, but as it was not granted till

15th April, Audrey and I moved into 'Summerseat' Upper Flat on 16th March 1910. Landlord Mr. Sherman (old Sanawar boy).

Some friends at Simla (not including Gondolier cast)

Kettlewells Lee's sister D.C. Simla.

Col and Mrs Rodwell (formerly 56th).

Mr and Mrs Trelawney (69th Punjabis) Central Hotel.

Dr Spooner, archaeological Dept (Central Hotel).

Stoddart, P.W.D. (Central Hotel).

Capt. and Mrs Steele (Central Hotel).

Major Elsmie DAQMG Frontier Section 56th.

Moberley DAQMG (56th).

Trotter – Staff Captain, Frontier Section (56th).

Major and Mrs Kaye DAQMG.

Capt and Mrs Lock R.E. Staff Capt. (met at Wana)

Maj. Gen and Mrs W du G Gray.

Major. and Mrs Ward (30th PI).

Col and Mrs James S & T Corps.

Col and Mrs Lukis IMS.

Major and Mrs Champain DAQMG.

Genl Drummond (IG, IS Troops).

Maj. Goodeneough.

Capts. Murray (30P), Reynolds (37th L), Harris, Crawford (Gordon Highlanders), Capt and Mrs Riley (25th P) Kriekenbeek, Major Robson (10th Jats), Tugwell, Capt. and Mrs Talbot (Ruth Creswell) 14th Sikhs, Pulley, Johnston (4th C) Attaches.

Major and Mrs Black, Capt Black, Capt Aspinall, Major Winter, Major Church, Maj Boileau (and Mrs), Capt Gibbon, Col Malleson, Col Wyngate in IB, Capt and Mrs Clark. Mr and Mrs Battye, Mrs Scallon, Major and Mrs James UMS, Miss Benjamin MD. Col and Mrs Moore AVD., Revd and Mrs Martin, Mr and Mrs Henry and Mr and Mrs Ker (Alliance Bank) Capt and Mrs Kensington RE, Maj and Mrs Twining RE, Mrs Hamilton (wife of Col H.)

Journey to Kashmir

4th May

Kashmir. Had 8 painting lessons with F. Swynnerton, Bownie Moon of Rs 25/- before leaving Simla. When the Champains came back to Forest Lodge, we moved into the upper flat of Summerseat on the Bishop Cotton School Road, also took Summerseat Cottage, landlord Mr Sherman. Moved in 17th

March. Stayed with Col and Mrs Moore AVD at Blair Atholl from 15th –17th April.

Left Simla on Sunday 17th April. Dropped Audrey at Dharampore for Sanawar.

Arrived at D.I. Khan 19th April in dust storm, in bungalow with Dalmahoy and Segar, also present :- Maj and Mrs Ridgeway, Capts and Mrs Perkins and Cochran, also two Campbells and Napier. I arrived with Padre Rintoul. Left D.I. Khan on 22nd April with Major Joohnston 1st B.L.

Arrived Pindi 23 April went to Imperial Hotel. Met Capt and Mrs Hogg (just married). Also Alex and Freddie Dalles with whom I had dinner in their house near Civil Lines. Audrey arrived from Sanawar on 26th (she was to have arrived on 24th but was seedy and could not come) and we left in a Bareilly cart with 4 ekks on 27th April. All the time in the plains it was wet and cool.

27th April		to Tret
28th	"	to Kohala
29th	"	to Domel
30th	"	Chakothi
1st May		to Rampur
2nd	"	to Baramulla

At Chakothi we met Miss Banham, a lady pedestrian who had walked twice round the world and is an Alpine climber.

The following is an extract of accounts-

My journey from Simla to Srinigar via D.I.Khan (E from Simla to Srinigar to D.I.Khan) and Audrey from Simla to Srinigar via Sanawar total about Rs 550 -0-0. This includes railway fares and luggage:- 170-0-0 (from E Simla to Darya Khan)

Pindi to Srinigar carriage	Rs 140-0-0
Sundries railway 'travelling	Rs 60-0-0
Sundries tonga journey	Rs 36-0-0
Hotel bill Pindi	Rs 3 5-0-0
Luggage by goods to Srinigar	Rs 24-0-0
Stores for Journey	Rs 30-0-0

In dunga house boat *Devonia* Mauje Amria, Rs 50/-p/m/ two cook boats Rs 15/- p.m. each engaged for us by Motamid Dunbar. Boat contains outside room, drawing room, dining room, passage and pantry, 2 bedrooms, 2 bathrooms and chabutra on top. We left Baramullla 3rd. May, arrived Srinigar 5th May.

6th May 1910 King Edward VII died.

22nd June

I left Srinagar on 19th May to look for Ibex and red bear beyond the Zoji La pass. Took with me Ikbala Shakari of Augurbagh near Gunderbal and son of Marndoo, tiffin coolie Sabana (good) and Kaidera and Aziza, Also our cook, a small tent d'abris for myself and a hired tent for servants, 4 ponies or seven coolies carried all kit.

Arrived Baltal (South side of Zoji La) 22nd May, crossed the pass, under deep snow with cold wind on 23rd. and reached Kohor Nullah 24th May. Four days shooting there, first day sat and watched herd of 21 ibex but could not get a shot, second day same direction saw nothing, third day tried hills on south of nullah but saw nothing, fourth day tried side nullah to north and saw herd of 13 ibex which went away but came back in the evening. I got a shot just before nightfall but too dark to see properly and missed. The next day I got 5 marmot, the 30th May was wasted owing to non arrival of coolies and on 31st May I went to Matayan bungalow and tried the nullah there for two days, I saw 6 ibex but could not get a shot.

On 2nd June, I moved to the Sukh Nullah and had 3 days shooting there, saw a white bear with two cubs twice but failed to get her. The first time she was frightened by a coolie who was following us and the second time she got away in a water course before I could get my rifle ready. I fired ten shots at her altogether but out of range, *(just as well)*. [This seems somewhat uncharacteristic.]

On the 6th June I returned to Baltal where the snow was gone and there was beautiful spring scenery. I met the Sparkings (State Engineer at Baltal which place I left on the 9th doing 21 miles, and 19 miles on the 10th to Chattargul. Stopped one day at Chattargul and returned to Srinigar on 12th June. Ikbala is an old Shikari, no longer active and a humbug.

There was deep snow everywhere and it was very cold though the sun burnt fiercely. I slept in my clothes all the tme except at Baltal and Matagau and was pretty uncomfortable. The trip lasting 25 days cost Rs 98–8–0 including carriage and shikarri's pay.

The following are some notes for a 4 months trip to Leh, authorized carriage hire:-

	Pony Rs	coolie Rs
1. Srinigar to Gunderbul	– 8 –	– 4 –
2. Gunderbul to Kangau	– 8 –	– 4 –
3. Kangau to Gund	– 8 –	– 4 –
4. Gund to Sonamarg	– 10 –	– 5 –

5. Sonamarg to Baltal	– 8 –	– 4 –
6. Baltal to Matagau	– 12 –	– 6 –
7. Matagau to Dras	– 8 –	– 4 –
8. Dras to Kharboo	– 10 –	– 5 –
9. Kharboo to Khargil	– 8 –	– 4 –
10. Khargil to Moulbeck	– 14 –	– 7 –
11. Moulbeck to Bot Kharboo	– 8 –	– 7 –
12. Bot Kharboo to Lamayaru	– 8 –	– 4 –
13. Lamajary to Murle	– 8 –	– 4 –
14. Murle to Saspul	– 8 –	– 4 –
15. Saspul to Nimoo	– 8 –	– 4-
16. Nimoo to Leh	– 12 –	– 6 –
	9–2-0	4–9-0

A special pass is necessary to go beyond Leh. The regulations for supply of grain and ata en route should be inspected before starting (office of British Commissioner, Leh).

Expenses should include Rs 60/- for special shooting licence (Rs30/- for shikarri and Rs 14 for 2 coolies). A pony for the 15 marches is Rs 9–2-0 and a coolie Rs 4–9-0 but by contract or arrangement shikarri they could be got cheaper.

The other expenses for 4 months would be:-

Hire of furniture (10 p.m.)	Rs 40-0-0
Tent hire (20 p.m.)	80-0-0
Carriage (12 ponies going and coming) say	240-0-0
Moves in Leh	50-0-0
Shikarrie pay and 2 coolies (30 and 14 p.m.)	176-0-0
Bungalow rent (on emergency)	30-0-0
Food (70 p.m.)	280-0-0
Servants pay (70 p.m.)	100-0-0
Stores	100-0-0
etcs	100-0-0
	1376-0-0

A large store (say 20 pairs) of socks for grass shoes should be taken.

The following are necessary or useful in camp:-

Quinine, permanganate of potash, castor oil, lead and opium (for internal trouble), boric powder, bandages, vaseline (for rifle), Rangoon oil, Llanoline

Cheap tobacco or cigarettes for baksheesh
Googles
Raisins for chapatties
Syram kettle and small lunch basket (can go in rucksack)
Treacle
Portable books to read
Tea for servants
Lots of chocolate
Spade and small hatchet and saw
Cheap rope amd some good spare rope
Flower vases
Nails, basket, meat
Kerosene oil for 1 lamp

We sat up for bear frequently and had 4 days bear drives with 60 coolies each day but only got one bear in the first day's drive. On that occasion Calvert wounded two bears (having fired at my bear) and I killed one of the wounded ones under an apricot tree on which Audrey was perched.

22nd September

On the 31st August – after 6 days rain – we moved camp up the hill under pine trees. On the 11th Sept. Calvert was recalled for detachment duty at Buxar Dewars owing to the death of an officer of this Regt. – Balderton.

The Tribes (Major 38th Dogras) were also in camp at Chattergul for July and part of August. I forgot to mention that at the end of July Seagram and Audrey and I made an expedition to the Gungerbal Lakes, following the pilgrimage road i.e. marching up the Chatter Gul Nullkah for 2 days, one day halt and two days march back via the Wangat Nullah and Naranag ruins. After that we went into Srinagar for a week and returned to Chattar Gul. Seagram left us at Srinigar.

16th October

We left Chattar Gul on the 27th Sept reaching Srinagar on the 28th and went into tour boat. We intended to return via the Pir Punjal route but the cholera was bad on the district and Dr. Neve advised us not to go. So we waited in the house boat till 18th and returned by the ordinary road as follows in a Bareilly cart with 3 ekkas:–

1910 (D.I.K.)

Srinigar to Uri 19th October. Rampore Dak Bungalow burnt down the day before.

Uri to Gahari 20th October. Fell on my head in Ghari dak bungalow and developed fever which lasted four days.

Ghari to Kohala 21st October

Kohala to Tret 22nd October

Tret to Pindi 23rd October, left Audrey at Lai Musa and arrived D.I.K. 26th October. We met Waters at Lala Musa going to Bombay to fetch his wife, and travelled in train with Thompson, the D.C. of Mainwali (knows Hildesleys).

People met in Kashmir:-

Mrs Losack (Kashmir General Agency)

Mr and Miss Gough

Dr A. Neve (Mission Hospital)

Col and Mrs Macleod (Residents)

Major, Mrs and Barbara Calvert (120th Rajputans inf.)

Major and Mrs Tribe, 38th Dogras

Mrs and Miss Pocklington, Miss Hargreaves, Capt. Stuart, Miss Moore, Miss Harrrington all in Nagera Bagh.

Capt and Mrs Ben

Capt C.D.Oliver, Asst. Political and Phelps game preservation.

Capt Renton 25th Punjabis

Col and Mrs Fairbrother

Enriques and Palmer 21st Punjabis

G.D. Campbell and Segar 40th Fus.

I had written on ahead for a tent to be supplied from the arsenal but owing to some mistake it had not arrived and I got quarters in the Crawford house, Mrs. Crawford being particularly nice and thoughtful. The 72nd Punjabis from Calcutta arrived at D.I.K. on the 31st October, and the 47th Sikhs left on the 2nd November.

12th November

On the 7th November I started on a trip along the Frontier to report on camping grounds, water supply and tracks for manoeuvres, the itinerary being:-

7th November by tonga to Potha thence by march to Kulachi where I was met by an escort of INCO and 6 men of the 1st Lancers.

8th November accompanied by the Tahsildar of Kulachi to Luni BMP post.

9th Novbr. Garah Manji B.M.P. post.

10th Novbr. with 20 rifles and 10 sabres from Jatta, 3 B.M.P. sowars.

I went over the border through the Shaeranna Dara to Chinjasm Kurram and Wachapastoo with pickets to Dotannis who are responsible for the Dara.

11th Novbr. marched to Jatta and thence by tonga to D.I.K.

1911 (D.I.K.)

8th January	Derajat Manoeuvres 1910				
Troops					
40th	10th December.	Regt alone marched to Potha			
19th Punjabis	11th "	"	"	"	Hathala
72	12th "	"	"	"	Rori
1st. Lancers	13th "	"	"	"	Zefer Khan Pass

21st. Kohat MB   14th Battle of Zafar Khan Pass. Regt. as savage enemy, then to Garrah Manji. Brigade concentrated in camp from 14th, to 18th Decbr., on 15th we put our field firing targets, 15th Brigade field firing. 17th savage enemy rearguard action. 18th savage enemy and Regt. alone to Kulachi. I went on with 100 men to dig wells but did not find sufficent water. 20th battle and to Hathala; brigade concentrated 21st drove back to D.I.K. in tonga with Col Crawford. Regt, arrived 22nd I shared 80 lb tent with Major Ridgeway. Tearing wind and sand storm day and night nearly the whole time we were out.

On 15 days leave to Sanawar from 23rd Decbr. to 6th January. Left D.I.K. midnight and Darys Khan by 3 a.m. train on 23rd Dec. Return journey to Kalka 1st class fare Rs 46/-0. In train we met Hadow (irrigation) and Coventry (forests) also Buster Brown of 47th Arrived Kalka morning of 24th Dec and walked thence to Sanawar.

At Sanawar met Mrs Hiliard, Mr and Mrs Barrow (retired, on way home) and Capt. Spencer RAMC (with KRR) Lunch at Kassauli club with Mr Sparke, to Kassauli to see old Mrs Toussaint. Went shooting 3 times with Beynon of brewery and Sanderson. New Year's Eve Dinner with Sanderson. Superintended shooting of team F Coy S.V.R. for Indo-Transvaal competition which they won with 941 points out of 1050.

Left Sanderson in heavy snowfall on 4th January via Dharmpore, shopped at Lahore on way back and reached D.I.K. morning of 6th January.

14th February

Left D.I.K. on 27th Jany with Battalion for training:-

27th to Saggu	11 and a quarter miles
28th to Yarik	11 and a half miles
29th to Pegu	15 miles

I commanded the 3rd. D.C. at training.

At Pegu also 21st Kohat and 28th Mountain Batteries for practice camp.

There also arrived for one night Sir George Roos-Keppel Chief Commr. Frontier Province[42] with Staff and a double company of 57th Rifles from Bannu.

Left Pegu on 12th February 26 and a half miles to Saggu. 13th Febry. marched to D.I.K.

26th March

Heard by mail this day of Father's illness, double pneumonia and congestion of lungs at age 74. 79 Recovering rapidly. Mails of 2nd and 9th April brought me letters from Father giving good news of himself.

12th April

General exodus from D.I. Khan, beginning of hot weather conditions, many friends gone.

14th April

Molloy went on leave. Took over duties of DAA and QMG Darajat Brigade.[43]

16th May

Left for Shekh Budin with Col. Arrived Shekh Budin morning 17th.

Saw Register containing entry of my baptism at Church.

In club with Col. Cox, Col Grant IMS (PMO) and Major Rattray GSO. Brig. Genl. GT Younghusband CB subsequently relieved Col. Cox as Bde Commander. Also in Shekh Budin, Major and Mrs Smithett (GSO Bannu Bde), Major and Mrs Murray RE, Major and Mrs Stewart fro Bannu, Mr and Mrs Drase (Post Office), Capt and Mrs Napier IMS, the Revd. K. Foster, Chaplain, Mr and Mrs Eldon (bandmaster). Two Sergeant Clerks (Edwards and Rice) from Darajat Bde, and three Sergeant Clerks from Bannu Bde. Major Rattray, GSO Darajat, H. Fraser Esqre, Sessions Judge, Revd. J.Williams, Chaplain, Wickham, DSP Bannu, Hicks DSP., D.I.K. Dalmahoy 40th (3 days) Ventris 21st Kohat MB (3 days) Major Molloy DAA and QMG, Capt Pearse S&T, Col Herbert 19th Punjabis, F.Phillips 21st MBRA, Capt MG Lee, 40th Pathans.

13th October

Left Shekh Budin with Napier IMS and lived in a quarter in a gunner's Bungalow at D.I.Khan. Went to Bannu at end of October for Delhi Durbar Assault-at-Arms. Stayed for two days in Tyrrell's quarters in the fort and had meals with the Smithetts 21st. Punjabis. I travelled with Subbedar Nalapa, we were both defeated in the inter brigade tournament.

1912

6th January

Major Rattray GSO went home on sick leave on the 23rd Octbr; Major Shea taking his place soon afterwards. Molloy being away at Delhi Durbar I continued doing the work of DAA and QMG till Decbr. 20th 1911 on which day I went on 15 days leave.

Father has been in bed nearly all the summer and still is with some sort of rheumatic pains. The Doctors cannot tell exactly what is the matter with him nor can they cure him. I went on 15 days leave with Captain, Mrs and Miss Cochran and Christopher on the 20th Decbr. till the 4th January. The Garrison Engineer lent us two of his boats with a crew each of six men, we also hired a small boat for shooting and took tents and supplies with us and had a very pleasant time, moving by river and camping on the banks and shot koolan, geese, partridges, and hare. The Cochrans made excellent arrangements and I ran the boats, shikarris and coolies. Our best camp for shooting was near a village called Kot Umar Jan on the left bank, but geese were also plentiful about 6 miles (by land) above that place. When going down the river about 15 miles can be made comfortably in a day. The Majis in this part of the world are most willing and hard working.

28th February

Left D.I.K. on 30th January with the Regiment. Marched to Darya Khan and thence to Calcutta in two troop trains. I travelled in 2nd train leaving Darya Khan at 6 p.m. with the right wing under Maclachlan, also Macpherson, Campbell, Cochran and Mackenzie IMS. Reached Majerhat station near Alipore at about 6 a.m. on 3rd February.

I stayed with the Regt. at Alipore from 3rd to 21st February. I met Mrs Sharpe and Mrs Aldersmith, also Capt. and Mrs Hamilton IMS in charge jail.

Left Howrah station at 9.11 p.m. on 21st February, reached Mussoorie[44] on 23rd Febry. meeting Captain E. Moore, RIR from whom I was to take over Adjutancy of the Mussoorie Volunteer Rifles. Stayed night at Zephyr Hall

Boarding House and left on 24th Feby. visiting E.I. Railways Schools at Jharrapani en route, arrived Meerut, Pir Bucksh Hotel on 25th February.

1st March

My weight taken at Wheler Club, Meerut this day was 11 stone 2 lbs.

Left Meerut morning of 7th March, spent the day with Charlie and Katie at Delhi and reached Lucknow on morning of 8th March. Put up at Imperial Hotel and made acquaintance of Col. T. Beere CDE. VD commdg. Mussoorie Volunteer Rifles.

Left Lucknow on the evening of the 9th March and reached Roorkee midday 10th March, put up with Capt. E.W.C. and Miss Sandes, Thomason College. Had dinner with Major Stansfield Bde Major. Met Major General; Keary and Capt. Nelson S.S.O.

Left Roorkee afternoon 12th March and arrived Meerut the same evening, Pir Bucksh Hotel. Dinner with Capt. and Mrs Godwin and Capt. Routh 56th also met Major Major and Mrs Ogilvie IMS.

21st March

Father died aged 79. Received a telegram at Mussoorie on 22nd March.

Left Meerut early morning 17th March arrived Aligarh the same day. In dak bungalow and meals with H. Cooper Esqre. Govt. High School. Also met Johnston, a judge, deaf.

Left Aligarh 18th arrd. Dehra Dun 19th March, had lunch with Genl and Mrs. and Miss Campbell and reached Mussoorie in the evening, stayed 2 nights at Zephyr Hall, Mrs Mier's boarding house and then moved to Bassett Hall, proprietor and manager D.J Lavelle Esqre, his wife an invalid and Miss Lavelle, also two Miss Brae's sisters in law.

> *Mussoorie Volunteer Rifles*
> *Formed 27th July 1871 at Meerut.*
> *In 1903 detachments were at Meerut, Rookes, Saranpore, Aligarh.*
> *Establishment in 1912–11 Companies (incl. 3 Reserve Coys.)*
> *Tyndall was appointed to the Corps as Adjutant 1 March 1912 to approx April 1915.*
> *Commanded by a Lieutenant Colonel.*

21st April

On 13th April left for Simla, dinner with Genl Campbell and travelled in train with Home a civilian. At Simla interviewed Genl. Peyton M.S. to C. in C.,

Colonel Lean, Inspector of Volunteers and Major Stoor A.M. S.

Left Simla 15th April, arrived Meerut 16th April, left Meerut 17th April, arrived Mussoorie 18th.

1st May
Left Mussoorie 26th April, arrived 27th left Meerut 27th, reached Mussoorie 28th April.

7th June
Left Mussoorie 4th June with Mrs. Dank and Deaconess May Gorton, marched to Sainjit bungalow (9 miles) in the morning and on to Lakhwar Dak bungalow (six and a half miles) the same evening. We returned to Sainji the evening of the 5th June and back to Mussoorie on the morning of the 6th June. It was very hot and the country was unlovely and we were all rather glad to get back.

17th August
Went to Rajpore 5th August and saw Mrs Dank and Stephen and Nanny off. They were returning to Khandwa.

Left Mussoorie 12th Agust reached Meerut morning of 13th stayed Dak bungalow, returned evening of 13th August reached Mussoorie 14th August. Heavy rain all the way up the hill from Rajpore.

My weight 10 stone 2 lbs.

31st August
Left Mussoorie 26th August, arrived Simla afternoon 27th, Royal Hotel Case 28th. Left Simla 3.15 p.m. arrived Mussoorie 2 p.m. 29th.

7th September
Left Mussoorie 3rd. Sept. arrived Simla 4th Sept for second visit, stayed Royal Hotel. Case compromised. Left Simla 6th arrived Mussoorie 7th Sept.

21st October
Left Mussoorie 30th Sept. halted 1st Sept. Meerut and on same evening to Delhi, spent night Delhi stn waiting room. Left Delhi early morning 1st Octbr. by BB and CI Muttra Nagda route, arrived Bombay (Church Gate Station) 8.30.

3rd. October and put up at Great Western Hotel. Met Audrey ex P & O SS *Peris* on morning 4th Drove round Malabar Hill in evening. Left Bombay with Audrey evening 5th October (Victoria Terminus) G.I.P. route, changed at Agra evening 6th October into through carriage and arrived Dehra Dun 10.30 a.m. 7th Octbr. and came straight up to Mussoorie.

On 12th October Mrs. Danks arrived again at Bassett Hall.

17th November

Left Mussoorie Monday 11th Novbr. arrived Aligarh 12th, stayed with F. Cooper Esqre.had 2 parades with 'E' Company and left on 13th for Meerut.

Train missed connection and I spent night at Ghazrabad station.

Arrived Meerut at Pir Bucksh Hotel 14th Novbr. had 2 parades with 'D' Company and left morning of 15th for Roorkee. Arrived Roorkee evening on 15th Novbr. stayed night with Capt. and Miss Sandes had one parade with T Company and saw armouries, returned to Mussoorie on 16 Nov. Saturday.

4th December

Left Mussoorie with Audrey on 26th Novbr. for a trip along the Tehri road. 26th Novbr. to Danaulti bungalow 16 miles, 27th to Kariagalli bungalow. 28th back to Danaulti, and 29th returned to Mussoorie. It was very cold and there was some snow and ice, we had meals on the road and cooked most of our own food and thoroughly enjoyed the trip.

1913

1st January

Left Mussoorie 4th Decbr. 1912, arrived Aligarh 5th Decbr. stayed with F. Cooper, went that day to a lunch given in honour of Sir James Meston L.G. of W.P., on the 6th shot snipe with Cooper on Shekli Gheel and had good sport, left on the 8th Decbr, for Meerut and stayed at Pir Bucksh Hotel dinner on the 8th with Major and Miss Puech, returned to Mussoorie on morning of 10th Decbr. On 12th Decbr. went to Rajpore to see Mrs Danks, returning to Khandura.

On the 16th Decbr. 1912 moved into North View. Audrey and I went down for a week in January. We left North View on the 19th January, spent one night at Aligarh with Cooper, motored out to the 'strong fortress of Aligarh' and saw the Salvation Army Settlement for criminal tribes[45] motored out to a native wedding in the evening, we motored to Meerut the next day and stayed one night at the Pir Bucksh Hotel. Went to Dehra Dun the next day and stayed two nights with Col and Mrs Ramsden and so home again.

My weight 11 stone 3 and a half lbs. back to normal again.

Left Mussoorie 25th February. Pir Bucksh Hotel 26th–28th for annual inspection of 'D' Company by Colonel Jacob GSO on 28th. Returned Mussoorie 29th February.

Left Mussoorie 6th March, stayed one night with the Ramsdens (Col R. at Lucknow for dentist) at Dehra Dun. Q(i) Tactical fitness exam at Dehra on 7th March. Passed with 189 out of total 300 marks. Went on from Dehra to Meerut on evening of 7th March for proficiency exam for members of 'D' and 'E' Companies on 8th March, Col. Creagh 128th Pioneers President. 7 out of 8 candidates passed. Returned to Mussoorie on 9th March.

Left Mussoorie on 11th March and arrived same day with Sandes at Roorkee stayed with them two nights for annual inspection of T Company on morning of 13th March by Maj. Genl. Keary. Returned Mussoorie 14th March.

8th April

Left Mussoorie on 28th March with Audrey and arrived the same day at dak bungalow Hardwar. Had a very pleasant week in this charming spot. Made the acquaintance of Perin PWD who took us out one day on the river Ganges down which we floated on inflated skins and afterwards saw the sights of Hardwar and the pilgrims bathing. I painted most of the time. Audrey went on to Ambala to Charlie and Katie Dallas on the 3rd April for Dorothy Turton Smith's wedding on the 8th April and returned to Mussoorie on the 11th April. I returned from Hardwar on the 4th April.

9th May

Left Mussoorie 28th April for shooting for Command and Provincial Medal at Meerut on 29th April. Returned Mussoorie 30th April.

21st August

Major, Mrs and Kenneth Ferguson stayed with us from 21st August for 10 days.

Bow Vernon and Helen Vernon arrived on 21st Septbr and stayed with us. Bow returned to his Regiment 27th Punjabis at D.I.K. on 7th Octbr.

Capt G.D. Campbell 40th Pathans stayed with us from 28th to 30th Sept. He was Staff Officer to Genl. Lean Inspr. of Volunteers.

9th October

I went to Meerut on 4th Octbr. stayed at Pir Bucksh Hotel making preliminary arrangements for Volunteer Camp, and returned on 7th Oct. to Mussoorie.

26th October

Went down to Dehra on Monday 20th on a board of examination for promotion exams. Also on the board Lt. Col. C. Norie and Major N. Macpherson 2/2 Goorkhas. I stayed in Dehra club and went in 3 miles to cantonments daily, lunched at 2nd G.R.Mess. Audrey and Helen stayed at North View. I returned on Saturday 26th.

13th December

Audrey, Helen Vernon and I went down to Rajpore together on 14th Novbr. from Rajpore. Audrey drove off in a mule tonga to stay with the Fergusons at Gangora. Helen and I drove to Dehra Dun Rly station and left together by the evening train. Helen going to stay with friends at Agra. I got out at Roorkee for Pur Camp. I rode out 16 miles on the 15 Nov. to camp and stayed with the 2/2nd K.E.O.Goorkhas for a month. Also in camp the 3rd. Bn. K.R.R.C., 1st and 2nd/9th Goorkhas, 21st and 26th M.Bs RA. Troop each of 13th Hussars and 18th Lancers and No 5 Coy S & M.

With 2/2nd Goorkhas:-
Lt Col C Norie DSO
Majors Niel Macpherson and 'Tiger' Harcourt
Captains 'Ned' Ridgeway and 'Boosey' Barton
Lieuts 'Hamish' Reid, 'Stuffy' Innis, Corse-Scott
Nigel Woodyat, Hind, Scoones. Also in General's Camp Capts Bailey and Chope. Brig, General Johnson Commanding and Major Walker R.F. Bde Major.

I had some practice for 'Q' exam and left camp on 10th Decbr. riding to Lhaksar and thence by train to Mussoorie on 11th. I rode up from Rajpore in heavy rain which turned to snow at Mussoorie.

1914

12th January

Left Mussoorie 6th Jany. arrived Meerut, Pir Bucksh hotel 7th left Meerut 8th via Delhi (where I called on 33rd P and Maclachlan, the Olgivies were out) to Aligarh. On my way up to Mussoorie on 10th I went round to see Col. Ramsden and had lunch with him.

27th January

Trip to Nagthat with Canon and Mrs Menzies.

Left Mussoorie on Monday 19th Jany. and walked with Audrey to Lakhwar 15 miles. On 20th Jany. 7 miles uphill to Nagthat P.W.D. bungalow. On 21st and morning of 22nd Jany shot at Nagthat, fine outing but birds very scarce. On 22nd returned to Lakhwar. On 23rd Jan. Canon and Mrs Menzies returned to Mussoorie and Audrey and I took breakfast and painted on the banks of the Jumna near the bridge. On 24th we returned to Mussoorie, a long and tiring climb after finishing the painting on the way.

Weight on return was 10 stone 11 lb.

4th February

Q ii examination, 1st try. Left Mussoorie on 28th Jan. arrived Meerut Pir Bucksh Hotel on 29th, exam held on Monday 2nd February. Board consisted of Brig. Gen. Edwards, Meerut Cavalry Brigade, Col Asquith RA, Lt. Col. Goshing 60th Rifles.

My force was 'V' R.H.A., 13th Hussars, 3rd. Skinner's Horse, 60th Rifles, one Battalion Reservists. My Staff Officer was Lieut. W. Nicholl 'V' R.H.A. I failed to pass.

Also in the Hotel, Major and Mrs Dundas, 3rd Gookhas, Dr Fitzgerald-Lee, Capt. Moore 2nd Bn. Royal Fusiliers.

I got back to Mussoorie on 3rd February.

4th March

I left Mussoorie on 5th Feby. and reached Roorkee on the early morning of 6th Feb for the inspection of 'I' Company by Major General Keary. Sandes put me up for the day and I had meals at the Sapper Mess. There was a big guest night that night at which the Bishop of Lucknow and Mr Norman Bennet (Commissioner for B.S.) were present. I returned to Mussoorie on 7th February.

Audrey and I left Mussoorie together on 20th Febry. I got out of the train at Meerut on 21st February and Audrey went on to Aligarh to Mr Cooper. I stayed at Meerut for the inspection of 'D' Company by Lt. Col. Goshing 60th Rifles on the 23rd February and joined Audrey at Aligarh on the 24th February. We stayed at Aligarh on the 24th February together at Mr. Cooper's till the 27th February and saw the horse fair, a dance and a concert being part of the Aligarh 'week'. Also at Cooper's Mr and Mrs D'arcy McCarthy (Court of Wards), Cole (Judge), Capt. Buckley IMS (Civil Surgeon Bulandsharh) and Miss Sim.

On the 27th February we went to stay with Capt. and Mrs Liepmann, 13th Rajputs at Agra. We saw the finals of the Highland sports that afternoon, and the tattoo at the Fort in the evening. They were both well worth seeing. The next morning Miss Thornton (also staying with the Liepmann's) showed us over the Taj which is indescribably beautiful.

On the 28th February we went to the Central Hotel, Delhi, but had most of our meals with the Ogilvies at Curzon House opposite. On the 1st March we had a splendid day with the Ogilvies and Major Keighley RE saw New Delhi in plan on the ground, with the 'radiating vistas' being laid out. We had lunch at the Kutah Miniar and tea at Tuglakhabad and did a round of about 30 miles passing the Purana Killa, Hamajon's Tomb, many other monuments and the ruins of six old capitals dating from about 1,200 A.D. The present Delhi is the 7th and the new one will be the 8th.

On the 2nd Audrey and I drove round and saw over the Fort and in the afternoon we drove with the Ogilvies over the ridge. Hadow the Policeman also took us for a very pleasant motor drive the first evening after dinner. We left Delhi the night of the 2nd March and got home on the 3rd March after a very pleasant trip. We had lunch with Col. Ramsden at Dehra Dun on our way home.

26th March

I left Mussoorie on 11th March arrived Pir Bucksh Hotel, Meerut on 12th March. 'D' company annual rifle meeting 12th an 13th March.

On the 16th March I went to Saharanpore on duty and back to Meerut.

On the 17th March Brigade Genl. Lean with GD Campbell inspected 'D' Company. In the evening I dined with Mr and Mrs Landale Johnston (Judge ICS) There were also at dinner Genl. Lean, Major Davis GSO., Col Rennie, Capt Carpendale and GD Campbell - also two ladies staying in the house.

I also had dinner one evening at the Wheler Club with Major De Labilliere M.A.D.

I left Meerut on 17th March and got back to Mussoorie on 18th March.

My weight 10 stone 12 lb.

August

Went home on leave in May. G.A. Lloyd, the Welch Regt. did my work and stayed with his sister, Mrs Shute (107th Pioneers) and Mrs Ogilvie as paying guests with Audrey at North View. My leave was granted in VII Meerut Division Order No. 323 of 1914. 3 months and 6 days leave, first 90 days on privilege leave, my leave being actually from 4th May to 7th August inclusive.

Left Mussoorie 3rd May travelled 2nd class to Bombay and left 6th May, 3rd. class in Messagerie Maritime SS *Sydney* it was fairly comfortable with decent passengers and a small quantity of kit. Arrived Marseilles 20th May and went straight to Wyton. I stayed most of the time in England at Wyton but went twice to Woodgates, once alone and once with Audrey also several times to London staying with Audrey at the Orchard and Bentinck Hotels.

I left London on the 20th July, travelled via Folkestone – Boulogne, stayed the night at the Hotel de Louvre at de la Paix, Marseilles (expensive). Left Marseilles 22nd July in M.M. SS *Dumbea* 2nd class. There was no sign or talk of war then. We heard of war between Austria and Servia at Port Said.

It was hot in the Red Sea and we heard more interestng telegrams at Aden. The monsoon in the Indian Ocean was bad. We arrived Bombay night of the 5th August. Many searchlights and signs of war. Commander Beatty R.I.M came on board and gave us all the news including declaration of war 4th August between England and Germany. Stayed at G.W.Hotel. Left Bombay 7th arrived Mussoorie 8th August.

November

Left Mussoorie 19th Novbr. to Meerut and stayed at No 57, The Mall with Revds. M.W. Ragg and Maynard. Graham Hanmer came to dinner one evening. I went to Delhi for the day on 21st Novbr. to the tailor. On 23rd Novbr. I went to Aligarh with Brig. Genl Iggulden and Capt. Skipwith and stayed the night with Cooper. Returned to Meerut on 24th. Dined with Graham at the Wheler Club evening of 25th and left by train after dinner arriving Mussoorie 26th November.

December

Left Mussoorie Wednesday 9th Decbr. to Delhi arriving 10th Decbr.

Spent morning at H.Q. Offices to see about my chances of going on service, and the rest of day with Ogilvies driving round New Delhi and Hamajon's tomb, in motor with them. Left the same evening and arrived Mussoorie 11th Dec.

Left Mussoorie 23rd December with Audrey by train to Mozuffarnagar, thence by rum rum to Nadeera Bungalow, Jaoli, Ganges canal, via Bijnor road as far as the canal 10 miles, then canal bank road 5 miles to bungalow. Shot black buck and pea fowl and did some sketching, spent Christmas there and left on Sunday 27th arriving Mussoorie 28th Dec. and had lunch with Col. Ramsden at Dehra en route.

1915

January

Left Mussoorie 18th January arrived Aligarh 19th Jan. Stayed with Cooper (Miss Cooper and Miss Greig out from England) Dug a model trench in Slater's Compound and put up notice in Club inviting residents to inspect it. Went to Gautieres dinner at the club on the 24th Jan. went for a shoot with Sister, Pike and Johnstone (of Pioneer Lock Works). We slept in a carriage in the station and left early in the morning by train for Dinhari, walked about 3 miles N.E. to Jheel (Lalpur Jheel about 7 miles further on) plenty of duck but very wild. Shot all day and returned to Saligarh by train (about 2 hours) in the evening.

Left for Meerut on 25th January, stayed at Pir Bucksh Hotel, Graham Hanmer and Mr Ragg and Maynard, left evening of 28th and reached Mussoorie 29th January.

February

Left Mussoorie 1st arrived Delhi 2nd February went to Army HQ Office to see about my chances of accompanying 40th on service, lunched at Harrisons in camp and left Delhi the same evening reaching Mussoorie on 3rd Feb. Owing to a piece of careless shunting at Delhi station I hurt my back while standing in the railway carriage talking to Capt Mansfield and when I got back to Mussoorie I had to go to bed for 7 days.

Left Mussoorie with Audrey on 18th Febry. arrived Aligarh 19th Feb. Audrey stayed with the Coopers, I stayed with Slater and Tozer. On the 20th Feb. went out to Tuppal by motor car (34 miles) with Slater, Tozer and Johnston. Cooper and Pike came out on 21st Feb. On 23rd Feb. field day with Police and W.P. Horse. Left Aligarh 24th. Arrived Mussoorie 25th Feb.

March

Left Mussoorie 3rd March with J.A.T. and arrived Hardwar the same day, stayed at dak bungalow till 8th March sketching. Police preparations on large scale for coming 'Mela'.

On 8th March we went to Dehra Dun and stayed with Colonel Ramsden till 14th March. Sketching. Met Mrs and Miss Hodges. Volunteer Proficiency exam with Harcourt 2nd Goorkhas on 12th March. We returned to Mussoorie on 14th.

Left Mussoorie on 19th March for Pir Bucksh Hotel, Meerut, arrived 20th March. Next morning met Graham and went over to stay with him.

Meerut Company's inspection by Brig. Genl. Thackwell on 23rd. Left Meerut the same evening and arrived Mussoorie on 24th March.

April

Left Mussoorie on 30th March with J.A.T. (sister Juliet Audrey Tyndall) to see her off at Bombay. Journey not too hot. Arrived G.W.Hotel on 1st April and did some shopping etc. Next day Good Friday. We hired Cook's launch in afternoon to the Caves of Elephants – 8 miles. Met Mrs Hilliard with her mother, Mrs Mackinnon, and the Graham family from Aligarh going by Audrey's boat. Saw J.A.T. off on Saturday 3rd April at the Ballad pier by P&O SS *Arabia*. Left Bombay same evening. Met Pie (Major, 98th infy.) in train of Blucher Dormitory. Arrived Mussoorie 5th April. Having vacated North View before we left Mussoorie, I returned to Himalaya Club.

Left Mussoorie 27th April, arrived Bombay 29th to Great Western Hotel. Met A.C.T on 30th April at 8.30 a.m. at Ballad Pier ex P&O SS *Caledonia*. We had tea at Yacht Club with Fowlers (Engineer, Malabar Hill) and left the same night 9 p.m. from Colaba station by B.B. & C.I.Rly. We travelled up in train with May Byatt, Molony 57th Rifles (wounded) and Mrs and Miss Herbert.

Subsequent Career of Tyndall

1915 to Retirement in 1925
(as reconstructed by the editor)

Captain Tyndall was still adjutant of the Mussoorie Volunteers when the Regiment embarked for Hong Kong in 1914 and was unable to free himself from this duty until after the Regiment had left for the Western Front in 1915, their having come to the notice of Lord Kitchener who remarked that it was a pity that such a fine body of men should be languishing in Hong Kong when there was a job to do on the Western Front.

Western Front France

1915

26th February
The Regiment was embarked for France at Kowloon on the SS *Basilan*, rather a rusty old tub by all accounts, with wives and families, one of them Mrs Cromie, was the wife of a Naval Officer who was subsequently murdered on the steps of the British Embassy in St Petersburg on the outbreak of the Russian Revolution.

1st April
The Regiment disembarked at Marseilles and marched through the town to base camp playing the 'Marseillaise'.

4th April
The Regiment left for unknown destination. They stopped at Lyons where officers were almost mobbed by crowds waiting to shake hands and offering paper flags marked 'Gloire aux Alliés'. They passed round Paris on 6th April Rouen on 7th, and reached Lilles railhead on 8th marching four and a half miles to billets at Robeca – there they were inspected by the Indian Corps Commander, General Sir James Willcocks (Willcocks' Weekend Wars on the Frontier) under whose command they were during the Mohmand Expedition of 1908. On 12th April they were at Paradis where they were inspected by Sir John French on 17th April.

All this led up to their involvement in the 2nd Battle of Ypres on 26th April in which they suffered 320 casualties (killed twenty-four, died of wounds ten, missing eleven, wounded 295) including Colonel Rennick who was killed, and experienced gas and spotter aircraft for the first time.

29th June

Major Tyndall reported for duty as second in command of units of the Indian Corps, including the 40th Pathans, stationed at Blessy near Neuve Chappelle.

His company was billeted in farm outbuildings. One morning the farmer announced his intention of killing a pig. Tyndall at once arranged to take his company on a route march; he kept them out all the morning – unfortunately when they returned the farmer was still cutting up the animal in the yard, giving rise to black looks, scowls and spitting in the Muslim ranks.

August and September

The Regiment had fresh spells of duty in the trenches near Neuve Chappelle and suffered some casualties.

At the end of September the Indian Corps was heavily engaged in the Battle of Loos, but the Regiment, although standing by, was not required to take part.

24th November

Inspection by the Prince of Wales who expressed the King's thanks to the Corps for their work on the Western Front.

The Indian Corps had suffered heavy casualties siunce 1914 – they were as follows:

Indian ranks only	killed	2,448
	wounded	14,557
	missing (probably killed)	3,198
	other deaths	667
	Total	20,870

In the autumn of 1914 there were literally no further reinforcements available from Great Britain for the Western Front. The Indians stepped into the gap.

14th December

The Regiment sailed from Marseilles on H.M.T. *Arcadian* – again to an unknown destination. Major Tyndall remained at Marseilles on the embarkation staff.

East African Campaign

1916

January

The Regiment landed at Mombasa in British East Africa on 8th January to join the East African Forces (see Appendix E) consituted to conquer the neighbouring Province of German East Africa.

General Sir Horace Smith-Dorrien had been designated Commander in Chief but had to be invalided home from Cape Town with pneumonia.

General Smuts was appointed in his place and proceeded to conduct the campaign with great efficiency in very difficult terrain which hampered operations at almost every step. There was bush so thick that visibility was often restricted to 100 yards; paths had to be cleared through elephant grass, thorny bushes and low trees, slowing progress sometimes to only 300 yards in one hour. Black cotton soil covered much of the land, and was passable when dry, with rain transport proceeded with the utmost difficulty, while a lot of rain made roads and tracks impassable and even porters sunk to their waists. Transport continually varied to suit different conditions - light railways, cape carts, AT carts, Motor Transport, pack mules, donkeys and many porters. The climate was debilitating and tropical diseases, malaria, dysentery etc. took a heavy toll of the troops. Water was always a problem and generally found in infrequent water holes. Lions and Rhinoceros caused a number of casualties.

The Commander of the German Forces (see Appendix E) was Colonel von Lettow Vorbeck who arrived in 1914. He was a machine gun expert, and his expertise took a heavy toll of our troops in the campaign

It was thought that Smuts, our former adversary in the Boer War, would fill his staff with South Africans, but this was not the case, and he followed Smith-Dorrien's general strategical plan for an advance from Nairobi around the north-west of Kilimanjaro and the other from east of Voi, with the Central Railway as the long term objective.

2nd March

Major Tyndall rejoined the Regiment, having been obliged to sail via Bombay before reaching Mombasa.

The native of India was not highly regarded in South Africa, and as a consequence the South African troops were not pleased at having to fight alongside Indian troops they regarded as coolies. They did not realize that they were recruited from quite a different class. An incident just prior to Smuts' arrival made them appreciate the first class fighting qualities of the Indians who pulled them out of a very difficult situation when the South Africans had attempted to retake Salaita just outside Taveta.

April

The Regiment, now including Punjabi Mussulmans and Dogras as well as Pathans, was allotted to the 2nd East African Brigade commanded by Brigadier General J.A. Hannyngton CMG DSO.

Smuts had been pressing forward towards Moschi in a two pronged advance as planned, one column from Longido round the western flank of Kilimanjaro and the other, composed mainly of South Africans from Maktau, which occupied Taveta on 12th March.

The Regiment advanced from Mombasa through Voi and Taveta and reached Moschi inside German territory on 10th April in heavy rain which exacerbated transport difficulties, and they remained at Moschi on the lower slopes of Kilimanjaro for the rest of the rainy season.

5th May

Battalion HQ of the Regiment was set up at Kafe and a bush aerodrome cleared. All ranks were suffering from malaria and other fevers.

There was much activity preparing for the advance down the Pangani Valley.

June

The column pushed forward down the Pangani Valley and on 9 June Mombo was occupied by a detachment under Major Tyndall. On 15th June Korogwa was taken and on 19th Handeni was occupied.

Smuts could recognize no difficulties except as obstacles to be overcome and urged Hannyngton's column onwards. One march of 41 miles was completed in 44 hours.

The German forces now abandoned the Kahe-Tanga line, making for the Central Railway on which they hoped to prolong resistance. However our forces were much depleted by sickness and short rations. Many carcases of horses and mules were strewn around, victims of horse sickness.

July

On the 23rd the Regiment was at Mombone and had suffered much from disease, but they continued to push forward and occupied successively Ngambo and Ragusi. At this point their total strength in East Africa was 1,089 but the number fit for duty was only 470 – such was the effect of disease.

August

The Regiment came under command of the Inspector General of Communications with HQ at Korogwe, and, with the Jhind Imperial Service Infantry, advanced to Kangatcon on 4th August, then to Manga forming Column 'A' under Lieutenant Colonel Mitchell. They had orders to work towards the coast, but Mitchell became ill and Tyndall took over as CO. They mopped up German units and crossed a crocodile infested river to reach Bagamoyo on the Indian Ocean on 24th August, where they enjoyed a well-earned rest with sea bathing, fresh fish and coconuts.

September

The capture of Dar es Salaam was considered essential as it was the Ocean Terminus of the Central Railway.

General Smuts ordered the Inspector General of Communications to advance on the town which was occupied, after a short bombardment, by 'B' and 'C' columns, the garrison having evacuated and retired south. The Inspector General gave orders to Tyndall commanding Column 'A', now consisting only of the 40th Pathans to move west of Dar es Salaam to Rufu to check on the railway bridge, and if it was found to be only partially destroyed, to remain and guard it, but if wholly destroyed to march on to Pugu Hill south of the railway near Dar es Salaam. In recording this action, one cannot do better than set down extracts from the report of Major Tyndall, officiating in command of the regiment. These are as follows :-

Dar es Salaam, 6th September 1916

August 31st. – Column left Bagamoyo 2 a.m. Drove piquet of one German white and ten Askaris out of Mbaua village, capturing personal effects. Camped at Mbaua 5 p.m.

September 1st. – Left Mbaua 2 a.m. Drove small piquet and some snipers off road. One Indian Officer (Subedar Najibullah, 46th

Punjabis, attached) and one man wounded. As reports showed that enemy were holding Rufu station, and as the ground in front of the station appeared to be quite open, I marched into the bush and, crossing the Central Railway to the west of the station, worked round to the south where attack formation was assumed. Moved three miles to attack formation through the bush and entered enemy position from the rear. The rear guard (probable strength 50) scattered in the bush on our approach. Their main body had left the day before. I examined Rufu railway bridge, one mile to the west of the station, and found it completely destroyed. I reported this fact to the Deputy Inspector-General of Communications. The enemy position is a very strong one round the two-storeyed railway station. Issued rations and cooked.

September 2nd - Left Rufu 5.30.a.m. At 8 30 a.m. my advance guard surprised and scattered a piquet of 30 men in a village, capturing their personal effects. On approaching Masinga Village I left the track and worked round in attack formation through the bush to rear of enemy's position. Enemy surprised and scattered, offering no resistance. Captured two German white and a few Askaris of 3rd. Schutzen Company, also a herd of enemy's cattle. Prisoners reported that they were confused by our rapid advance, and movements of small parties of the enemy reported in the vicinity showed complete demoralization. Camped at Masinga, issued rations and cooked.

September 3rd. Left Masinga 4 a.m. Cut telegraph wire running from west to Dar es Salaam. At 2 p.m. received reliable information that enemy were holding two positions in front of me, close together, one at Kola on the road and one at Kasinga to the south. I left the road, and left the transport at this spot with orders to 2nd Lieutenant Berkeley (Quartermaster) to put out piquets from his escort of 20 rifles and to wait there for further orders. Advanced through bush to attack formation, keeping my left 300 yards from the road and my right thrown back as the position of Kasinga was unknown. My intention was to capture Kola, and then Kasinga, and to return to Kola for camp. After advancing for one hour in this way met a patrol of 12 German whites with some Askaris. Captured one white and wounded one Askari; remainder fled. I then learnt that both Kola and Kasinga were on my right, and after advancing some distance, I sent Major Lawrence with 1 company and 2 machine guns to Kola, and advanced as rapidly as possible on Kasinga with remainder of column.

Major Lawrence had a sharp fight at Kola village, and accounted for all the German whites at that place (1 killed, 2 wounded and captured, and 10 unwounded captured, all of Dar es Salaam Landsturm). On our side one Indian officer (Jemadar Mainu) was slightly wounded. The absence of more casualties was due to the fact that the fight took place in long grass and neither side could see the other. The Germans surrendered when Major Lawrence had approached to 25 yards distance.

With the remainder of the column I surprised and captured a large convoy and supply depot at Kasinga, capturing 9 German whites (Departments) and some Askaris with about 2,000 porter loads of European and African rations, or probably one full month's rations for two companies. In addition clothing and supplies of all kinds were captured as well as another herd of cattle. Two patrols to Major Lawrence failed to get through the enemy. The second patrol lost 2 killed and 1 wounded. The third patrol reached him. As it was getting dark, and I had to deal with captured supplies, I decided to call in Major Lawrence's party and the transport with 2nd Lieutenant Berkeley to Kasinga, and to halt there for one night. Both parties arrived safely at Kasinga at 7 p.m. by which time I had driven away small parties of the enemy who were hiding in the bush in the vicinity of Kasinga, from which place Kola proved to be 2 miles distant.

My first patrol to the Quarter Master with the Transport reached him safely.

There was no water in this neighbourhood except in the tanks carried on hand carts, which were captured from the Germans. This was barely sufficient for a small drink for everyone in the camp. I ordered no fires as the enemy were in the vicinity.

I consider that the spirit shown by the Dogras at Kola and the manner in which Major Lawrence led them and brought them back through the bush in the dark to Kasinga was most creditable. I attach on a separate sheet an account of the good work of Sepoy Charnel Singh for which I strongly recommend him for reward. (The exploit for which Sepoy Charnel Singh – Major Lawrence's orderly – was mentioned in this report occurred at the capture of Kola. Major Lawrence had called on a German to surrender, and he did so holding up his hands. As Major Lawrence approached him, however, the man lost his head and, snatching up a rifle, aimed at Major Lawrence. Sepoy Charnel Singh with great promptness and presence of mind shot the German through the head before he could fire.)

September 4th. At daybreak collected the captured supplies and burnt them. I was only able to carry away a small quantity. There remained a quantity scattered about the bush which I had not time to collect as we were without water. Marched at 8 a.m.

At 11.30 am. received news of enemy in Farsi village. I extended my vanguard across the road and sent a company to work round the flank. This manoeuvre resulted in the complete surprise of a small party of the enemy, 3 German whites and 5 Askaris of the Landsturm being captured.

At 1.30 p.m. I camped at Farsi, the men having had no food and very little water for 24 hours and very little rest.

September 5th. – Marched to Motoni and camped there. Received orders from Deputy Inspector General of Communications by runner to advance on Dar es Salaam. Marched to Dar es Salaam.

September 6th – I should like to express my gratitude for the very able assistance of Lieutenant Percival, Intelligence Department, and Intelligence Agent Burkitt, who were most successful in gaining information of the enemy, and also roads, distances and water.

I also take this opportunity to mention the excellent work of 2nd Lieutenant and Acting Adjutant R.T. Thornton and of 2nd Lieutenant and Acting Quartermaster H. Berkeley.

Following the above operation the Commander of the Column, Major. H.S. Tyndall was awarded the Distinguished Service Order, and Lieutenant Thornton the Military Cross.

The 40th Pathans marched into Dar es Salaam with the largest number of POWs, including twenty-seven German whites.

During these operations, a Greek Sisal Planter at Rufu complained that the Sepoys had looted twenty-three chickens from his outhouses. The Indian Adjutant was instructed to find and return them, but he misunderstood his orders and detailed men to go and collect twenty-three more chickens from the farm. This done he brought the chickens to the bewildered British Adjutant for orders as to disposal. They were straightway sent back to the Greek who, not having counted his chickens since losing the first twenty-three, received them gratefully!

Smuts now ordered that the Royal Navy should land garrisons at ports further south, and Tyndall was placed in charge of the landing parties.

13th September

Makindami was occupied under cover of a number of Naval vessels, including the flagship HMS *Vengeance* and cruisers *Hyacinth*, *Challenger* and *Talbot*.

17th September
A Force of the 40th Pathans was disembarked at Lindi.

Report made to Deputy Inspector for Communications at Dar es Salaam (Colonel C.V. Price CMG) by Major Tyndall commmanding detachment of the 40th:

> Lindi 'I have the honour to report as follows on the action near Lindi on 27th September. As local information appeared to be withheld and unreliable, I went on 25th September in *Echo*, guardship, Commander Charlwood, to reconnoitre a creek in the direction of Mrweka where there appeared to be some enemy. Finding that the *Echo* could get within range with her 12 pounder gun, I asked Commander Charlwood to proceed again on 26th September and shell vicinity of Mrweka, which he did at a range of 4,500 yards.
>
> Information also pointed to enemy further west, various places and numbers being mentioned.
>
> My plan was to reach round and come in on Mrweka from the west, and to be picked up and taken back to Lindi by the *Echo* from the place where she had fired on 26th. The tide allowed *Echo* to remain in position at this spot from 12 noon to 4 p.m.
>
> Consequently, at 2 a.m. on 27th September, I took 100 rifles with 4 machine guns, which was the force available after deducting garrison and necessary duties at Lindi. I did not take my Hotchkiss gun as I was unaware of the nature of the country and the tracks. I took porters carrying water. I marched for some 15 miles west and then turned south so as to come round behind where Mrweka appeared to be. Further information was not obtainable, though natives were interrogated. Piquets of enemy were chased out of 2 shambas with telephone wires, of which there appeared to be a fair number. As caution in advancing was necessary, I did not reach the enemy's position till noon.
>
> The bush was dense but at this point the firing line was crossing an open sandy plain with mangroves on our right flank, to cover the advance, when fire was opened on the firing line from concealed trenches in front and in the mangrove at 300 yards.
>
> From an enemy Askari captured here I learnt that the enemy in front were in telephone and trolly communication with larger parties to the west and that, having heard of our approach that morning through their telephone piquets, they had brought up reinforcements

by trolly line. Their strength was more than mine, and their position a strong one on the ridge running east and west with low sited and concealed trenches. The original firing line was after a while extricated from their position and brought up to high ground. Before this they had been lying in the open under close range MG and rifle fire. The conduct of the men was very steady. The plucky behaviour of Captain Murray, 2nd Lieutenant Whigham Teasdale and Subedar Jan Gul (attachd. from 26th Punjabis) deserves very particular mention. The rifle shooting of the enemy was bad.

The enemy had suffered considerable casualties but by 5 p.m. I could find no way of getting round them. As the porters with the water had run away and as the *Echo* would no longer be in her position I decided to return the way I had come

During the preliminary stages of withdrawing the enemy were pressing and the good work of the 3 officers above mentioned was very noticeable, especially that of 2nd, Lieutenant Whigham Teasdale, who moved a machine gun to threatened points and personally worked it under very heavy fire.

At this point a counter attack by about 20 men led by a German Sergeant was made on one of my (limbered up) machine guns as it was changing position. The German Sergeant was killed. It was not, however, till afterwards, when it was too late to return, that I learn that the MG with its team was missing. Up to the time that I left Lindi on September 28th (wounded) 3 of the team and the gun were still missing. I have instructed Major Lawrence to send out patrols and report to you if the gun and team are brought in. I returned to Lindi at midnight with the patrol without further incident.

My casualties were :- One man believed killed.

One British Officer and 13 ORI wounded.

The wounded were all removed to Zanzibar by HMS *Princess*.

Notes on Report

Two of the missing men of MG team subsequently came in but gun not recovered. Another man. Naick Sanam Gul, with broken leg, was also brought in by the enemy under a flag of truce.

Enemy's casualties : four German Europeans and ten Askaris killed.

Major Tyndall wounded in thigh and sent to Zanzibar Hospital. Major Lawrence assumed command of detachment.

In addition to fighting for five hours had marched nearly forty miles in just under twenty-four hours. Teasdale awarded MC. Sepoy Aijal Indian, Meritorious Medal.

Major Tyndall came out of hospital shortly afterwards.

30th September

HQ Wing of Regiment was landed from HMT *Edavana* at Kilwa Kiswani, a small port dominated by a ruined Portuguese Fort. Kilwa Kiwindje, connected by road ten miles to the south, became the Regiment's base of operations.

6th November

HQ Wing of Regiment marched to Mitole where it remained till 28 November.

During this period Subedar Mehrab Din (an Afridi) carried out a very successful three days' patrol and captured two prisoners (a wounded German White and an unwounded Askari) at Kilwa Kiwindje. He also shot a lioness at Mitole, having ordered his patrol to fix bayonets, but not to fire – at least unless he missed, he was a keen 'shikari'!

December

The enemy, whose main forces had been esconced in the Uluguru Mountains since September, had been driven south by Brigadier General Beyes' Mounted Brigade, and by a Belgian Column from the north-west .

They were concentrated more or less to the north of the Rufiji, but they also had units in the Mtumbi Mountains and were trying to invest Kibata. It was near here that the 40th Pathans were engaged in the action on Gold Coast Hill occupied by the Germans.

On the 15th December Gold Coast Hill was captured by the Gold Coast Regiment which was then heavily shelled by the enemy. They were reinforced by Major Tyndall with seventy-five men. The Gold Coast Regiment were ordered to withdraw, by which time they had lost two British Officers killed and seven wounded, thirty ORs killed and eighty-six wounded. Major Tyndall remained with 150 rifles, two MGs and four Naval Lewis Guns. For a week the Regiment held Gold Coast Hill under very difficult conditions. Heavy shelling continued, and then the men were becoming exhausted with malaria and insufficiency of rations – half the sentries being visited would be found lying down in the rain, sick from malaria or other ailments. Ten men were sent down daily. On 22nd December the ridge was evacuated. Regiment casualties – eight O.R.I, killed, two MG Porters killed and two wounded.

29th December

Lieutenant Colonel Mitchell left the Regiment to command a battalion of his own regiment and handed over command of the 40th Pathans to Tyndall who later became acting Lieutenant Colonel.

January

By the beginning of the month the Germans had evacuated Kibata. The 40th Pathans were at Kitambi where they remained until 11th January when they advanced on Ngarambe. They stayed there for a month and engaged in some very lively patrol activity.

28th February

The Regiment marched into Kitambi where full rations were available for the first time for many months.

2nd April

The Regiment moved to Chemera. Of the HQ party Lieutenant Colonel Tyndall was the only British Officer fit for duty.

12 April. News was received that the Germans were threatening Kilwa Kiwindje in force with nine companies numbering 1,200 men.

As the 40th Pathans was the nearest unit, they received orders to march south-east to delay or stop the German advance. It was not only the rainy season but the heaviest rainfall for nine years, and the column led by Lieutenant Colonel Tyndall, with 300 Indian ranks and five MGs (including the Gold Coast Regiment), made a long and miserable march in very wet and extremely difficult conditions when it was sometimes impossible even for porter transport to move, but they reached Rumbo after a few days and this lay between the Germans and Kilwa Kiwindje.

18th April

Tyndall led his column, now reinforced with 150 rifles of the 2nd Battalion King's African Rifles out from Rumbo in an attack on the German position which was found to be impregnable. Major Murchison was shot through the heart and killed. It rained all day and when retreating they found that the Ngaura River, which they had paddled across on the advance, had become a swollen, rushing torrent. However, they luckily found a fallen tree and this materially assisted a very good, well timed and controlled withdrawal.

Casualties were twenty-seven killed and sixty-nine wounded. The Germans had also suffered heavily, and there were thirty European Germans in hospital.

In the event the enemy did not reach Kilwa Kwindje with its stores and ammunition, so the action fought by Tyndall's column achieved its object. It was one of the most remarkable actions in which the Regiment had taken part. They remained at Rumbo for the rest of the month.

June

Lieutenant Colonel Tyndall was awarded the Croix de Guerre.

Many in the Regiment were sick and short of clothing. These were taken out of the Brigade and sent to rest in local Line of Communications. On 23rd June Tyndall, not in very good health, went on leave to Durban feeling he could be spared for a short time while the Regiment was resting.

In the meantime the Germans were being pushed south and the Regiment took part unexpectedly in the action at Narumgombe to which the enemy had withdrawn. All the British Officers of the 40th became casualties.

November

Lieutenant Colonel Tyndall was invalided back to England.

The East African Force had been constituted to conquer the Province of German East Africa. This it eventually did, together with the Belgian and Portuguese Forces. It did not however, round up and destroy the remnant of the German Forces. The German C.-in-C., realizing that the war would be won or lost in Europe, resolved to keep his forces in being till the end of the war, and so he fought skilful delaying actions which had this result.

Sea Power had played a great part. Naval Blockade dented the German stores and ammunition, at the same time facilitating transport for us and our occupation of coastal bases.

British Casualties- 4,000 killed or died of wounds.

5,500 died of disease.

1918

7th February

40th Pathans embarked at Dar es Salaam for return to India on Bibby Line SS *Warwickshire*.

24th February
40th Pathans disembarked Karachi and reached Fatehgahr base on 24 February.

April
Major Tyndall was a Company Commander.

Lieutenant Colonel Glassfurd CMG, DSO was Commandant.

The Regiment was stationed successively at Fatehgarh, Rawalpindi and Campbellpur.

1919

Third Afghan War

May/June
During the Great War the Amir Habibullah had maintained Afghan neutrality and enabled most Indian troops to be sent abroad. However he was murdered in February 1919 and succeeded by Amanullah, his third son, who was anti-British and felt insecure on his throne.

Pathans on the Indian side of the Durand line and Indian Congress Politcians engineered riots and Afghan troops crossed the border on 3rd May and took up position at Bagh on the British side of the border. Britain declared war on Afghanistan on 6th May.

The Regiment only played a small part in this short campaign being part of the 2nd Infantry Division in the North-West Frontier Force commanded by General Sir A.A. Barratt.

Most of the action was in the Khyber but the Afghans and the tribesmen did not cooperate well and Amanullah had soon had enough.

On 3rd. June the armistice was signed.

1920

March
This month witnessed the unveiling of the Regimental Memorial on the banks of the Indus near Attock.

Tyndall took over command of the Regiment from Lieutenant Colonel Glassfurd

1921

11th July

Lieutenant Colonel H.S. Tyndall DSO, Commandant of the Regiment. The old 40th was now designated as the 5th Battalion of the '14th Army Group'. From the beginning of 1923 '14th Punjab Regiment', with five active battalions and a training battalion. There was much reorganization at this time.

1922

February

On 3rd February the Battalion entrained at Nowashera for Karachi where they embarked on British India Steam Navigation Co's SS *Vasna* on 22 February for Iran reaching Basra on 28th February under command of Lieutenant Colonel Tyndall.

At Basra they were transferred to a river steamer for the journey to their destination, Amara. Two barges, on which the men lived, were lashed to the steamer. In the 'Narrows' of the Shatt-el-Arab the barges were used to assist the steamer in rounding corners by cannoning off them. This was the normal method of navigation.

The Shatt-el-Arab stretches as far as Quma, reputed site of the Tree of Knowledge, when the Tigris proper is entered. It was a desolate looking spot, and a British soldier is reported to have said, 'If this 'eres the Garden of Eden it wouldn't take no Angel with a flaming sword to keep me out.'

Amara lay about eighty miles upstream. The battalion was stationed in a cantonment on the opposite bank of the river to the town. The battalion lines were in old hospital huts with mud and wattle walls and reed thatched huts.

The Mess and Officers' Quarters were in the same type of buildings.

June

King Feisal of Iraq visited Amara and the Regiment turned out a Guard of Honour of 100 men with a pipe band.

Lieutenant Colonel Tyndall and Majors Murray and Hill were invited to dine with the King. Communication was difficult as the King spoke no English, although he spoke fluent French, so Tyndall was able to converse in that language. Major Pulley acted as interpreter in Arabic.

It was a very hot night and Feisal, being a strict follower of the Prophet, had always forbidden the consumption of alcohol in his presence. The only drink available was tepid curdled milk! As soon as the King had left, however, the Arab

Governor, not being so strict in the tenets of his faith, produced iced whisky and soda, much to the relief of the British present.

The unsettled condition of Turkey following the end of the Great War, and the liberation of Mesapotamia from Turkish rule by British and Indian troops, gave rise to some doubt as to the direction of events (hence the presence of the 40th Pathans in Iraq). The League of Nations had recently made Mesapotamia the nucleus of a new territory (Iraq) to be administered by Great Britain under mandate. In the meantime Kemal Attaturk was busy freeing Turkish soil of the Allies, and there had been friction with Turkey over settlement of the northern boundary near Mosul-Vilayet which resulted in a concentration of troops in that area.

August

The Treaty of Lausanne recognized the new Government of Turkey and established boundaries. Military forces in Iraq were then greatly reduced and at the end of August the Battalion received orders to return to India.

Just prior to departure, a herd of milk cows belonging to the battalion was put up for auction, but the Arabs would not bid in the hope of getting them free. At the last minute the gangways of the river steamer were lowered, and it was announced that the cows were going to India. Immediately lively bidding ensued and the cows were sold for a fair price.

The Battalion sailed on the SS *Vasna* and reached Bombay on 15th September 1923.

September

'C' and 'D' Companies were detached to Shaiba near Basra where there was an aerodrome on which was stationed No. 84 Squadron of the RAF.

October

The Royal Air Force took over control of Iraq, occupying an area previously known as Mesapotamia (The land between the two rivers – Tigris and Euphrates) an ancient cradle of civilization.

The Air Officer Commander in Chief was Air Marshal Sir John Salmond, who inspected the battalion on one occasion.

1924

Ahmedabad

The Battalion took over the lines and Mess of the 99th Deccan Infantry who were disbanded in the New Year. The cantonment lay in park like country about four miles from the city of Ahmedabad, the eighth largest city in India, and the centre of the cotton industry.

The surroundings were pleasant, and in many ways, Ahmedabad with its good shikar and tranquil life, far from the orbit of inspecting generals and so forth, was a survival of that earlier and more leisurely India which, by that time, had almost entirely passed away.

Five months after the arrival of the battalion in Ahmedabad, Lieutenant Colonel H.S.Tyndall DSO, Croix de Guerre, proceeded on a year's leave to England, pending retirement after twenty-eight years service with the battalion. His departure was marked by a great demonstration of affection by all ranks who spontaneously lined the road leading to the railway station holding torches.

Notes

1 Rawalpindi was then a major British military outpost – in the foothills of the Himalayas. Later it was the temporary capital of Pakistan (1959–1970) during the building of the new capital, Islamabad.

2 Tonga, near enough to a small pony trap – sometimes called a Tum Tum.

3 Abbottabad. About fifty miles north of Rawalpindi. Named after Colonel James Abbott, described by Henry Lawrence as 'gentle as a girl in thought' but acted differently. In the Second Sikh War (1848–9) he had led a band of mounted Yusufzai irregulars that forced the surrender of the entire Sikh Army. Now and again he blew transgressors from the mouth of a cannon *'pour encourager les autres'*.

4 Dak bungalows were situated on the outskirts of all military stations and were permanently staffed usually by a man and woman who could cook and look after guests who were often greeted with, 'I make you nice chicken curry', There was no booking requirement as most of the time they were empty and used generally for one or two nights only.

5 Second Lieutenant Tyndall joins 40th Pathans. The adjutant received a wire from Harnai (nearest railway station) – 'please arrange carriage' or words to that effect, signed 'Tyndal'. The 'tindal', the Quarter Master's factotum, was on leave at that time and due to return about then. A wire was sent back 'No dak available for tindal'. The result was that Tyndall had to walk the whole distance of 110 miles according to Regimental Records ; although Tyndall states that he had a riding mule, the records state that the mule carried his baggage.

6 In March 1897, while Tyndall was on leave, the 40th Pathans had received orders to move to Rawalpindi, being relieved by the 25th Bombay Rifles. The move gave the opportunity for a route march in fours with the adjutant's wife accompanying on horseback; covering a distance of over 200 miles, pipe and srinai bands played the column onwards. During the entire march through the Zhob and Gomal valleys no pickets were put out and none were stationed round the camp at night; a tribute to Sir Robert Sandeman, the Governor General's agent for Baluchistan 1877–1892, who had gained the respect of the Baluchis and the other wild tribes in the area; his legacy of peace however, would not last much longer.

7 Maisar. In June 1896 a Hindu clerk had been murdered at a levy post in N. Waziristan. The murderer was never found and the wrangling over the 2,000 rupees fine led, a year later, to a visit by the Political Agent, Mr Gee, accompanied by a military escort of about 250 men under the command of Lieutenant Colonel Bunny. After a courteous reception, in the tradition of Pathan hospitality, the troops came under heavy attack and Colonel Bunny and all the British officers were wounded. The Indian officers saved the situation and enabled the force to retire. A punitive expedition, the Tochi Field Force, of two brigades, was sent in July 1897.

8 The Corps of Guides was created in 1846 by Henry Lawrence, their main function being to guide regular units in the field and to provide intelligence. The task of raising the Guides was given to a keen young political agent named Harry Lumsden who also held a Lieutenant's commission.

Lumsden soon turned his force of one cavalry squadron and three companies of infantry into a crack fighting unit. The scarlet tunic was discarded, to the horror of the British Military Establishment, in favour of khaki which of course was far more suitable for fighting in the hills – or anywhere else for that matter. They were recruited mainly from Pathans, but also from Sikhs, Gurkhas, Punjabis, Muslims and some Hindus. Yusufzais and Khattaks were the main element of the Pathans. By the 1850's and 60s they had expanded to a strength of 1,000 and become the frontier's corps d'élite, still led by their original leader, now General Sir Harry Lumsden.

The mess was deserted because the guides had already left for Malakand. On 27th July the infantry commanded by Lieutenant Lockhart covered 32 miles in 17 and a half hours in fierce heat and choking dust. An officer at the Darghai post told Winston Churchill that they shouldered arms with parade precision as they passed the guard, went on up the steep ascent to the pass and went straight into action.

9 Night attack on 26 July. The Mad Mullah's hordes had descended suddenly on the Malakand position on the night of 26 July. Major Harold Deane, the political agent, had reported to Brigadier General Meiklejohn, who commanded the Malakand garrison, that the tribesmen were gathering and an attack was imminent. A telegram was sent to Marden ordering the guides to march without delay and the COs were briefed by the General. Nevertheless, the seriousness of the situation was not fully realized; the officers sat down to dinner still in their polo kit and there was talk of a small skirmish. At the dead of night the bugle sounded, the officers seized their swords and belts and the storm broke. A night attack is always alarming for defending troops and the attack on the Malakand bore all the elements of surprise, darkness, rugged terrain and an unknown number of ferocious enemy to cause maximum confusion among the defenders – hence Tyndall's reference to the indescribable condition of the camp.

It can be said that the situation was almost certainly saved by the prompt action of Lieutenant Colonel McRae who, with Major Taylor, collected as many men of the 45th Sikhs as possible (half the battalion was at Chakdarra) and ran along the old Buddhist Road to a narrow defile which commanded access to the camp. If the enemy had got there first they would have streamed through and overwhelmed the camp, but the Sikhs just won and held the position against 1,000 tribesmen for a week. During the night of 28/29 July Lieutenant H.B. Ford of the 31st P.I. and Lieutenant H.L.S. Maclean of the Guides were severely wounded. A remarkable and gallant action by a medical officer, Surgeon Lieutenant V. Hugo, saved the life of Ford who was dangerously wounded in the shoulder and bleeding to death when Hugo came to his aid. The position was under heavy fire from the enemy, nevertheless the doctor struck a match and examined the wound. As the match sputtered out amid a hail of bullets he saw that an artery had been severed, he seized it and, literally holding a man's life between his finger and thumb, remained under fire for three hours. Ford had long since fainted from loss of blood. When the enemy broke into the camp Hugo bore Ford to a place of safety without relaxing his hold on the artery. His arm was paralysed with cramp for many hours after his ordeal was over.

10 Chakdarrah was another strong point set up to guard the road to Chitral. Its defence must rank with that of Rorke's Drift, Fort Chitral and other epics of Empire; a handful of defenders holding out against desperate odds – about 200 Sikhs

commanded by Lieutenant Rattray against an enemy who grew daily in numbers which reached a total estimated at 14,000. On 27 July a small force of cavalry, the 11th Bengal Lancers under Captain Wright, had managed to break through by what seemed a miracle and became a much needed reinforcement for the hard pressed garrison. Assaults by the enemy continued without ceasing, in many cases scaling ladders were brought to the walls of the fort before the attackers were driven off. Communication with Malakand was almost impossible as the signal tower was under constant fire from the enemy. Finally a signaller managed to heliograph two 'Help us' messages.

It was fortunate that General Sir Bindon Blood had arrived at Malakand on 1 August to take command of the operation. He saw at once that the key to the situation was a hill with a prominent spur beside the position on the Buddhist Road held by Colonel McRae and the 45th Sikhs. He ordered Colonel Goldney, with a force of 300 men – 250 from 35th Sikhs and 50 from 38th Dogras – to capture the hill.

At dawn on 2 August the Chakdarra relieving column set off down the graded road, at the same time Colonel Goldney advanced to take the hill which would bear his name. He got within 100 yards without being seen, then they charged and cleared the hill of the enemy. This began a general evacuation of the tribesmen from the hills and high ground, and the way to Chakdarra was open.

When the fort was relieved on 3 August the garrison had been fighting for five days without sleep, for the last eighteen hours without water. Casualties were twenty killed and wounded. The enemy lost about 2,000.

11 VCs awarded to Colonel Adams and Lord Fincastle. Lieutenant Colonel Adams of the Guides Cavalry led a group of horsemen in pursuit of tribesmen, who had fled after the 'Gate of Swat' had been forced by General Sir Bindon Blood's troops. His group included Lieutenant Lord Fincastle, the *Times* correspondent and Lieutenant Maclean. Captain Palmer, who commanded the leading squadron, and Lieutenant Greaves of the Lancashire Fusiliers, acting war correspondent of the *Times of India*, galloped ahead and attacked the enemy. They, however, turned on them savagely and after a fierce clash of arms both fell to the ground wounded. They were lying at the foot of the hill surrounded by tribesmen and all would have been lost had not Colonel Adams and Lord Fincastle with Lieutenant Maclean and two or three Sowars not dashed up to their assistance and carried them back to safety, in the course of which Lieutenant Greaves was killed and Lieutenant Maclean mortally wounded. Lord Fincastle's horse was shot.

12 The Swat Valley is beautiful and fertile. There was formerly a large Buddhist settlement here and there are numerous ruins of once thriving cities. It must have been one of the few peaceful spots in these wild mountains. When Tyndall was there, however, the gentle Buddhists had long since disappeared to be replaced by savage tribes.

13 The Haddah Mullah was a pious and mystical but turbulent priest who had, thirteen years previously, quarrelled with the Amir of Afghanistan and raised the Mohmands against him. The Amir had summoned him to Kabul, but the Mullah had wisely declined and remained in the independent Mohmand territory where, a notorious Anglophobe, he was a considerable nuisance on the frontier. He had attacked the

Chitral Expedition in 1895 and was now inflaming the tribes to holy jihad against the British.

14 Colonel Fred Batty of the Guides had been mortally wounded when his battalion of 12th/13th Guides Infantry had been holding a bridgehead on the Swat River during the Chitral Expedition.

15 Mohmand Valley. As a result of the action at the west end of the Mohmand Valley involving the Guides, the 35th Sikhs and the Buffs – a punitive expedition before proceeding to Narwagai – the HQ for Brigadier General Jeffreys, commanding the 2 Brigade, was left in the plain in the middle of the valley at Bilot. Due to garbled orders and loss of contact in the darkness General Jeffreys was left in a situation where there were no other troops but a gun battery and thirty sappers later joined by the 12 Buffs. They were heavily attacked all night and might have been wiped out altogether if help hadn't arrived in time. General Jeffreys was wounded in the head and Captain Watson's hand was smashed by bullets.

16 Khan of Jhar was one of four friendly Khans in the Mohmand country covering Dir and Bajauer. Like the Khan of Narwagai he was constrained by fear to display a friendly attitude towards the Sirkar, and received moral support from British agents. The Khan of Dir was the most important and he received material assistance from the British Government in pay and certain allowances of arms and ammunition; he raised levies and kept the Chitral Road in repair. The Khan of Khar was perhaps the most honest and trustworthy. However the population remained hostile to the British, although they submitted sullenly to their rules.

17 Winston Churchill, then a lieutenant in the 4 Hussars, had taken special leave to act as war correspondent for the *Daily Telegraph* during the Malakand Campaign. 'Like most young fools,' he wrote many years later, 'I was looking for trouble'.

18 The Tirah was Afridi and Oraksai country, both fierce and independent tribes whose territory had not previously been entered by the British or by anyone else. The building of a line of defensive forts along the Samana hills overlooking the vales of Tirah by the Indian Government in 1891 had alarmed both them and the Amir Abdur Rahman who considered himself their spiritual leader and de facto temporal leader of this grey area. The Afridis, therefore, were ripe for rebellion, at the instigation of the Afridi Mullah Sayid Akbar, who was conspiring with the Mad Mullah, and were at the centre of the uprising in 1897. The Afridis and Oraksais together mustered 40,000-50,000 men. It was decided to send a large force comprising the two divisions and supporting troops under Lieutenant General Sir William Lockhart, in all 35,000 men. It was the largest army to take the field since the Mutiny, and the best equipped. Infantry regiments had the Lee Metford rifle, the first bolt action weapon used by British Forces. Nevertheless, this impressive force had a severe mauling from the tribesmen, particularly in the Bara valley where it 'looked more like a rout than the victorious withdrawal of an punitive force', and the Tirah force was only saved from annihilation by the British mountain guns. Lockhart only succeeded in finally subduing the tribes in the Khyber Pass after five months.

19 A jirgah was normally a deputation consisting of representatives from a tribe who might not necessarily voice official or majority opinion; in fact very often it was formed of some minority, e.g. peace terms might be agreed on the morning and the

camp rushed that night. The jirgah which Tyndall describes in this case was no doubt the full durbar at which General Blood, with Major Deane, the political officer, received the full submission of the Mohmands. They gave security for their rifles which had not yet been surrendered. They were informed that as they had suffered severe punishment, no fines or further penalty would be exacted. They were also offered medical aid for their wounded but declined, fearing a stratagem.

20 Mian Mir was subsequently known as Lahore cantonments. It was very unhealthy and the Regiment went into cholera camp Shah Kai. There were twelve cases of cholera of whom eight died.

21 Sister.

22 Fiancée.

23 Exercise and sport, played a very important part in the lives of the British in India. It was an obsession which stemmed from the fear that unless one kept fit one would catch 'some dreadful disease or other'.

   Polo was first played by planters in East Bengal in about 1840 and very soon spread across India. It was almost obligatory for army and ICS officers.

24 Lieutenant B.EM. Gurdon was an officer of the Indian Political Department who had distinguished himself at the Siege of Chitral in 1895 for which he had been awarded the DSO.

25 The Pathans coveted rifles greatly and were prepared to risk their lives to steal one. The most extreme precautions had to be taken to prevent losing a rifle. Men usually slept with rifles chained to them.

26 Ekka – a small one horse vehicle (Hindi – ekka = unit).

27 A wing of the Regiment was on detachment to Dera Ghazi Khan under Captain Rennick and Lieutenant St George. One of the first gramophones to arrive in India was sent to the mess there.

28 Lord Curzon had arrived in India as Viceroy on 3 January 1899; of quick, enquiring mind, he had long prepared himself for this post. He was just thirty-nine and the youngest ever to be appointed to this high position.

29 China – Boxer Rebellion 1900.

   They were going off to join the China Expeditionary Force which was dispatched in June 1900, at first replacing garrisons in Hong Kong and Singapore (already sent to China) and then, as the British contingent of the CEF totalling 10,000 men, proceeding to China.

   The Boxers were one of a number of secret societies which grew rapidly into a vast and dangerous association of brigands which the Government soon found beyond its powers of control. However they professed great loyalty to the throne, and their war cry was, 'Exalt the dynasty and destroy the foreigners'.

   Lawlessness and violence increased against foreigners who were blamed for all ills, particularly Catholics and Protestants, and there was a wholesale massacre of Chinese Christians.

   Tientsin was attacked in June 1900.

   The International garrison consisted of the following:

Austrians	50
British	393

French	50
Germans	110
Italians	40
Japanese	50
Russians	1,800
United States	43
Total	2,536

The city was relieved on 13/14 July, and the legations in Peking on 16 August. This virtually brought the troubles to an end, but China was forced to accept treaty ports for foreign trade.

(A rough translation of Boxer from Mandarin Chinese is ' Righteous Harmonious Brigade': yi, righteousness + he, harmony + tuan, brigade.)

30 Indus – low water in cold weather, in hot weather the river could be anything from eight to ten miles across.

31 A Wing of the Regiment under Captain Rennick and Lieutenant St John, had been on detachment to Dehra Ghazi Khan.

In July of this year Wings were abolished as administrative units, and designated double companies, although still used for describing a half battalion.

32 Caretaker, night watchman.

33 Subjects taught; map reading, compass bearings, written and verbal reports, observation of the enemy, moving under cover, retiring from heights in mountain warfare, observation of tracks, semaphore and physical training.

34 Bhustie – water carrier.

35 No doubt wife and daughter of General Elles who commanded a division in the Malakand Campaign.

36 The North-West Frontier Province came into existence in 1901 on the insistence of Lord Curzon who had been opposed to the administration of the Frontier by the Punjab Government, a situation which presented certain anomalies and led to delays and disagreements, where a subordinate government lay between the Indian Government and a volatile area, difficult to control, whose security was vital to the whole of India. Hence the concern of Turton and Kitty.

37 Muhammedanism used to be the general and inaccurate, if not offensive, term for Islam. It is offensive because it gives the impression that Muhammed shaped this religion. In Muslim eyes God inspired Muhammed his prophet to preach Islam to his people – derived from the word 'salam' which means primarily 'peace' but in a secondary sense 'surrender'. Its full connotation is 'the perfect peace' that comes when one's life is surrendered to God.

Hassan and Husein were actually grandsons of the prophet, sons of his daughter Fatima and Ali; their descendants, the Shiites insist, are the only legitimate caliphs or leaders of Islam; while the Sunnis, the majority sect, accept the first four caliphs as the rightful successors of Muhammed.

38 Later General Sir Frederick Campbell KGB DSO DL, Colonel of Battalion.

39 Juliet Audrey Tyndall – sister.

40 The battalion marched 150 miles to DIK or 'Dreary Dismal' Khan. The Indus was crossed, as it was cold weather and low water, by a bridge of boats. In hot weather

the river could be anything from 8 to 10 miles across.

41 Tyndall was now Brigade Intelligence officer and had been ordered to make a road recce and military report in the Tank area in aid of plans for the relief or support of Wana Garrison in event of extensive tribal uprising. These sketches and reports were subsequently used to correct 'Route to Waziristan', some being incorporated in 'Military Report on Waziristan'. They were based at Jandola fort in the Mahsud country, and the marches were very hot in summer, with twenty or thirty men falling out; by contrast it was very cold in winter.

42 Sir George Roos-Keppel was one of the great men of the Frontier. He had succeeded Sir Harold Deane (political officer in the Malakand Campaign) as Chief Commissioner of the North-West Frontier Province in 1908. He was tough and hot tempered but regarded with great affection by the Pathans whose language he spoke fluently.

43 They were dealing with Wazir raiders in 'heat that made your eye brows crawl' – chief among these were the Mullah Powindah, Jagga, Jalotai and Kamil. The raiding of villages was particularly bad at this time, but it was forbidden to take punitive measures on account of financial stringency. When it got too bad a mobile column was dispatched, consisting of two companies of infantry, a squadron of cavalry and a section of a mountain battery. The shepherds, who were the chief sufferers, were always ready to bring news of the raiders who were sometimes caught.

44 Mussoorie – near Dehra Dun, East of Simla, in the hills.

45 The Criminal Tribes of India. – entire families were devoted from the cradle to the grave to a life of crime. A child who was born to a family within these tribes automatically became a criminal, the caste system making it impossible to do otherwise, because they could not change caste. The sub Himalayan region of North India was the favourite habitat of these tribes. Some of them were said to be direct descendants of pre-Aryan dwellers of the country.

The government had for many years been trying to control them. In 1908 Booth-Tucker of the Salvation Army was requested by the Commissioner of Rohil Khand, a member of the Government of the United Provinces, to open a settlement at Gorakhpur. Activities such as carpentry, dairy farming, irrigation, stone quarrying and agriculture were introduced. This was a success and a number of other settlements were opened soon afterwards.

From *By Love Compelled* by Solveig Smith.

Appendix A

Service Career of Lieutenant Colonel H.S. Tyndall DSO born 16 July 1875 first commissioned 16 January 1895

1895	Attached 3rd Battalion, Rifle Brigade.
1896	Attached 40th Pathan Regiment of Bengal Infantry.
1897	Attached 38th Dogras, Malakand Field Force for six months.
1900	Quarter Master 40th (Pathan) Regiment of Bengal Infantry
to	Quarter Master 40th Punjab Infantry.
1902	Quarter Master 40th Pathans.
1903-04	Assistant Instructor Army Signalling, Northern Circle.
1904-05	Adjutant 67th Punjabis.
1905-08	Adjutant 40th Pathans.
1909–10	Attache, Intelligence Branch AHQ.
1912–15	Adjutant, Mussoorie Volunteers.
1915–18	In France and East Africa with 40th Pathans.
	Company Commander, 2nd i/c and Offg. Commandant.
	Wounded East Africa, DSO and Croix de Guerre.
1919	2nd i/c 40th Pathans in 4th Brigade.
	2nd Division, Third Afghan War.
1921–25	Commandant 5th Battalion, 14th Punjab Regiment.

Colonel Tyndall died on 2 February 1942 in Worthing, Sussex.

Appendix B

5th Battalion (Pathans)
14th Punjab Regiment, formerly 40th Pathans.
('The Forty Thieves')

'40' has been preserved in identity of Regiment since 1780.

The Regiment is directly descended from Shahjehanpur Levy raised by Lieutenant E. Dandridge in 1858, and became 40th Bengal Infantry in 1861, predecessor of the 40th Pathans.

1780	40th Battalion, raised to operate against the Mahrattas in Gwalior.
1781	33rd. Battalion
1784	33rd Battalion disbanded owing to financial stringency. Hiatus.
1802	2nd Battalion, Marine Regiment (Hamilton-Ki-Paltn).
1803	2nd Battalion, 20th Regiment.
1824	40th Native Infantry Volunteers.
1858	Shahjahanpur Levy, reconstituted after Mutiny.
1861	44th Regiment of Bengal Native Infantry. 40th Regiment of Bengal Infantry.
1864	40th (Shahjahanpur) Regiment of Bengal Native Infantry.
1885	40th Regiment of Bengal Infantry.
1890	40th (Baluch) Regiment of Bengal Infantry.
1892	40th (Pathan).
1902	40th Punjab Infantry.
1903	40th Pathans.
1922	5th Battalion, 14th Punjab Regiment.
1934	5th Battalion, (Pathans), 14th Punjab Regiment.

Appendix C

Some of the more prominent Personalities
mentioned in the Diary

2nd Lieutenant G.A. Preston, who always seemed to have a new joke, joined the Regiment from the Royal Scots, and was known as 'Goldfish' because of two little tails on the tunic of his Royal Scots uniform.

In 1919 as a lieutenant colonel he was appointed Military Governor of Kars in Armenia. He was killed on horseback about 100 yards from the Residency in an unexplained accident.

Lieutenant Colonel Rennick died of wounds in the Ypres Salient in 1915.

Lieutenant Ridgeway became Brigadier General R.T.I. Ridgeway CB. He was wounded at Loos on the Western Front, and retired in 1920.

Lieutenant J.C.P. Craster, as Captain Craster, was killed leading an assault during the Tibet Expedition in June 1904.

Lieutenant Colonel F. Campbell DSO was Commandant of the Regiment 1899–1906. He commanded the 40th Pathans during the Tibet Expedition of 1904, and was the inspiration and moving force behind the assault and capture of Gyantse Jong, the key to the defence of Tibet.

In 1920 he retired to Scotland as General Sir Frederick Campbell KGB, DSO, DL. In 1932 he was appointed Deputy Lieutenant of the County of Argyll.

Appendix D

The Malakand Field Force

On 30th July 1897 the following order was officially published:

> The Governor-General in Council sanctions the dispatch of a Force to be styled 'The Malakand Field Force' for the purpose of holding the Malakand, and the adjacent posts, and operating against the neighbouring tribes as may be required.'

> Commanding – Major General Sir Bindon Blood KCB

1st Brigade

Brigadier General W.H. Meiklejohn CB, CMG

1st Border Royal West Kent Regiment
24th Punjab Regiment
31st Punjab Regiment
45th (Rattray's) Sikhs
Sections A and B of No. 1 British Field Hospital
No. 38 Native Field Hospital
Sections A and B of No 50 Native Field Hospital

2nd Brigade

Brigadier General P.D. Jeffreys CB

1st Border, East Kent Regiment (The Buffs)
35th Sikhs
38th Dogras
Guides Infantry
Sections C and D of No 1 British Field Hospital
No.37 Native Field Hospital

Sections C and D of No 50 Native Field Hospital.
Divisional Troops.

4 Squadrons 11th Bengal Lancers	1 Squadron 10th Bengal Lancers
22nd Punjab Infantry	2 Companies 21st PI
10th Field Battery	6 Guns No. 1 British Mountain Battery
6 Guns No. 8 Bengal Mountain Battery.	6 Guns No. 7
No. 5 Company Madras Sappers and Miners	Sect. B of No 13 British Field Hospital
No.3 Company Bombay " "	Sect. A & B of No 35 Native Field Hospital
No 34 Native Field Hospital	Sect. B of No 1 Native Field Hospital.

Total 6,800 Bayonets
       700 Lances and Sabres
        24 Guns.

Appendix E

East Africa

ORDER OF BATTLE – APRIL 1916

British and South African Forces
    Commander in Chief- General Jan Smuts.
    First Division – Major General A.R. Hoskins CMG DSO
1st East African Brigade –   Brigadier General S.H.Sheppard DSO
                                    (CRE in Tibet in 1904 and associated with
                                    Lieutenant Colonel Tyndall DSO
                                    commanding the 40th Pathans in assault of
                                    Gyantse Jong)
2nd East African Brigade – Brigadier General J. A. Hannyngton CMG DSO

    Second Division – Major General J.L. Van Deventer
1st.South African Mounted Brigade – Brigadier General M.Botha
3rd South African Infantry Brigade – Brigadier General C.A.L. Berrange CMG

    Third Division – Major General Coen Brits
2nd South African Mounted Brigade – Brigadier General B. Enslin
2nd South Afiican Infantry Brigade – Brigadier General P.S. Beves
    Also Scout Corps, 4 Howitzer Brigades and RFC.

German Forces
    Commander in Chief – Colonel von Lettow Vorbeck
30 Field Companies
10 Schutzen Companies
Total – about 2,200 European Germans
10,000 Askaris
1,500 Ruga-Ruga

Armed with M71 rifles plus some hundreds of British .303 Lee Enfields, machine guns and ammunition.

Transport consisted entirely of porters who took their women about with them.

Bibliography

Books

Allen, Charles. *Plain Tales from the Raj*, Futura, Macdonald & Co. 1976
— *RAJ, a Scrapbook of British India, 1877–1947*
Barthorp Michael, *The Northwest Frontier, British India and Afghanistan, AP Pictorial History 1839–1947*, Blandford Press, 1982
Birdwood, Field Marshal Lord, *Khaki and Gown*, Ward Lock & Co. Ltd, 1942
Burnaby, Fred. *A Ride to Khiva*. Cassell Patter & Galpin, 1877
Caroe, Sir Olaf. *The Pathans*. Oxford University Press, 1958
Churchill, Winston S., *TheMalakand Field Force*, Longmans Green, 1898, Octopus Publ. Group (Leo Cooper), 1989
Elliott, Major General J.G., *The Frontier 1839–1947*, Cassell, 1968
Enriquez, C.M., *Pathan Borderland*, Thacker Spink & Co., Calcutta.
Fletcher, Arnold, *Afghanistan, Highway of Conquest*, Cornell University Press, 1965
Fraser-Tytler, Sir W.K., *Afghanistan*, Oxford University Press, 1950
Gardner, Brian, *The East India Company*, Rupert Hart-Davis, 1971
Greeen, Colonel Sir Henry, *Advance of Russia in Central Asia*, Harrison, 1873
Mason, Philip, *A Matter of Honour, the Indian Army, its Officers and Men*, Macmillan, 1986
— *The Men who ruled India*, Pan Books, 1987, Jonathan Cape, 1985
Miller, Charles, *Khyber*, Macmillan Publ. Inc., New York, 1977
Norie, ??first name?? *Military Operations in China, 1900-01*, Intelligence Dept., War Office, 1903
Roberts P.E., *History of British India*, OUP, 1927
Robertson, Sir George, *Chitral*, Methuen, 1898
Robertson, Captain W.R., *Official Account of the Chitral expedition 1895*
Ross, Frank E., *Central Asia, Personal Narrative of General Josiah Harlan, 1823–1841*, Luzac & Co., London, 1939.
Shelvankar, K.S., *The Problem of India*, Penguin, 1940
Trench, Charles Chenevix, *The Frontier Scouts*, OUP, 1986
Warburton, Sir Robert, *Eigheen Years on the Khyber 1879–1898*, John Murray, 1900
Waters, Major R.S., *History of the 5th Battalion (Pathans). 14th Punjab Regiment (later 40th Pathans)*, James Bain Ltd, 1936

Periodicals
Journals of the Royal Society of Asian Affairs
The Raleigh Lecture on History – from Alexander Burnes to Frederick Roberts
  – Survey of Imperial Frontier Policy, J.L. Morrison, 1936

Index